INTRAPRENEURING

INTRAPRENEURING

*Why You Don't Have to Leave the
Corporation to Become an
Entrepreneur*

GIFFORD PINCHOT III

1817

HARPER & ROW, PUBLISHERS, New York

Cambridge, Philadelphia, San Francisco,
London, Mexico City, São Paulo, Singapore, Sydney

Library of Congress Cataloging in Publication Data

Pinchot, Gifford.
    Intrapreneuring: why you don't have to leave the corporation to become an entrepreneur.

    Bibliography: p.
    Includes index.
    1. Entrepreneur. I. Title.
HB615.P46   1985   658.4′2   83-48800
ISBN 0-06-015305-9

85 86 87 88 89 10 9 8 7 6 5 4 3 2 1

To Bob Schwartz

who inspired me to conceive of ways to
make intrapreneurs at home in large organizations

To Norm Macrae

who planted the seeds in Bob's mind

Contents

INTRAPRENEUR: Any of the "dreamers who do." Those who take hands-on responsibility for creating innovation of any kind within an organization. The intrapreneur may be the creator or inventor but is always the dreamer who figures out how to turn an idea into a profitable reality.

ENTREPRENEUR: Someone who fills the role of an intrapreneur outside the organization.

Memo to the CEO

Although not addressed to you, this book will be read by your people who may well start the revolution without you. The revolution that's coming will have many people working almost entirely *for themselves* within the corporation. Does that mean that they will work any less enthusiastically for you? Just the opposite. For the first time you will be able to stimulate and direct rapid, profitable innovation. That's why it is in your best interest to read this book too.

Generally, when you or any CEO calls for innovation, very little happens. This is not because of a lack of good ideas but because of the difficulties your people have in implementing them. If you are not hearing good ideas, it is because they are blocked or sanitized before they reach you. Worse, if employees' good ideas aren't being implemented, these potential innovators are probably leaving to become entrepreneurs—in many cases to become your competitors.

The stagnation of innovation in large organizations is the almost inevitable result of the currently fashionable systems of analysis and control. This book outlines another way of controlling innovation which is both more frugal and more effective because it is based on the way innovation actually happens.

When I look at successful innovation in companies as diverse as Hewlett-Packard, General Motors, Bank of California, 3M, General Mills, Du Pont, or AT&T, I always find small independent groups of imaginative action takers working to circumvent or even sabotage the formal systems that supposedly manage innovation. These courageous souls form underground teams and networks that routinely bootleg company resources or "steal" company time to work on their own missions. They make new things happen while those trying to innovate by the official route are still waiting for permission to begin.

These corporate risk takers are very much like entrepreneurs. They take personal risks to make new ideas happen. The difference is that they work within large organizations instead of outside them. I call them "intrapreneurs"—my shorthand for intracorporate entrepreneur.

Intrapreneuring is a revolutionary system for speeding up innovation within large firms by making better use of their entrapreneurial talent. It can allow you to hold onto your best innovators by providing them with the opportunity to make their ideas happen without having to leave your company.

Intrapreneuring offers a sound way to respond to the business challenges of the 1980's and beyond. New competition at home and abroad is rapidly demonstrating that our large firms must innovate or die. But just when innovation has become an essential competitive weapon, many large companies are being gutted by a new kind of competition which saps their ability to innovate—competition for their intrapreneurs.

Venture capitalists and other investors are bidding away your best innovators and with them your ability to turn good ideas into new profits. Fortunately, keeping your intrapreneurs is not as difficult as it seems.

When your people read this book they will know how to make more intelligent demands on you and your firm. They will ask you to support sensible systems designed to give greater freedom to intrapreneurs. You may feel you have already granted strategic and financial autonomy to your divisions and reduced the power of corporate staffs. CEOs who have fostered decentralization often feel that they have done their part and that the rest is up to their division managers. But remember that the prospective intrapreneurs in your company, like independent thinkers anywhere, pose a threat to those who feel comfortable only with the status quo. The environment you create must support freedom not only for division heads, but also for the people far down the hierarchy whose hands-on innovation efforts have often been blocked by those marvelous modern systems of analysis and control. Unless you tell them you expect freedom for intrapreneurs, your barons may feel it is their duty to continue applying the management tools that disempower their intrapreneurs.

Intrapreneurs will make all the difference between your firm's success and failure. The cost of losing entrepreneurial talent is more than just losing a skilled technologist or effective marketer. Intrapreneurs are the integrators who combine the talents of both the technologists and the marketers by establishing new products, processes, and services. Without them innovation remains potential, or moves at the glacial pace of bureaucratic processes that no longer suffice in an environment filled with entrepreneurial competition.

What do you need to do when your people read this book and realize they could be intrapreneurs? Try this:

1. *Clearly state your vision of the company's future so that your intrapreneurs can work on creating innovation that directly relates to the strategy of the company.*
2. *Look at every level for intrapreneurs with ideas—not just for ideas alone; an idea without someone passionate about it is sterile.*
3. *Replace red tape with responsibility.*
4. *Reward intrapreneurs with new career paths that fit their needs.*
5. *Advise managers that in the game of musical chairs caused by the removal of layers of unnecessary management, safety of a sort as well as the greatest opportunity lies in becoming an intrapreneur.*

There is a revolution about to happen in your corporation. Let it start with you.

DISCOVERING "THE DREAMERS WHO DO"

Why would anyone choose to be an intrapreneur if he or she could become an entrepreneur just as well?

I first asked myself this question in 1978 during a seminar at Bob Schwartz's School for Entrepreneurs in Tarrytown, New York. Of the four great opportunities for entrepreneurs that Bob mentioned, one seemed a contradiction in terms and the paradox attracted me. Quoting his friend, Norman Macrae, who in 1976 had written in the London *Economist* that "successful big corporations should devolve into becoming 'confederations of entrepreneurs,' "* Bob suggested that—if anyone could figure out how to make it work—the opportunities awaiting entrepreneurs *inside* large corporations could be tremendous.

The idea was jarring: The independent entrepreneur and the "organization man" seemed irreconcilable opposites, at least until Bob exploded some of the myths about the personalities and motivations of entrepreneurs. This new perspective gave me the first clue as to how established firms might make a place for what I came to call "intrapreneurs." From the standpoint of a company, the benefits of having intrapreneurs are obvious: Intrapreneurs introduce and produce new products, processes, and services, which in turn enable the company as a whole to grow and profit.

But back then it was less clear to me exactly how to design a system and culture within a large organization that would allow a place for someone like the entrepreneur.

---

* "The Coming Entrepreneurial Revolution: a survey," *The Economist,* Dec. 25, 1976, p. 42. Norman says he dreamed up the idea with his friend, John Diebold, at John's Institute of Public Policy Studies.

Needless to say, the resources of a large corporation can be attractive to a would-be innovator. Corporations can provide manufacturing facilities, networks of supportive suppliers, a depth of proprietary technology, all kinds of personnel resources, and marketing clout. Such advantages, however, are often offset by bureaucratic systems that inhibit intrapreneuring. These inhibitions are compounded by the popular image of the entrepreneur as a money-hungry empire builder, a personality antithetical to the culture of the big company.

But this image was among the myths Bob's school challenged. I learned, to my surprise, that the primary motivation for most entrepreneurs is not the acquisition of wealth. Many do become wealthy, but they do so almost by accident in the course of pursuing some vision of what their customers, and the rest of the world, might need or want. Since their ventures must be financially successful if they are to satisfy their customers' needs, money becomes an important way to measure progress—but in and of itself, it is rarely the purpose of the venture.

Entrepreneur Howard Vollum, cofounder of Tektronix, explains that when he started out he had no idea the company would become large; much less the largest employer in Portland. "I would have been quite satisfied with a small company," he said. "I wanted to provide the tools needed by those of us who were coming home from World War II. We discovered we could not go back to what we were doing before the war. We were hooked on electronics, but the tools we had to work with were antiquated. In the beginning I just wanted to build the best oscilloscopes in the world."

Indeed, entrepreneurs are primarily motivated to satisfy a personal need for achievement, usually by bringing the world new products and services that are meaningful to themselves as well as to the market. Understanding this, I realized that the entrepreneur's commitment to action and drive to introduce new products rapidly was precisely what large organizations need. I was heartened by the fact that the primary goal for most entrepreneurs is not the acquisition of great personal wealth, for I saw little opportunity for accord should the entrepreneur within the corporation require the same multimillion-dollar payoffs an independent entrepreneur might receive upon launching a successful new business. Given this insight, the corporation's challenge to attract, motivate, and retain intrapreneurs appeared a solvable problem: Rewards for intrapreneurs would have to include something more directly related to intrapreneurial needs, in addition to salary and bonuses. I learned through conversations with dozens of new entrepreneurs that most leave corporations not primarily because they find their pay and benefits insufficient but because they feel frustrated in their attempts to innovate. They need empowerment to act as much as they need material compensation.

When entrepreneurs succeed in independent businesses, they earn much more than wealth and prestige; they earn the freedom to act. The capital earned in the ventures empowers entrepreneurs to take risk, adopt a larger time frame in which to try new ideas, and pay for their own mistakes without having to justify them to a boss.

Corporate entrepreneurs, despite prior successes, have no capital of their own to start other ventures. Officially, they must begin from zero by persuading management that their new ideas are promising. Unlike successful independent entrepreneurs, they are not free to guide their next ventures by their own intuitive judgments; they still have to justify every move. They have difficulty taking the long view because they never know whether their projects will be capriciously killed. How different this is from successful entrepreneurs who have capital of their own and thus can do as they choose.

Intrapreneurs' inability to use the earnings from one success to fund the next is among the greatest barriers to intrapreneuring. It is however a poor reason *not* to be an intrapreneur at least once, because success as an intrapreneur gives you the experience and track record to more easily succeed as an entrepreneur. Failing to empower successful intrapreneurs prevents corporations from benefiting from their seasoned innovators, who leave or become ineffective.

We know for certain that the entrepreneurial personality is to some degree intolerant of authority, and this makes it hard for intrapreneurs to beg for permission. I have seen intrapreneurs grow frustrated as they watched the corporation earning millions from their last business ventures while they remained unable to launch their next. What was needed if intrapreneurs were to remain inside the corporation, I concluded, was something that would function like capital does for the entrepreneur.

What I devised was a new system of rewards including "intracapital," a fund set aside by the corporation for use by a specific intrapreneur to start new businesses on behalf of the corporation. Originally, the purpose of the intracapital system was to reward past success with a tangible kind of freedom in the form of seed money for future ventures.

I then spent several weeks imagining how such a system might work. In the fall of 1978, four weeks after Bob Schwartz issued his challenge, I outlined the basic principles of such a system and coined the word "intrapreneur." Within three months I had sold my manufacturing firm and begun studying the intrapreneur and intrapreneuring in depth. At the time I was proud of the system I had created, but Bob and I agreed that corporations were not ready for it. That was just before the Japanese competitive scare hit, and American management was still too set in its ways to consider changing. Yet I knew the time would come for intrapreneurs.

To prepare for that time, I went to work for a new product consulting firm to see how new products and new services were handled in many different firms. I found myself bringing good ideas to firms that already had enough. Their real problem was that their intrapreneurs were prevented from implementing the ideas they already had, so bringing in more ideas solved the wrong problem. I decided again to dedicate myself to helping companies lower the barriers to implementing their people's own ideas by finding ways to encourage and empower the army of frustrated intrapreneurs which was their greatest resource for innovation.

Since deciding to work full time removing the barriers to new ideas within large corporations, I have divided my time among three tasks:

- Helping audit and improve the environment for intrapreneurs in companies such as AT&T, Du Pont, 3M, Martin Marietta, and Xerox. (None of the specific information in this book comes from my studies of these companies as a consultant. I have taken the basic principles gathered from in-depth studies, and found examples of these principles in other firms.)
- Making case studies in order to better understand the care and feeding of intrapreneurs everywhere.
- Speaking to anyone who will listen about what I have learned.

After I agreed to write about intrapreneuring, it turned out that the publisher and I had different books in mind. They had expected one on how to succeed as an intrapreneur despite the system. I had hoped to explain how managers could create an environment supportive of innovation and intrapreneuring.

This book addresses both subjects, because understanding the basic barriers to intrapreneuring is useful both to would-be intrapreneurs and to their managers. In fact, most of the book is devoted to explaining how corporations and intrapreneurs interact, not to prescribing what to do about it.

Even when I direct my words specifically to intrapreneurs or to managers, I want the other group to listen in. By addressing intrapreneuring from both points of view, I hope to raise the level of dialogue about innovation and to make intrapreneurs, managers, and their organizations more effective.

Right now, our society honors entrepreneurs, senior executives and inventors, but rarely intrapreneurs. If big companies want to quicken the pace of innovation and be cost effective at it, they must honor and empower intrapreneurs. Through this book, I hope to encourage and point the way for both intrapreneurs and those managers who want to help them flourish.

—Gifford Pinchot III
January 1985

An Intrapreneurial Honor Roll

The following intrapreneurs played a hands-on and courageous role in driving the innovations and businesses listed with them into being against obstacles that easily justified quitting. Each would be quick to say that he or she had a lot of help, which is inevitable because they are not just inventors or idea people. In making a business happen, they had no choice but to depend on others.

HULKI ALDIKACTI	The Pontiac Fiero sports car
AVA ALLEN JIM GEORGE JIM MAYS	NBI's separate supplies business
ALVIN BOESE	3M—the nonwoven industry
DICK BRATT	Norton—abrasives from waste
PAGE BURR	Kollmorgen—Multiwire® automatic wiring process and Multiwire® interconnect boards
A. B. COHEN	Du Pont—Riston® printed circuit materials
BRIAN EHLERS	Apple's computer graphics tablet and plotter
P. D. ESTRIDGE	IBM's personel computer
ALEC FEINER	AT&T—the Ferreed switch, System 75 and Horizon® PBX
GENE FRANZ PAUL BREEDLOVE	Texas Instruments—Speak-n-Spell®
ART FRY	3M—Post-it® Note Pads

RUBEN GUTOFF JOHN WELCH	General Electric's engineering plastics business
RICHIE HERRINK	IBM—corporate training
MALCOLM HODGE	TRW—optical fiber connectors
CHUCK HOUSE	Hewlett-Packard—The "electronic lens" CRT display
H. K. (BUD) HEBELER	Boeing—energy and environment business
LEE IACCOCA	The Ford Mustang
JUDITH DARIEN KLEIN	Exxon Enterprises—management development and training for entrepreneurial start-ups
MICHAEL KRANFUS	Ford—the SVO Mustang
STEPHANIE L. KWOLEK	Du Pont—Kevlar® aramid fiber
LEW LEHR	3M—health-care business
WILL LEWIS	G.E.'s Clinton Job Corps Training center
BERNIE LOOMIS	General Mills—Kenner Toys such as Star Wars® and Strawberry Shortcake® lines
DICK NADEAU	Du Pont's automatic clinical analyzer, the ACA
HUGH PARKS	Martin Marietta—Copperhead (laser guided missile)
MICHAEL PHILLIPS	Master Charge and Bank of California's CDs
JIM RUSH	G.E.'s Gemlink® microwave data communications system

MATT SANDERS	Convergent Technologies—Workslate® and innovative work stations
JOHN L. WEBB	Xerox—the 2600 and other innovative copiers
JOHN DAGNEAU	Atlantic Cement's cement dust business
STUART SANDO DICK CLOVER	Intel's bubble memory business
CLARENCE L. (KELLY) JOHNSON	Lockheed—the first U.S. tactical jet fighter (1943), the Starfighter, the U-2, the SR-71

Please send recommendations (names, affiliations, and accomplishments) of intrapreneurs who should be included in future Honor Rolls to:

The International Institute of Intrapreneurs
Box 111 Cedar Swamp Road
Deep River, Connecticut 06417

BOOK I

THE INTRAPRENEURS

CHAPTER 1

The New Intrapreneurial Spirit

Good news! While much of American industry may have lost ground to international competition, our entrepreneurial sector is the envy of the world. Japanese businessmen who came to the United States twenty years ago to study the miracle of American management come today to study our venture capital system.

However you measure it, U.S. entrepreneurial activity is growing. Business start-ups, which averaged 1,800 a day in 1950 and 4,000 in 1960, increased to an estimated 12,000 a day in 1983. From 1970 to 1980 small new businesses added 20 million new jobs, while the *Fortune* 500 companies added none. *Fortune* 500 companies *lost* 3 million jobs from 1980 to 1983, while companies less than ten years old added 750,000.*

The vigor of our entrepreneurial spirit is the United States' greatest business treasure. Our childhood fantasies still have more to do with taming the frontier and breaking free from tyranny than with advancing steadily toward the heights of vast organizations. Unlike the Japanese or most European nations, we lack a homogeneous culture and the manners for deference to authority. This makes it very difficult for most of us to accept the role of respected cog in a vast industrial machine. But we do have a spirit of self-reliance, adventure, and willingness to try new things. The result is that while we are poor at regimentation, we have a full measure of the entrepreneurial spirit.

In this time of rapid economic and technological change, the entrepreneurial spirit can be a unique and important advantage, but only if we learn to use it. Intrapreneurship is

* David Birch, Director, MIT Program on Neighborhoods and Regional Change, Cambridge, Mass.

a method of using the entrepreneurial spirit where many of our best people and resources are: in large organizations.

For a while things looked bad for the entrepreneurial spirit in the United States. Much of our society deplored bigness in the 1960s, yet almost everyone imagined a future of fewer and larger organizations. In 1870, 80 percent of working Americans were self-employed. Today only 7 percent are, although according to Milton Stewart, editor of *Inc. Magazine*, seven times that number would like to be.° Although the tide has turned back toward smallness, half of us still work in organizations of over 100 people.†

Our society is caught in a tug of war between bigness and smallness. We yearn for the personal satisfaction, independence, and freedom of small organizations. But we cannot return to being a nation of small proprietorships, because the tasks of modern society are too complex. Although we have greatly overestimated the advantages of bigness, tasks like making automobiles, building space shuttles, and even distributing soap are still more efficiently done on a relatively large scale. *What is needed is a way to have the advantages of both bigness and smallness at once.*

Among the many ways to combine the large and the small are joint ventures, R&D partnerships, licensing, marketing agreements, and, above all, the voluntary interaction of large firms buying from smaller ones. One time-honored method is subcontracting. On large-scale projects and complex products, a big firm becomes the system's integrator, and many smaller firms produce components and supporting services. For example, major aerospace projects are orchestrated by firms that parcel out the task to numerous smaller subcontractors, and even the subcontractors have subcontractors. Big firms work the big picture and small firms sweat the details.

In automobiles, the Japanese have learned to use subcon-

° *Inc. Magazine*, May 1981, p. 7.

† David Birch, Director, MIT Program on Neighborhoods and Regional Change.

tractors better than we do. Instead of holding them at arm's length and buffeting them with an antagonistic purchasing system, they establish long-term relationships of mutual service and trust. Only with such mutual trust can large firms such as Toyota depend on such small entrepreneurial suppliers, who routinely drive onto the assembly floor to deliver inventories just in time to keep the line going.

We too can build an environment that honors a more cooperative relationship between customer and vendors, and it will be very valuable to do so. In addition, many organizations profit from the virtues of smallness, like flexibility and the feeling of ownership within the walls of the company. What they need is employees who behave like entrepreneurs.

Many organizations are working on encouraging intrapreneurs. 3M's chairman, Lew Lehr, said in 1983:

> For many years the corporate structure [at 3M] has been designed specifically to encourage young entrepreneurs to take an idea and run with it. If they succeed, they can and do find themselves running their own business under the 3M umbrella.
>
> The entrepreneurial approach is not a sideline at 3M. It is the heart of our design for growth.[*]

This approach is not limited to 3M. Jack Welch, General Electric Company chairman, announced in 1982 that he was "trying to reshape GE . . . as a band of small businesses . . . to take the strength of a large company and act with the agility of a small company."[†]

Nor is interest in intrapreneuring limited to the United States. Anders Wall, president and chief executive of Beijerinvest of Sweden, a major European conglomerate that includes Volvo and many other concerns, said this in 1980:

> Today we must support people with ideas and initiative—

---

[*] Lew Lehr, "Dreaming in Color: The Engineer as Entrepreneur," speech given at University of Nebraska, April 2, 1983.

[†] "GE's Wizards Turning from the Bottom Line to Share of the Market," *Wall Street Journal*, July 12, 1982, p. 1.

5

the entrepreneurs—because they are *agents of change* and our hope for the future. Experience shows that successful companies are those who have *initiated* change in technology, marketing or organization and managed to *keep a lead* in changes over competitors. Therefore, entrepreneurs are needed not only to start new business ventures on a small scale, but also to put life into existing companies, especially the large ones.

The trouble is entrepreneurs and large companies do not seem to get on well together, although they should need each other. The entrepreneur needs the resources of a large company to try his ideas on. The large company needs the innovative force and initiative of an entrepreneur. But the entrepreneur likes to be his own boss and the organization of a large company usually gives little room for independence.°

For a brief time we believed that carefully planned new-product processes could replace the disorder of entrepreneurial passion. Study after study has proved this false. Innovation almost never happens in large organizations without an individual or small group passionately dedicated to making it happen. When such people start up new companies, they are called entrepreneurs. Inside large organizations we call them intrapreneurs.

The importance of intrapreneurs is most evident after they leave. Ed Roberts, of MIT's Sloan School of Management, followed 39 innovators who left a single Route 128 corporation to found enterprises of their own. Roberts and his colleagues found that after five years nearly 85 percent of the new businesses were flourishing. In fact the combined sales volume of the 33 remaining entrepreneurships was two-and-one-half times that of their founders' ex-employer.†

The importance of intrapreneurs is evident even in failure:

° Speech to the Swedish-American Chamber of Commerce, New York City, April 23, 1980. Courtesy of the Foresight Group and Mr. Anders Wall.

† Ed Roberts, personal communication.

When Texas Instruments studied fifty or so of its new-product introductions, both successful and unsuccessful, a startling fact emerged. Every *failed* product—without exception—lacked a zealous volunteer champion. What was missing was the intrapreneur. In fact, the more we look at innovation, the more we find intrapreneurs.

As companies mature, the simple-minded entrepreneurial devotion to product superiority, effectiveness, and efficiency is usually displaced by a maze of bureaucratic systems. That is no longer good enough. The more rapidly American business learns to use the entrepreneurial talent inside large organizations, the better. The alternative in a time of rapid change is stagnation and decline. As we free ourselves from small-minded consistency and double-checking, the world will once again see that freedom works. In fact, in the new economic era we are now entering, it may turn out that nothing else will do.

THE COMING INNOVATION AGE

I am not one of those who believe that the United States will cease to be an industrial power by ceding all brutish businesses to the Third World and becoming a mere purveyor of information. In fact, I fail to understand how we will ever manage the balance of payments without making large quantities of physical goods, both for use at home and for export. Certainly we cannot maintain our competitive advantage in the world by spending even more time satisfying the needs of information-hungry bureaucracies.

Central to our strength is the willingness of our entrepreneurial types to combine strong conceptual skills with "dirt-under-the-fingernails" action. Few other nations have such a bent for practical genius. It is true that we are spending and will continue to spend more time thinking and less time pounding, wrenching, and cranking, but that does *not* mean that thought and information will become our major products.

Consider what happened as we moved from the agricultural age to the industrial age. The United States remained a major agricultural producer despite the industrial revolution, but the way we grew crops changed. Today a larger and larger portion of agricultural value is created by industrial means. Farm labor has become a tiny part of a giant complex of industries that make tractors, agricultural chemicals, fuels, veterinary medicines, and rubber boots. A similar change will occur in the industrial sector as we enter what is called the Information Age. The information explosion will not eliminate industrial production in the United States, but it will change how it is done and change the factors that produce industrial success.

In the future, the products made in advanced nations will derive less of their value from either blue-collar labor or capital goods and more from the quality of thought and innovation that go into them. This will occur because our competitive advantage will be based on doing things differently and better or producing products that no country with lower-cost labor has yet learned to make. As information on how to make existing products and to operate existing processes becomes increasingly well-distributed in the Third World, old and unchanging industries will migrate from the advanced nations to countries with cheaper labor and raw materials. This apparently grim fact puts us on an innovation treadmill: We must continuously innovate just to stay where we are. Indeed, the faster the rest of the world learns to adapt and change, the faster we must innovate to stay ahead. Nor is acquisition the answer to our dilemma. We are being forced out of a world of stable businesses that can be bought and sold as if they have enduring value as they are. We have entered a world of constant change where certainties don't exist and productivity in innovation is becoming as important as productivity in production. But this is no cause for alarm. Not only is the world of innovation more fun, but it is a world in which America's entrepreneurial and intrapreneurial talent can prove the decisive advantage.

Calling these times the "information age" draws attention to the nature of the changes taking place but gives few clues to most companies on how to respond. Not all companies can produce computers, telecommunications, and data bases. There are many whose basic business is not selling, transmitting, and storing information. Such companies may feel like second-class citizens in the information age and may make counter-productive responses such as high-tech glamor acquisitions or loss of hope and self-esteem. They will find that the best response they can make to the explosion of new information is to find ways to use it to be better at the kinds of businesses they already know—in other words, to innovate. For these companies, this is more productively called the innovation age.

Most people sense that we need to give greater freedom in our large organizations to produce more innovation, but they also fear that the price of loosening controls will be chaos. Simultaneously giving greater freedom and getting greater coordination and cooperation may seem like a paradox, or at best a utopian dream. But the history of humanity is a rocky climb toward ways of working together that produce simultaneously more cooperation and more freedom.

The sullen acquiescence of pharaoh's slaves was good enough to build the pyramids, but that same literal-minded slave labor could never have accomplished John F. Kennedy's goal "to put a man on the moon by the end of the decade." Higher levels of cooperation engaging mind, heart, and soul are possible only among those who are free.

Freedom for employees wasn't always important. Norman Macrae, an editor of the London *Economist* and an early champion of intrapreneuring, explains:

> During the Henry Ford manufacturing age about forty of the world's 159 countries grew rich because they were temporarily able to increase productivity efficiently by organizational action from the top: i.e., executives sat at some level in the offices of hierarchically run corporations and arranged how those below them on the assembly lines

could most productively work with their hands.

This method of growing rich has now run into two rather fundamental difficulties: a "people problem" because educated workers in rich countries do not like to be organized from the top; and an "enterprise problem" because, now that much of manufacturing and most of the simple white collar tasks can be gradually automated so that more workers can become brain-workers, it will be nonsense to sit in hierarchical offices trying to arrange what people in the offices below do with their imaginations.°

The Innovation Age is actually a natural partner of the information age. Despite all the new information we have, there is a bottleneck—not from creating information nor storing it nor even from gaining access to it—the bottleneck is in using new information to do new things.

For a brief time as we automated production, it did look as if we were to become a nation of clerks dedicated to shuffling more and more paper about less and less action. Fortunately, this dismal view is false. New knowledge creates the opportunity to do new things in new ways that make old ways obsolete.

Our new efficiency in creating and distributing knowledge means we live in an age in which the ability to innovate effectively has become the primary determinant of business success. When the competition is innovating well—creating new or improved products, services, or processes—one must innovate or die. But this means organizations must give their employees freedoms that are more akin to those of entrepreneurs.

We are poised on the brink of another great leap forward in effectiveness by achieving higher levels of both freedom and cooperation—and therefore productivity. The experiments in intrapreneuring spontaneously appearing in many of our more progressive firms are harbingers of a new and more

° "The Coming Entrepreneurial Revolution: A Survey," *The Economist*, December 25, 1976, pp. 41–42.

effective pattern for working together, a pattern by which organizations can comprehend and manage the complexity of our times. No one yet fully understands that emerging pattern, but we are all contributing to it as it unfolds.

In the future intrapreneurs will do an increasing portion of the corporation's work. The large corporation will become an umbrella under which numerous small intrapreneurial groups interact in voluntary patterns too complex and synergistic to be planned from above.

THE STATE OF INNOVATION IN LARGE FIRMS

Innovation does not mean invention. Invention is the act of genius in creating a new concept for a potentially useful new device or service. In innovation, that is just the beginning. When the invention is done, the second half of innovation begins: turning the new idea into a business success. This second step may be called implementation, commercial development, new-venture creation, or any of a host of other names; it is as essential to innovation as thinking of the idea in the first place.

The Implementation Crisis

You might think that larger organizations would be stodgy in thinking up new ideas but, because of a wealth of management talent, would be very good at executing them. It turns out, however, that just the reverse is true: Our large organizations are producing large numbers of good ideas but generally are unable to implement them.

A prime beneficiary of large organizations' inability to implement innovation is the venture-capital community. There is a frequent pattern in which exciting new technologies are developed in large firms but their implementation bogs down in a morass of analysis, approvals, and politics. When such opportunities are rejected by a large firm, the dissatisfaction often drives the would-be intrapreneur into entrepreneurship. Ed De Castro couldn't get Digital Equipment, to back his revolutionary new computer, so he left and formed Data General, which became the fourth largest U.S. computer manufacturer and a major competitor of Digital Equipment. Steve Wozniac couldn't get Hewlett-Packard to take an interest in small computers. He very reluctantly left to join Steve Jobs, who couldn't sell a similar idea to Atari. They formed Apple Computers. Both their former employers probably wish they had listened to these entrepreneurs when they were trying to be intrapreneurs. Both have belatedly entered the personal computer market.

The "raids" of venture capitalists on both the people and technologies of large firms have become so frequent that Gordon Moore, chairman of Intel, calls them "vulture capitalists" who are hurting U.S. product-development efforts by luring away key employees. George Pake, group vice president for Palo Alto Research Center at Xerox, is concerned about small firms exploiting new technology but not creating it. "If you take these people away [from large companies] where will the advances of the 1990s come from?"[*]

Whether for good or ill, the lure of entrepreneuring has increased markedly in recent years. The official venture capital "war chest" has grown rapidly (Figure 1-1). More importantly, ordinary individuals have begun investing in entrepreneurial enterprises. Unless large firms find ways to make intrapreneuring more rewarding there is a grave danger of selectively losing their best innovators.

The meaning for large companies of this explosive growth of entrepreneuring is twofold:

1. **There will be a rapidly growing number of sophisticated new competitors for all or part of any business.**

   They will segment markets minutely and take away every niche that the company doesn't actively defend.

[*] *Business Week,* April 18, 1983, p. 89.

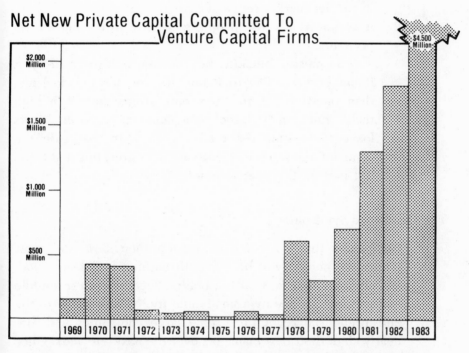

Net New Private Capital Committed To Venture Capital Firms

Figure 1-1 The ways of managing innovators that worked in 1975 will not work in 1985. There is 200 times as much venture capital available that enables them to leave and start their own businesses.

These competitors will attack with new technology. They will be more sophisticated and better funded than most entrepreneurs of yore. To defend against these focused attacks, companies will need large numbers of intrapreneurs to apply new technologies and operate responsively in smaller market segments.

2. **A corporation's best people will leave to become entrepreneurs.**

Businesses outside the glamour industries are not immune. According to Peter Drucker, a good deal less than one-third of the new entrepreneuring is in high tech.° Even in high-tech companies creative engineers leave to become real-estate tycoons. In that case the company doesn't have another competitor, but it still has lost part of its power to innovate.

The Deadwood Syndrome

Companies that don't learn to keep their best and most innovative people will be left with nothing but dead wood. We all know that most of the really effective work in middle management is done by a small minority. Now, because of the entrepreneurial revolution, some large companies will lose nearly all of their best managers over the next ten years. Once the exodus starts the remaining good people despair and the rate of selective departure accelerates. Soon, without realizing it, the company is staffed by the walking dead. Many corporate giants of today will be gone in thirty years. Finding a way to motivate and keep intrapreneurs is the most important strategic issue of our times.

Behind the success of venture capitalists is a very simple fact: They offer both intrapreneurs and investors a better deal than large companies do. Investors are taking money from the stocks of more mature companies and pouring it into venture capital funds. They are moving billions of dollars because the

° *Harvard Business Review*, vol. 62, no. 1, Jan.–Feb. 1984, p. 60.

returns are better with the venture capitalists. The returns are better because venture capitalists are managing innovation more profitably than most of the large corporations with whom they are competing for funds. They can outperform the corporations, in many cases with cast-off ideas those corporations developed, because they have a fundamentally better approach to the management of innovation. When large companies learn to be more effective in implementing their own ideas, they will become more than competitive with venture capital.

The Venture Capital Laboratory

The differences between corporate venture groups and private venture capital groups put in bold relief the effect of corporate cultures and systems on innovation. Corporate venture groups were very popular in the 1960s and early 1970s; in fact, between one-quarter to one-third of the *Fortune* 500 companies established venture groups during that period. But very few of them from that period remain in operation today.*

The failure of corporate venture groups is at first surprising, because intelligent people set out to imitate the successful pattern of venture capitalists. In addition to money, they had the resources of the corporation to draw on. But, as it turned out, being inside the larger corporation also produced a different way of operating.

The difference begins with the method of selecting investments: In selecting a project to implement, most large companies focus on an exhaustive analysis of the business concept and business plan. Sensible though this sounds, venture capitalists, whose sole business is the commercial phase of innovation, have found through experience that this is a poor way to select investments. Instead, the venture capitalist follows the maxim: **"I'd rather have a Class A entrepreneur**

* Norman Fast, "A Visit to the New Venture Graveyard," *Research Management,* March 1979, p. 18.

with a Class B idea than a Class A idea with a Class B entrepreneur."

The reason the venture capitalist bets more on the person than on the idea is because a business plan changes more rapidly than does a person's character. The reason corporations have such trouble with innovation is that most planning systems fail to take into account the unpredictability of innovation. They are too inflexible to allow quality intrapreneurs to turn on a dime as circumstances change.

We are trained to plan as shown in Figure 1-2.

First, one sets a goal, then over an extended period one plans how to achieve it. Finally, having wasted nothing but paper, time, and market research, one takes action based on a fully formed plan. One expects, of course, *minor* variations from the plan, but managers are judged competent to the degree that they minimize these variations.

How different this model is from the actual pattern of innovation, as shown in Figure 1-3. Innovations do not proceed smoothly from defining goals through planning to implementation of the plan. Despite the apparent rationality of later recountings, *innovations never happen as planned* because no one can accurately plan something that is really new! Instead, the early stages of innovation consist of groping toward a vision, counting one's progress by what can be learned from mistakes, until at last one grasps a pattern worth repeating.

Scotch tape was first developed to seal cellophane around insulation bats in refrigerated railroad cars. Despite a lengthy effort and close contact with potential customers, there were no sales in this market at all. But Dick Drew, the tape's inventor, was persistent. He found he could sell it to retail merchants to close cellophane packages. Though successful, all involved agreed its sales would never reach $1 million per year. Then six months after Dick introduced cellophane tape to this second market, Du Pont found a way to heat-seal cellophane and the tape's second raison d'être disappeared. But by then the product had an unpredicted life of its own, one that no one could have predicted. Merchants continued

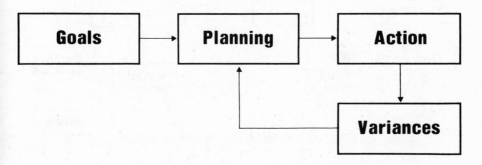

Traditional Planning Cycle

Goals → **Planning** → **Action** → **Variances**

Figure 1-2

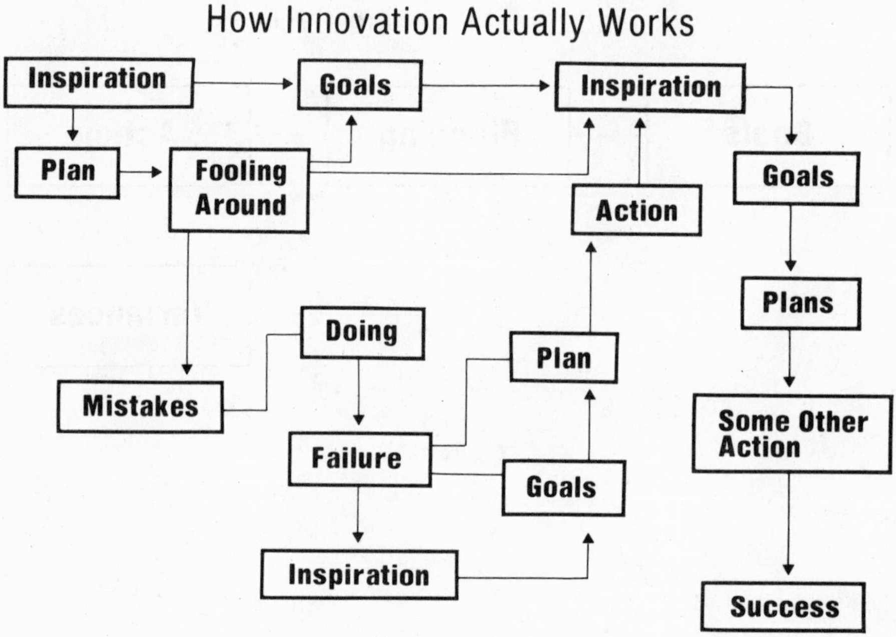
How Innovation Actually Works
Inspiration
Goals
Inspiration
Plan
Fooling Around
Goals
Action
Plans
Doing
Plan
Mistakes
Some Other Action
Failure
Goals
Inspiration
Success

Figure 1-3

to use it to seal paper packages. But the real surprise was that Depression-era families began buying it to fix and patch everything from books to falling plaster. From a series of failures, there emerged a highly profitable business.°

Credit for this success goes not just to Dick Drew, but also to the flexibility he was given to continue trying. Flexibility is an important ingredient missing in many corporate environments.

The venture-capital system is effective because it empowers the entrepreneur to act swiftly and decisively in response to new information. Intrapreneurs and entrepreneurs are hands-on people who deeply experience their new businesses. Their judgments are informed not just monthly by reports and presentations but daily by such subtleties as the smile of a customer or a passing remark from three years before. To benefit from their experience-driven intuition, one must give intrapreneurs freedom to act. Seasoned investors have learned to get the best of entrepreneurs' intuition by choosing good people and letting them run their own businesses. They look for people who are so deeply—even irrationally—committed to making their ventures succeed that almost no amount of surprises and setbacks will stop them. Considering the normally erratic path of innovation, this investment strategy makes more sense than depending primarily on the quality of the original plan, which generally becomes obsolete the moment it begins to be used.

Corporate America is now becoming aware of both the threat and the good example of entrepreneurs. Corporations are dividing businesses into smaller units, freeing those units from unnecessary controls, and empowering intrapreneurs to act. The results have been promising.
• Decentralization and encouragement of intrapreneurship allows Hewlett-Packard to produce eight new products per week.

° *Our Story So Far: Notes from the First 75 Years of 3M Company,* Minnesota Mining and Manufacturing Company, St. Paul, Mn., 1977, pp. 71–74.

- Five years ago the automobile industry was hopelessly bureaucratic. Now important experiments have led to intrapreneurial teams developing cars such as Fiero and Ford S.V.O.'s Mustang.
- National Cash Register's Entry Systems Division has become so entrepreneurial that 50 percent of its revenues come from products introduced within the last year.

Events everywhere are helping corporations to realize the need for intrapreneurs. The information explosion is encouraging businesses to move away from hierarchical systems to systems in which innovators act as equals with others who form an informal support system. This shift into intrapreneuring has its parallel in developments in computer systems. First there was the mainframe, one per corporation, as befitted highly centralized, hierarchical organizations. Then minicomputers were introduced and dispersed at the division level paralleling divisional autonomy. Now personal computers have emerged everywhere focusing on local tasks. Intrapreneuring is the organizational analog of the personal computer revolution. Computer systems now serve users rather than data processing executives. Similarly, intrapreneuring decentralizes the corporation and shifts attention from the hierarchy to the individual.

Even the type of leaders emerging in the Innovation Age will differ vastly from the managers who got us where we are today. Older virtues will re-emerge as more important than the powerful analytical skills we have only recently learned to use. Analytical tools will become subordinate to courage, intuition, and the ability to place trust wisely. Top management will face the formidable task of integrating the efforts of a number of visionary leaders—each of whom is balancing the needs, ambitions, and results of a small army of restless intrapreneurs—with the need for corporate stability.

If you are an intrapreneur, you already know the importance of your role, so don't let yourself be sold short. Take the responsibility for making the system support the imple-

mentation of your vision. Make sure you get the freedom you
need to do your job. The corporation needs you as an
intrapreneur, not as a disgruntled and inactive cynic. Most
important, if you are truly an intrapreneur, don't allow yourself
to be shoved aside. There is a crying need for you—if not in
your present company, then in another, more enlightened
one.

THE INTRAPRENEUR'S TEN COMMANDMENTS

1. Come to work each day willing to be fired.

2. Circumvent any orders aimed at stopping your dream.

3. Do any job needed to make your project work, regardless of your job description.

4. Find people to help you.

5. Follow your intuition about the people you choose, and work only with the best.

6. Work underground as long as you can—publicity triggers the corporate immune mechanism.

7. Never bet on a race unless you are running in it.

8. Remember it is easier to ask for forgiveness than for permission.

9. Be true to your goals, but be realistic about the ways to achieve them.

10. Honor your sponsors.

PROFILE

CHUCK HOUSE: Growing from
Employee to Intrapreneur

Chuck House's career as an intrapreneur illustrates the problems most intrapreneurs encounter and overcome, even in companies with extraordinarily supportive cultures. Hewlett-Packard is a company with a well-deserved reputation for tolerating independent action. As Lew Randall, a Silicon Valley venture capitalist, pointed out, "There is probably no other company of its size in which it is so easy to bootleg a new project." But life is not easy for intrapreneurs anywhere, not even at Hewlett-Packard. So Chuck House discovered. He was twenty-six and had been with the company only a few years. In typical intrapreneurial style, he overcame dozens of "insurmountable" barriers and, with the help of a dedicated team, got a product into use in record time.

Since becoming an intrapreneur, Chuck has been involved in one way or another with the beginnings of nearly 20 percent of Hewlett-Packard's major product lines. Although he stresses that at Hewlett-Packard everything is done by teams, that is not a bad record of innovation for one person in a company with 6,000 people in the research labs alone.

Yet Chuck's intrapreneurial success was not the result of any unusual role in the company; quite to the contrary, his career has proceeded along rather traditional company lines. But between those lines we can see the personal style of the consummate intrapreneur.

Chuck's first project to become an intrapreneurial venture— as opposed to a standard Hewlett-Packard project—was the moon-lander monitor, which used a cathode-ray tube similar to a television picture tube but able to reproduce rapid events a TV could not capture. The project allowed NASA scientists, peering at the new monitors, to follow telemetry data readouts and watch the historic pictures of the first moon walk with decent resolution.

Among the monitor team members sharing pride in the success at Cape Canaveral on July 20, 1969 was Chuck's close friend and colleague, Milt Russell, a veteran designer of the display monitors used in computer systems. His designs included the high-speed SAC monitors in the Cheyenne Mountain NORAD headquarters, which in the days before the first space walk were awkwardly large, the tube stretching back over four feet behind the picture screen. Milt had been trying to solve this size problem— using an electronic lens to give a wide-angle dispersion of the image over a short distance—and to produce a compact high-speed monitor much like the familiar TV set.

This idle experimentation might have gone nowhere without a boost from the Federal Aviation Administration which asked for bids on building a new control tower monitor. One of Chuck's senior managers thought the electronic lens might give Hewlett-Packard the design advantage it needed to win the competitive bidding. He was looking for volunteers to take on this challenge. At the time, Chuck was a frustrated oscilloscope designer upset because people weren't listening to his ideas. His concern was particularly focused on the observation that people were buying Hewlett-Packard oscilloscopes and then using them for something else. This "misuse" seemed to Chuck like an arrow pointing to a broader market, but no one would listen. The FAA project was an opportunity to prove his point. Here was a project intended to extend oscilloscope technology into a new kind of market.

Observing the use of a product for something else entirely is a powerful message to intrapreneurs. In order to pursue a corollary market, however, one must break through the "collective wisdom" about "what business we are in." In companies where the official use of a product or service is generally well thought of, the new use often seems insignificant or "wrong."

Therefore, successful intrapreneurs must often find ways to graft their new ideas onto existing management goals and percep- tions. Because Chuck's enthusiasm now matched up with some-thing Hewlett-Packard wanted, he had no difficulty getting a three-month, two-person exploratory project approved.

He met with Milt Russell, and together with a few others excitedly began to build a display using the electronic lens. Their screen had just as large an area, yet was half the size and weight of other monitors and twenty times as fast. Better still, it used a fraction of the power required by others, but produced a brighter display.

Despite all these advantages, the monitor was a failure. Just hours after completing the prototype, the team saw it would never meet FAA specifications, which demanded a very high resolution picture so air traffic controllers could read the code numbers that identified each airplane they were monitoring. The Hewlett-Packard prototype failed to reproduce the minute numbers.

Some people might have tried to improve the technology to meet FAA specifications. Others might have given up, which is in fact what Chuck's supervisors encouraged him to do. But Chuck did neither. Moreover, he refused to spend an indefinite amount of time fighting for permission to improve the product, for a very simple reason: It seemed useful to him as it was.

Like most successful intrapreneurs, Chuck was able to see success in apparent failure. Having begun with a broad vision of a market need and not just the FAA's request for a monitor, he was not deterred from his purpose by that single failure. He believed in using oscilloscope technology to build displays for other uses. Now he had a prototype with unique properties that he liked. He decided to find out what it was good for by taking it to potential customers and asking them. At that moment he crossed the threshold from engineer to intrapreneur.

It was winter in Colorado, where Hewlett-Packard had stationed him, and he longed for the California sun, so Chuck decided to conduct his own market survey in California. In those days the roles in Hewlett-Packard were traditionally defined, and engineers were not expected to conduct market research. Furthermore, because the project had failed to reach its technical goals, Chuck's boss resisted spending any more money on it. But Chuck persisted, arguing that it was prudent to invest $2,000 looking for other applications before killing a technology whose development had already cost over $75,000. His prototype did, after all, produce faster, lighter, brighter, and more energy-efficient displays. The budget finally approved was more frugal than Chuck had hoped for, but his California trip was on. He loaded his family into his VW and shipped the monitor by air. At each stop along the way he checked his family into a motel, removed the front seat on the passenger side, drove to the airport to pick up the monitor, then transported it to potential customers in the space the front seat normally occupied.

All this was in violation of a cardinal Hewlett-Packard rule: You do not show prototypes to customers. The rule was based on company security. Employees had to keep valuable technology secret until it appeared in finished form. Chuck felt he was abiding by the spirit of the policy if not the letter. He reasoned that there was no sense in being careful with a technology that was going to be scrapped. In two weeks he lugged the prototype to forty computer manufacturers and potential end-users, asking each one what it might be good for and how it needed to be improved. By hooking up the prototype to his potential customers' equipment and working with them, he could see the monitor's real potential as well as its flaws.

Returning to Colorado armed with the new market data, he was able to get permission to continue with a team for eighteen months. Chuck immediately realized that the team's commitment to the project was essential to its success. He explained his broad vision of the monitor project to them: the opportunities he saw in "misuses" of oscilloscopes as displays and what he had begun to learn about their potential customers when he lugged his first model about in his car.

He had the wisdom to let the team share in building the detailed vision of what they would work on together. Milt Russell, who had come from GE's defense group, saw great potential for monitors in defense work and took the group to visit defense installations and talk to customers there. Tom Bohley had just come from the University of Missouri; his wife Abby was a nurse, so Tom saw medical applications. The team worked on applications for operating rooms and nurses' stations. Al DeVilbiss, who had been at the Jet Propulsion Laboratory before joining Hewlett-Packard, wanted to work on applications for the Space Center, which particularly excited Chuck as well. Mankind was about to realize one of its great dreams, and Chuck wanted to be part of that dream.

Their time in the lab refining the product was interspersed with valuable on-site meetings with potential customers, trying a monitor for a particular application and expanding their understanding of customer needs. Often the only useful market research for something new is watching the customer try it out. The team found that interest in their new, less expensive, high-speed monitor was strong wherever they went.

Then came the annual division review, when senior management, including Messrs. Hewlett and Packard themselves, visited every division and reviewed its progress.

To Chuck's great disappointment, his monitor project suffered a disastrous review. The marketing people had done some telephone surveys and found that few of their customers were interested in "a somewhat blurry display," regardless of price, size, or weight. They projected a total market of thirty-two units. Chuck argued that the marketing had failed to understand his strategy for marketing the product. They had called only upon oscilloscope customers, the only customers they knew. New applications required new customers, Chuck explained. Besides, the device was difficult to describe: because it was new, only demonstrations could uncover its salability. Moreover, an angry House concluded the marketing manager's estimate of only thirty-two monitors sold was off by at least 6 percent, because the man hadn't surveyed Chuck's father who promised Chuck he would buy two himself.

Unfortunately in 1966, people seldom understood that intrapreneurs take responsibility for all aspects of creating their new business. To the Hewlett-Packard management Chuck House was an engineer who, by straying over into marketing, was operating beyond his expertise. They could easily see from his agitation and tone that he was "prejudiced" and so rejected his opinions in favor of the objective marketing experts.

We now know that intrapreneurs almost always do their own market research, and that it is generally more thorough and more effective in finding new markets than that provided by uninvolved marketers. We know enough now to call the passion that was then called "a lack of objectivity" by a more apt name: "commitment."

Not only did Chuck encounter resistance from his own division's marketing group, but he also locked horns with the chief corporate engineer who was a great supporter of a competing technology then in its early stages of development in the central labs. This situation plagues intrapreneurs. (One of Xerox's more successful intrapreneurial groups calls it the "Pretty Girl Over the Hill Syndrome," wherein people reject the intrapreneur's workable prototype on the basis of a comparison to promises from a project idea that may never succeed.)

After the presentation, in a meeting with Chuck's senior division manager, Dave Packard made it clear that he wanted Chuck's project aborted for three reasons: First, the division's own marketing didn't support it; second, corporate technology gave it a negative vote; and third, the division was in the middle of a struggle for supremacy in its base business—oscilloscopes—and shouldn't be distracted by such a diversionary project. Packard's verdict was blunt: "When I come back next year I don't want to see that project in the lab!"

Chuck's boss's superior, Dar Howard, brought him the bad news. However, despite Packard's rejection (which must have implied some criticism of Dar), he was still supportive. But as he put it, "What defense can we create for continuing the project?" Chuck's response: "If we have it in production before he returns, Packard won't find it in the lab."

Dar looked at him in disbelief, "But it is a two-year project; we could never finish it in one year!" Undeterred, Chuck replied, "Give me ten minutes and I'll see if the team thinks it can be done." The team's commitment was so great that Chuck came back in 10 minutes with their agreement to accept the challenge. Letting the team decide this matter for themselves helped create the unity necessary to accept the sacrifices of a crash program.

It was not a banner day for rational management when Dar decided to let the team continue in the face of Packard's unequivocal command. But he was that kind of leader, courageous and willing to back his own people all the way. The project went underground, but continued in double time.

Not surprisingly, the marketing people continued their fight against the project. But the team had come too far to give up easily, and the race was on. More than once Chuck turned to his potential customers, prevailing upon them to call the Hewlett-Packard decision makers and plead his case. When his immediate boss, John Strathma, examined the divergence of Chuck's data from the findings of the marketing department, he visited five of Chuck's potential customers to check on their reported interest in the monitors. Fortunately, the results of those checks confirmed Chuck's stories; he had been very careful not to exaggerate the truth.

When Dave Packard returned a year later, the monitor was on the market. No trace of it remained in the lab, but it pretty clearly wasn't dead. "I thought we decided to kill this idea!" he exclaimed, somewhere between amusement and impatience. It took courage to remind him of his exact words and to point out that they had literally complied with his instructions of the previous year. By then the sales numbers were encouraging and it was, after all, gratifying to have Hewlett-Packard equipment in use at the space center. By not staying mad but rather celebrating a courageous intrapreneur, Packard took another step in creating the Hewlett-Packard culture, which values courage and independent action over obedience.

Chuck House and his team built three versions of the product and all achieved glory in their first year. The moon monitor was used to support man's first trip to the moon. The medical monitor was used by DeBakey in the first artificial heart transplant. Even the large-screen oscilloscope designed for use in schools for classroom demonstrations appeared as a featured part of a technology system for special effects which won an Emmy award. Not a bad start for a young man who had defied the system and the role he had been given to transform his vision into a marketplace reality.

Chuck left the project after completing the third-generation product and reaching a little over $10 million in annual sales. The initial product lasted ten years without redesign and always had excellent margins. More important, it was the first nonoscilloscope graphics use of the electronic lens, which eventually found its way into nearly half of Hewlett-Packard's instruments.

Chuck attributes his success at intrapreneuring to three factors. Throughout, he was able to keep the project alive by staying in touch with the market. Several times he resurrected the project by calling on enthusiastic potential users for endorsement. His company might not believe him, but when the Ford Motor Company called his boss to plead his case, Chuck's credibility increased enormously.

Second, he feels that intrapreneurs need undisputed integrity. "It is important not to oversell your ideas to your company because you are asking for an audit. And if you don't pass the audit you won't get a second chance." Third, the intrapreneur needs sponsors who endorse and support him whenever a test of wills occurs. Chuck says, "You cannot carry the day by facts alone; you need someone more powerful to take the chance with you and shield you." These are common intrapreneurial patterns:

1. Chuck didn't give up.
2. He took the rough prototype to market soon after it was done.
3. He did the market research himself.
4. He had sufficient intrapreneurial commitment to combine work and personal life.
5. He learned rapidly from failure.
6. He rebounded with a revised plan because his vision for the business was far broader than a single product idea.
7. He had observed that a "misused" product is often a sign of an unfilled niche and remained open to new applications.
8. He saw strengths, not weaknesses, in a new and different product. He explored new uses for those differences himself.
9. He ignored direct orders to kill the project.
10. He let the whole team decide whether or not to take the risk and attempt the "impossible."

In addition Chuck was aided by three positive traits of his employer: The Hewlett-Packard tradition that allows engineers to pursue their dreams in small project teams proved stronger than

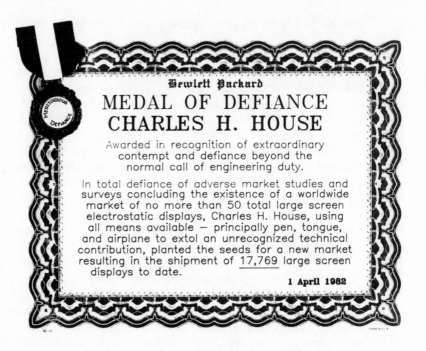

Hewlett Packard

MEDAL OF DEFIANCE
CHARLES H. HOUSE

Awarded in recognition of extraordinary
contempt and defiance beyond the
normal call of engineering duty.

In total defiance of adverse market studies and
surveys concluding the existence of a worldwide
market of no more than 50 total large screen
electrostatic displays, Charles H. House, using
all means available — principally pen, tongue,
and airplane to extol an unrecognized technical
contribution, planted the seeds for a new market
resulting in the shipment of 17,769 large screen
displays to date.

1 April 1982

a direct order by a founder of the company. Marketplace success is given more credence at Hewlett-Packard than the need for absolute obedience from employees. Hewlett-Packard has numerous "sponsors" throughout its technical management ranks, and as one of them, Dar Howard stepped forward at a critical time when the project was about to be cancelled.

The combination was a winner.

TEST

Are You an Intrapreneur?

Answer "Yes" or "No" to the following questions:

1. Does your desire to make things work better occupy as much of your time as fulfilling your duty to maintain them the way they are?
2. Do you get excited about what you are doing at work?
3. Do you think about new business ideas while driving to work or taking a shower?
4. Can you visualize concrete steps for action when you consider ways to make a new idea happen?
5. Do you get in trouble from time to time for doing things that exceed your authority?
6. Are you able to keep your ideas under cover, suppressing your urge to tell everyone about them until you have tested them and developed a plan for implementation?
7. Have you successfully pushed through bleak times when something you were working on looked like it might fail?
8. Do you have more than your share of both fans and critics?
9. Do you have a network of friends at work whom you can count on for help?
10. Do you get easily annoyed by others' incompetent attempts to execute portions of your ideas?
11. Can you consider trying to overcome a natural perfectionist tendency to do all the work yourself and share responsibility for your ideas with a team?
12. Would you be willing to give up some salary in exchange for the chance to try out your business idea if the rewards for success were adequate?

If you have answered yes more times than no, the chances are you are already behaving like an intrapreneur.

CHAPTER 2

Who Is the Intrapreneur?

For years everyone defined corporate success as moving up the hierarchy. Then companies recognized that individuals could make major contributions—without becoming managers—by inventing or making technical breakthroughs. Many innovative companies—IBM, Tektronix, 3M, and Texas Instruments among them—thus created a second career path through which inventors could win prestige and salary increases without assuming management roles.

Some people, however, have talents that neither of these career paths can develop. For them, intrapreneurship offers a third career path to bridge the gap between manager and inventor. Intrapreneurs, like entrepreneurs, are not necessarily inventors of new products or services. Their contribution is in taking new ideas or even working prototypes and turning them into profitable realities. When the ideas have become solid and functioning businesses, so that even the least imaginative of accountants can clearly see their value, intrapreneurs tend to grow bored. At this point, they often need proven managers to maintain and develop the businesses while they go back to building new ventures for others to manage.

The roles individuals assume in a business life cycle can be placed on a spectrum starting from one end with idea people and inventors and moving through intrapreneurs in the middle to professional managers at the other end. (See Figure 2-1, page 34.)

The difficulty most large organizations have with innovation comes directly from trying to proceed without empowering intrapreneurs. Without them, attempts to innovate look like the diagram in Figure 2-2 (the blank in the center shows that several vital steps are omitted between the creation of ideas and their delivery to market).

Who is the intrapreneurial man or woman responsible for the birth and youth of a growing business?

As you can imagine, the set of skills that defines the intrapreneur is different from that of either the traditional corporate ladder climber or the newer individual contributer. Few of the innovations that large organizations need can be implemented by a single person. More than inventors, intrapreneurs need team-building skills and a firm grasp of business and marketplace reality. While they don't need the political skills of senior managers working through multiple layers of management, they clearly must be leaders. And more than professional managers, they must make rapid decisions in the absence of adequate data. They must be comfortable groping toward a successful business pattern without much guidance from above.

Although the tasks of intrapreneuring push people into certain patterns, there is no set formula for determining in advance who can be an intrapreneur and who cannot. People become intrapreneurs when circumstances drive them to an act of will: the decision to make a new business concept into a reality within their company despite the barriers and risks. While intrapreneurs tend to be young, many are also in midlife career crises or nearing retirement. The intrapreneur of Boeing's 200-foot wind-power generators, for example, was a sixty-three-year-old aeronautic scientist whose hobby was windmills. Even though the opportunity to expand his personal vision on a socially significant scale appeared close to his retirement, Wayne Weisner suddenly became a first-time intrapreneur.

While Ed Roberts of MIT's Sloan School of Management found that most technical intrapreneurs are well educated°(but not necessarily Ph.D.'s), half of 3M's most famous intrapreneurs never went to college. Some intrapreneurs are geniuses and others have relatively ordinary intelligence. No functional

° "What It Takes to Be an Entrepreneur . . . and to Hang on to One," *Innovation*, no. 7, 1969, p. 47.

The People Behind The Life Cycle Of A Business

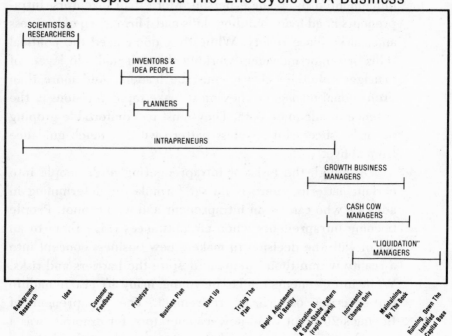

Figure 2-1

The Innovation Gap

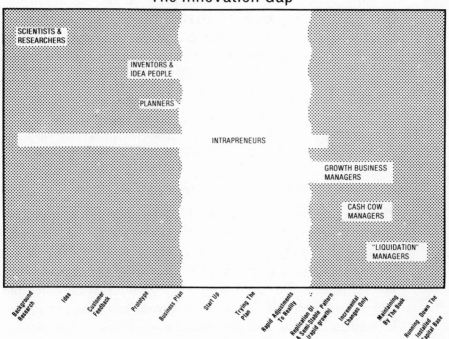

Figure 2-2

area has a monopoly: some come from marketing and others from engineering. Ava Allen cofounded NBI's supplies division after coming from a position in the personnel department. Background, age, and functional discipline just don't matter if the will to do new things is strong.

Being an intrapreneur is in fact a state of mind. This state of mind is not necessarily set in early childhood; it can be developed at any point in life given the desire and opportunity. Ohio State University psychologist Albert Shapero's findings from his studies of entrepreneurs apply equally well to intrapreneurs:

> Many individuals . . . become entrepreneurs even though they don't have the supposedly requisite characteristics or motives. . . . People who have not shown any prior tendency to become entrepreneurial often do so as a result of their experiences and life situations. No test will assure you that an individual will be an entrepreneur before the fact.[*]

Therefore, as you consider the characteristics of the intrapreneur that follow, don't wonder, "Am I this way?" Ask yourself if you wish to become *more* intrapreneurial.

As companies move out of the industrial era and into the Innovation Age, the speed of change demands that the constant search for a better way must be everyone's job. As you move beyond the known and into doing new things, deference to authority becomes less and less useful. Instead, you have to have the courage to let your own imagination and judgment tell you what direction to take as you explore the unknown. When you take that step, you leave the realm of the traditional employee and become an intrapreneur.

[*] "The Entrepreneurs: Corporate Heroes or 'Lousy Managers'?" *The Wharton Magazine,* vol. 3, no. 1, Fall 1978, pp. 34–35. Copyright © 1978 by the Wharton School of the University of Pennsylvania.

THE VISION

Einstein said that he rode into the theory of relativity on a beam of light. Intrapreneurs ride to the discovery of successful ventures on the strength of their vision. Hulki Aldikacti, the intrapreneur behind Pontiac's highly successful new Fiero sports car, had an almost tangible vision of what he wanted to build. "My hobby is sculpture and the process of building a new car is very much like carving a sculpture. First you make a total picture in your mind of what it will be, then you build it." Hulki built his vision from a lifetime of building, driving and loving cars. "I critique every car I drive," he says. "When something is wrong—perhaps I can't see the instruments clearly—then I resolve never to design a car that has that flaw."

In the early stages of building the Fiero, Hulki built a wooden mock-up of the passenger compartment. To get a better feel for what the car would be like, he sat in the driver's seat during his coffee breaks, imagining what it would be like to drive the finished car.

This behavior is absolutely typical of intrapreneurs. Since one of their most basic tools is daydreaming, their natural inclination in any spare moment is to play over a new business opportunity in their mind's eye, considering the many different ways to go forward and the barriers they might encounter along each path. Because they foresee the barriers, intrapreneurs can plan ways around them before becoming locked into a death struggle with an unworkable situation.

While building his vision of the Fiero, Hulki used a trick to reduce the chaos of possibilities. He imagined certain kinds of people as the customers, specifically young people. He therefore concentrated on his children away at the University of Michigan. By personalizing the customers, he got more emotional about it. That, Hulki says, "is all to the good."

For Hulki a car is not just a way to get around—it is a

psychological experience composed of many such minutia as the way the door closes; the power of the motor; the sounds and vibrations, both good and bad; how the seat supports you; the feel of the steering. All these must work together. It is the intrapreneur who composes them into a harmonious experience.

In some business circles visionaries are belittled as impractical dreamers. Quite to the contrary, imagination or vision is perhaps the most concrete of mental tools. The better a person's imagination, the more concrete a plan he or she can produce. Great artists and inventors generally have extraordinary powers of imagination, without which they could not do their jobs.

All Europe mourned when Beethoven lost his hearing, yet he went on to write what many consider his finest works. Like many great composers, he could hear the music in his mind and test different ideas without playing them on an instrument. Although he was deaf, his power of imagination was great enough for him to "hear" an entire symphony. More than half the population can sound a melody line in their heads without having to hum it. A tiny percentage can sound four-part harmony in their minds. But Beethoven had the capacity to "hear" eight-part harmony and the textures of a ninety-six–piece orchestra. What enabled him to be such a great artist was in part his extraordinary ability to visualize— or in this case "hear"—his work before it had actually been performed.

A similar degree of visionary power exists in the great inventors. Nikola Tesla, for example, the inventor of three-phase electric current, new turbines, and a variety of other things, explained how he turned his ideas into working machines: He would build a model of a new invention in his mind. He would set the model running, then push it to the back of his mind and go about his business. Weeks later he would bring it back to the forefront of his mind and check the bearings for wear. If the model wasn't right, he redesigned it mentally and sent it back for more mental testing until it worked perfectly. Of course, we have only Tesla's word for his mental processes, but observers noted that, having finished inventing something and designing it in his head, Tesla could visualize the measurements and how the parts fitted together and could construct each part of the invention without using plans or drawings.* Engineers know it is impossible to do this without having made general drawings first to see exactly how all the parts fit together. Impossible, that is, unless one has the incredibly precise, concrete, and visionary capability of a Tesla.

THE NATURE OF INTRAPRENEURIAL VISION

The visionary capabilities of a musician differ from those of an inventor in kind but not in degree. One hears music, the other sees machinery. Likewise, the visionary skills of intrapreneurs differ from those of inventors in kind, but not in degree. Intrapreneurs do not necessarily need a highly developed mechanical or technical imagination, but they will be helped by an ability to imagine business and organizational realities in the way their customers will respond to innovation.

Matt Sanders, who has tried often enough so that he has had both successes and failures in launching new products, describes the early phase of creating a new product: "At the same time that you are putting the product concepts together, you are also trying to mentally design an organization that accommodates the product. It's every bit as much a conceptual problem as the product itself. How am I going to get the business from here to there?"

As Fiero's Hulki says, "When you think about how to make a product, it's not for the customer only. You have to think of ways to do better for GM, too."

The intrapreneur's vision is not just a vague idea of a

---

* Inez Hunt and Wanetta W. Draper, *Lightning in His Hand: The Life of Nikola Tesla*, Omni Publications, Hawthorne, CA, 1964, p. 128.

goal, nor is it just a clear picture of the product or service. It is a working model of all aspects of the business being created and the steps needed to make them happen. Intrapreneurs spend a lot of time building and testing their mental models. They see the marketing and production, the finance, the design, and the people as an integrated system. Their vision of each of these areas may not be as good as that of a professional marketer, manufacturer, or financier, yet the intrapreneur is of irreplaceable value in a wider role—the ability to see how a business as a whole could work and then to act with courage and decisiveness to make it happen.

This ability to visualize the steps from idea to actualization is one of the basic and learnable skills of intrapreneuring. You can practice it by taking a few of your ideas and fleshing out your vision of how each could be made to happen using the appendix on Intraprise Plan Guidelines. In doing so you will develop the habit of thinking your ideas through as businesses. And one of them might catch fire and seem so workable and important that making it happen becomes your next step.

BECOMING THE CORPORATE HYBRID

In the beginning no one else understands the intrapreneur's ideas well enough to make them work. As a result, others say it can't work. Intrapreneurs thus find themselves crossing organizational boundaries to do what are officially other people's jobs. Bank of California market researcher Michael Phillips wanted to launch a new investment vehicle, a certificate of deposit for consumers. To get it going quickly, he found himself writing the operations manual that explained to branch offices how to process the new CDs—clearly a task for operations, not market research.

When intrapreneur Art Fry, the inventor of Post-it Notes (those now familiar yellow pads with the gently adhesive backs), was told by the marketing division his idea wasn't wanted by customers, he did his own market research. When

40

manufacturing told him Post-it Notes were impossible to make, he worked out the production technology himself. No problem, no matter how far from his supposed area of expertise as a lab person, fell outside his responsibility, because Art was an intrapreneur.

A product-line manager in the marketing organization at Tandy Corporation was unsuccessful when he proposed the development of a personal computer to sell in the Radio Shack stores. His intrapreneurial response was to build, with the help of a few coworkers, a prototype of such a machine. He presented his vision again, this time with a well-developed prototype. The result: Radio Shack became a dominant player in the personal computer marketplace.

The intrapreneur is the general manager of a new business that doesn't yet exist. Intrapreneurs frequently have marketing or technology backgrounds, but once they take on the role of intrapreneur they belong to neither. The intrapreneur must cross the barriers that divide the organization into functions, such as marketing, engineering, research, manufacturing, sales, and finance, and take responsibility for all aspects of the business he or she wishes to start.

THE NEED TO ACT

Intrapreneurs are naturally action-oriented. Rather than plan endlessly, they almost immediately start doing something to realize their plans. One of the most consistent traits of the intrapreneur is an unwillingness to accept no for an answer. Our case histories of success are filled with the likes of Chuck House and Hulki Aldikacti, who defied direct orders and went on building their dreams. Were it not for an almost unstoppable need to turn vision into action, the intrapreneurs who have brought us most of the new ideas we now enjoy would still be waiting for permission to begin.

Intrapreneurs Dick Nadeau and Bill Truitt were asked by their boss to explain their new idea to the plastics department.

They received mixed reviews. "The plastics people said it was a brilliant idea, but they thought we would have great difficulty accomplishing it—in fact, they said they thought it was impossible," says Nadeau.

On the way back to their offices, Truitt asked Nadeau what they should report back to their boss. "Tell him the truth," said Dick. "Tell him they thought it was a brilliant idea."

PURSUING THE PLEASURES OF MUNDANE WORK

Intrapreneurs don't stand on ceremony or have standards about what sorts of work are beneath them. They do the mundane work that is part of every new project. As entrepreneur Howard Head of Head Ski Company described the start-up situation, "When the floor needed sweeping, I swept it. When the sales force needed a rousing speech, I gave it. I did whatever needed to be done."

To only a slightly lesser degree, that is the lot of the intrapreneur. Unlike managers, whose job is largely to delegate, intrapreneurs can often do things faster by doing them themselves. Instead of making elaborate drawings and waiting six weeks for machinists to bring them to life, they make sketches and then machine the parts themselves. Instead of thinking up ways to make their services to the company into profit centers, and then wishing it could happen, intrapreneurs print brochures and solicit new customers.

This tendency to prefer hands-on work gets the job done and helps intrapreneurs to stay quite literally in touch with all aspects of their intraprise. Their ability to make quick decisions and, when necessary, to consider sweeping changes of plan in terms of their impact on all aspects of the business depends on their being in touch.

COMBINING VISION AND ACTION

Most occupations require a predominance of either vision or action, as shown in Figure 2-3. Workers are too often told that their visions are not valued and all that is required or desired of them is to do the things that they are told to do. They often become dreamers at home and on the job. But their dreams, if they concern work at all, tend toward insubordination and revenge. The separation between their dreams and their actions is a prescription for alienation.

The separation between vision and action, and the alienation it produces, is also evident at higher levels in the corporate structure, where company planners dream the dreams of corporate growth that are then given to line executives for execution. In Figure 2-3 I have placed executives further up the vision scale than workers because in practice their job calls for more than just managing the execution of plans—they must imagine the means to do so.

Intrapreneurs are both thinkers and doers, planners and workers. They have to be, because no one will realize their dreams for them, nor would they wish them to. Until they make their visions real, no one ever understands their significance.

The vision of the intrapreneur is not just quantitative or theoretical. Successful intrapreneurs often mention that they have a feeling for the business they are forming that can only come from hands-on involvement. Their visions of what could be are rich because they are grounded in action.

As repetitive work is gradually taken over by machines, the human role will increasingly be to visualize improvements and to make them happen. If we are to be efficient at this innovative task we must more closely couple vision and action, allowing as often as possible for the thought to flow directly to the deed. As the basic task of all employees thereby becomes more intrapreneurial, supervisors will learn to en-

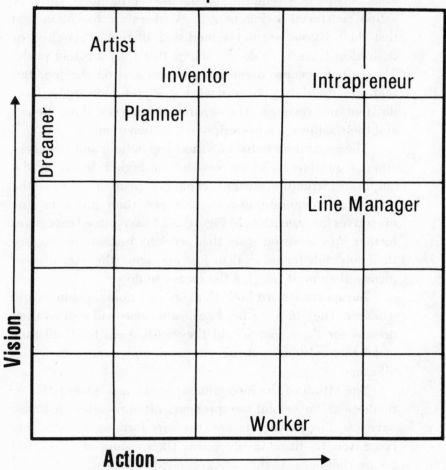

Figure 2-3

courage the more mundane forms of intrapreneurship. From small daily improvements to breakthroughs, innovation will flourish and alienation will decline.

DEDICATION

One of the most significant questions every intrapreneur must ask is whether success is worth the price. When night after night your peers go home on time while you stay, you have to wonder about your good sense. "It's crazy to work this hard, but I love it," says intrapreneur Joe Tanner. Joe was a researcher at Du Pont who loved developing new products, but his boss told him that he would never be promoted without an advanced degree. He thought of getting out of research and becoming a venture manager, but he observed that at Du Pont people were generally venture managers only once. After that they were given staff jobs that seemed boring to Joe. So he left and joined a neighboring Du Pont spin-off company, Gore Associates, that seemed to offer more room for an enterprising young man without a Ph.D.

At Gore he took on the task of turning the breathable waterproof fabric called Goretex into a business supplying clothing manufacturers. He built that business, but as it grew he was eventually replaced by someone with stronger skills in managing an established business. He quit. After a brief stint at a small family concern, Joe healed his wounds and is back at Gore starting another division, this time in industrial coatings. He talks about the prospects in glowing terms, conveying a dedication that clearly explains why he cheerfully works long hours.

One of the reasons traditional product development systems can't compete with intrapreneuring and entrepreneuring is that they are too bureaucratic to encourage dedication or give it full rein. When traditional managers divide marketing and technology, vision and action, and a host of other functions into separate jobs, intrapreneurs are denied the commitment,

45

completeness, responsibility, and excitement that inspire total dedication.

The dedication of entrepreneurs is frequently so extreme that they have almost no time or attention for other aspects of life. Their divorce rate is higher than among middle managers. One entrepreneur was able to joke about this problem. He explained that he set aside one hour every week to spend with his wife so she wouldn't be totally excluded. With typical understated humor, Peter Drucker said, "Entrepreneurs are the most boring dinner companions I know. All they want to talk about is their ventures. They never want to talk about anything interesting like, for example, me." Dick Nadeau says, "The price of [intrapreneuring] is that you let everything else go. Sometimes I wondered if I made the right choice—if I should have spent more time with my family. But then again I don't know if you really have a choice. I am an involved person and I can't change that."

As a potential intrapreneur you must consider how dedicated you are willing to be, and how you will balance that dedication with the rewards you hope to get, which may be less than many entrepreneurs. You will have to find ways to sustain the dedication without becoming cynical when people block your best efforts instead of helping. On the other hand, it may be possible for you to maintain some balance between work and personal life by taking advantage of the resources of the corporation.

The legends of 3M almost all speak of the dogged dedication of the intrapreneur. When his bosses told intrapreneur Phil Palmquist to stop working on reflective coatings because that wasn't his job, he continued four nights a week from 7:00 P.M. to 11:00 P.M. Soon he had a product 100 times brighter than white paint. Among other things, it now lights up roadway signs at night when your headlights shine on them. In a more extreme case, George Swenson, another 3M intrapreneur, was fired when he wouldn't stop working on a new roofing material. He continued working on the project despite the fact that he was no longer employed. Once he had it working, the company relented and rehired him. By treasuring such stories, 3M encourages others to try to innovate despite opposition.

But there is a less glowing side to this. Intrapreneurial dedication can be combined with a tendency to put objectives before people. The average intrapreneur is not what Blake and Mouton of managerial grid fame described as a 9:9—that is, a person totally committed both to people and to production and able to satisfy both commitments without sacrificing one or the other.

Although concerned intrapreneurs exist, when a conflict arises their priorities generally lie on the side of getting a quality job done on time rather than on meeting people's needs. This attitude does not derive from disrespect for their people; it is just that they do not consider their own or anyone else's comfort nearly as important as getting the job done. They expect the impossible of themselves, and consider almost no sacrifice too great. They expect almost as much of others as they do of themselves. They tend to be puzzled by people who work with less than total dedication and who have standards that fall below excellence.

Dick Nadeau was, according to many, the undisputed intrapreneur of the Du Pont automatic chemical analyzer. The ACA was created when a competing company, Technicon, had just developed highly efficient continuous-flow equipment for preparing large batches of standard blood chemistry profiles. Du Pont wanted to enter the market with a different idea for an automated machine that would do single blood chemistry tests as needed. According to his former boss, Don Sutherland, Dick ran the project despite the fact that he was not in charge of it. As Don says, "Dick did not let anything stand in his way, he just drove the thing. He drove his bosses, the manufacturing organization, and the marketing. The people who worked with him built shields around themselves in order to cope with this guy. And I think it was the only way it was going to happen. The secret of Dick's success was his unswervable focus on the business objectives of the ACA."

Managers must be willing to put up with a lot to let effective intrapreneurs do their work. Dick gave Du Pont what has become a $300 million business. That is worth a few bruised sensibilities. Now that he's gone, they even miss him. As one Du Pont executive said wistfully, "Where is Dick Nadeau when we need him?" There are intrapreneurs like Art Fry of 3M whose gentleness of manner and concern for others is palpable. If people get in his way, he goes around them. The difference is merely one of style.

PUTTING INTERNAL PRIORITIES FIRST

The intrapreneur's theme song ought to be "I Did It My Way." Although they are guided by their customers, intrapreneurs also feel the need for their project's completion personally.

When Michael Kranfus, head of the SVO (Specialty Vehicle Operations)—Ford's performance car skunkworks—set out to build a new Mustang to compete with the likes of BMW, the Ford bureaucracy had some difficulty dealing with his design philosophy. Michael stresses the importance of building a car that "feels right." "If you can't sit in a car and know whether it feels right or not," he says, "you shouldn't be building cars." Using an informed posterior rather than formal market research, Michael and his team built a car so good that it was simultaneously on the cover of *Road and Track, Car and Driver,* and *Motor Trend,* which hailed it as better than the BMW.

Most intrapreneurs become successful pursuing ventures that have become deeply and personally meaningful. They believe that the world needs the product they propose, that it will be a valuable contribution. Matt Sanders, an intrapreneur from Convergent Technologies, says this:

> Everyone says that you ought to start a business, be your own boss, and make a pile of money. I think those things are great, but it doesn't make you want to get up every day and do the things you need to do to start a business.

The only thing is believing in what you are doing from a personal viewpoint. You are driven by a sense of wanting to see it when it's all done and a successful, profitable business.

Dick Nadeau echoes this sentiment. "During the building of the ACA, I turned up my nose at a lot of offers for far more money in other companies. What drove me was not the money, but the psychic income of seeing a possibility out there in the market and watching it grow—of watching the people grow with it.

"The ACA was something really new. Du Pont wasn't known in the clinical testing field before and there was great pleasure in seeing it become what it is today."

Venture capitalists have a special name for entrepreneurial candidates who are dedicated to becoming wealthy by whatever means rather than to a specific enterprise. They call them "promoters," and avoid them like the plague. They lack the long-term commitment needed to overcome the inevitable times of trouble. Venture capitalists have become adept at testing for true commitment and dedication. They ask trick questions, offering the entrepreneur a chance to abandon the venture and jump into another, supposedly more lucrative project. They like to observe the entrepreneur over time before investing. Unlike promoters, whose new ideas come and go like the clients in a brothel, real entrepreneurs and intrapreneurs stay married to their ideas, often keeping and improving the same vision for years. The equivalent of promoters in the world of intrapreneurs have given intrapreneurs a bad name by lacking follow through. One way of making sure you do not become one is to address only ventures that have a powerful personal meaning.

SETTING SELF-DETERMINED GOALS

Intrapreneurs are self-determined goal setters who often take the initiative to do things no one asked them to do. No one, for example, told Chuck House to test market the rejected

FAA monitor for other purposes. One consequence of this goal setting is that intrapreneurs, like entrepreneurs, are self-appointed to their tasks. As this characteristic becomes more widely recognized, the appointment of intrapreneurs to their projects will surely go the way of the arranged marriage.

The goals intrapreneurs set for themselves are concrete and measurable. They are set in weekly increments initially and range, with objectives, through five- to ten-year plans. "A prototype in three months, three customers in six, and full-scale production at a rate of $5 million per year in sixteen months—by the end of three years we will have a $30 million business and 10 percent profit": these would be but a fraction of the timed and measurable goals an intrapreneur would use to direct and judge his or her progress. You can increase your chances of intrapreneurial success by practicing self-determined goal setting.

SETTING HIGH INTERNAL STANDARDS

The inner-directedness of entrepreneurs extends not only to goal setting but also to setting quality standards. When Art Fry was making Post-it® Note Pads, he finally got the quality to the point where others thought it was good enough. He remained unsatisfied, driving himself and those around him to find new processes and new formulas that met his own personal standards of excellence. In his eyes this has been a successful strategy. "Competitors can't maintain our quality, and so we remain the dominant vendor." Intrapreneurs gain little satisfaction from adhering to standards imposed by others, and may ignore them. They are famous for neglecting documentation. At the same time they will set for themselves very high internal standards in the areas they consider important. This constant striving for excellence, when combined with a good measure of impatience and a lack of respect for tradition, seems to produce superior new products and services in almost unrealistically rapid times.

OVERCOMING (NOT AVOIDING) MISTAKES AND FAILURE

Successful intrapreneurs tend to be confident about their skills and the prospects for their businesses. "If you dwelt on the possibility of failure, you would never start," says Dick Nadeau. "The [intrapreneur's] question is how to make it work, not whether it will."

Even when it is obvious to everyone around them that they have failed, intrapreneurs often see it differently. With a background of optimism, they confront failure not as a personal disaster but as a learning experience. Two major factors contribute to this tendency to view failure positively:

1. They don't admit they are beaten, and view failure as a temporary setback to be learned from and dealt with, not as a reason to quit.
2. They see themselves as responsible for their own destiny. As a result they don't tend to blame their failure on others, but rather to focus on the part that was under their control and wonder how they might have done better.

Dealing with mistakes and failure is very important to the intrapreneur, because doing new things is bound to lead to mistakes and even major blunders. You can work on adopting an intrapreneurial attitude toward these events by asking, when something goes wrong, what *you* can learn from it.

MANAGING RISK

The confidence to assume personal risk is a touchstone by which venture capitalists test entrepreneurs. Some demand that their entrepreneurs accept reduced salaries and even take second mortgages on their homes or deplete their savings to invest in the venture. They do this not so much to reduce their own exposure as to test and enlarge the commitment of the entrepreneur. The theory is that when everything you own is on the line, it is hard to walk away if suddenly the going gets rough or you get a better offer. The head of new ventures for one of the ten largest U.S. firms was so taken by this principle that the question "Would you take a second mortgage on your home for this idea?" has become his way of asking about the depth of intrapreneurial commitment.

Given the rewards usually available to intrapreneurs, a second mortgage is too much to ask; but intrapreneurs also have to take risks to push forward new ideas. Some companies are experimenting by formally asking intrapreneurs to take risks, much as venture capitalists ask their prospective entrepreneurs to do. For example, Intel asked the intrapreneurial group that developed its highly successful bubble memory to forgo their Intel profit sharing in exchange for a bonus system based upon the group's performance. This meant going for more than four years without profit-sharing checks while their peers received very significant bonuses. But their abstinence paid off when the bubble memory group achieved its objectives. Its participants received bonuses that put them well ahead of their peers who took no risk.

LOYALTY TO LONG-TERM BUSINESS OBJECTIVES

The goals intrapreneurs set for themselves include five- and often ten-year visions of what the business will become. To be sure, their plans include concrete measurable goals for the shorter term, but their short-run actions are always guided by the long run.

Once when things weren't going well, the powers that be put a one-month hold on Art Fry's Post-it Notes project. Art immediately exploded, "We can't do that, it will cost us a million dollars!" His boss, amused but suspecting Art had something up his sleeve, asked, "How do you figure that,

Art?" "Well," replied Art, "in a few years we'll be selling more than a million dollars a month of these things. If we wait a month now, we'll miss one of those million-dollar months later."

Art's quick response to the proposed delay illustrates the way he references every business decision to its long-term business significance. Many business leaders bemoan the lack of long-term thinking in American business management. Short-term thinking is not surprising when managers are judged on quarterly returns, but we can count on our intrapreneurs to consider the long run. Intrapreneurs struggle to meet targets set not by outsiders but by their own internal priorities, which are driven by the need to achieve their long-term goals. They will use what freedom they have to ensure the corporation's future growth.

Most of the peculiarities of the intrapreneurial personality can be understood by considering the pressures of combining in one person both a strong visionary and an insatiable doer who cannot rest until his or her vision is made manifest on earth as it is in his or her mind. These pressures not only explain their drive but also their intolerance of being told what or how to do. While they are open to information and ideas, they have all the orders they can stand from their own internal imperatives. The drive to realize the vision explains their dedication and willingness to perform any task, no matter how mundane, if that is what is needed to make the intraprise succeed. The characteristics of the intrapreneur are compared and contrasted in the table that follows.

WHO IS THE INTRAPRENEUR?

	Traditional Managers	Traditional Entrepreneurs	Intrapreneurs
Primary Motives	Wants promotion and other traditional corporate rewards. Power-motivated.	Wants freedom. Goal-oriented, self-reliant, and self-motivated.	Wants freedom and access to corporate resources. Goal-oriented and self-motivated, but also responds to corporate rewards and recognition.
Time Orientation	Responds to quotas and budgets, weekly, monthly, quarterly, annual planning horizons, the next promotion or transfer.	End goals of 5–10-year growth of business in view as guides. Takes action now to move next step along way.	End goals of 3–15 years, depending on type of venture. Urgency to meet self-imposed and corporate timetables.
Action	Delegates action. Supervising and reporting take most of energy.	Gets hands dirty. May upset employees by suddenly doing their work.	Gets hands dirty. May know how to delegate, but when necessary does what needs to be done.
Skills	Professional management. Often business-school trained. Abstract analytical tools, people-management, and political skills.	Knows business intimately. More business acumen than managerial or political skill. Often technically trained if in technical business. May have had former P&L responsibility in corporation.	Very like the entrepreneur, but the situation demands greater ability to prosper within the organization. Needs help with this.
Courage and Destiny	Sees others in charge of his or her destiny. Can be forceful and ambitious, but may be fearful of others' ability to do him or her in.	Self-confident, optimistic, courageous.	Self-confident and courageous. Many intrapreneurs are cynical about the system, but optimistic about their ability to outwit it.

Attention	Primarily on events inside corporation.	Primarily on technology and marketplace.	Both inside and outside. Sells insiders on needs of venture and marketplace, but also focuses on customers.
Risk	Careful.	Likes moderate risk. Invests heavily, but expects to succeed.	Likes moderate risk. Generally not afraid of being fired so sees little personal risk.
Market Research	Has market studies done to discover needs and guide product conceptualization.	Creates needs. Creates products that often can't be tested with market research—potential customers don't yet understand them. Talks to customers and forms own opinions.	Does own market research and intuitive market evaluation like the entrepreneur.
Status	Cares about status symbols (corner office, etc.).	Happy sitting on an orange crate if job is getting done.	Considers traditional status symbols a joke—treasures symbols of freedom.
Failure and Mistakes	Strives to avoid mistakes and surprises. Postpones recognizing failure.	Deals with mistakes and failures as learning experiences.	Sensitive to need to appear orderly in corporation. Attempts to hide risky projects from view so can learn from mistakes without political cost of public failure.
Decisions	Agrees with those in power. Delays decision until gets a feel of what bosses want.	Follows private vision. Decisive, action-oriented.	Adept at getting others to agree to private vision. Somewhat more patient and willing to compromise than the entrepreneur, but still a *doer*.

WHO IS THE INTRAPRENEUR? (*Concluded*)

	Traditional Managers	Traditional Entrepreneurs	Intrapreneurs
Who Serves	Pleases others.	Pleases self and customers.	Pleases self, customers, and sponsors.
Attitude Toward the System	Sees system as nurturing and protective, seeks position within it.	May rapidly advance in a system, then, when frustrated, reject the system and form his or her own.	Dislikes the system but learns to manipulate it.
Problem-Solving Style	Works out problems within the system.	Escapes problems in large and formal structures by leaving and starting over on own.	Works out problems within the system, or bypasses it without leaving.
Family History	Family members worked for large organizations.	Entrepreneurial small-business, professional, or farm background.	Entrepreneurial small-business, professional, or farm background.
Relationship with Parents	Independent of mother, good relations with father, but slightly dependent.	Absent father or poor relations with father.	Better relations with father, but still stormy.
Socioeconomic Background	Middle-class background.	Lower-class background in some early studies, middle-class in more recent ones.	Middle-class background.
Educational Level	Highly educated.	Less well educated in earlier studies, some graduate work but not Ph.D. in later ones.	Often highly educated, particularly in technical fields, sometimes not.
Relationship with Others	Hierarchy as basic relationship.	Transactions and deal making as basic relationship.	Transactions within hierarchy.

PROFILE

MICHAEL PHILLIPS: Intrapreneuring in a Service Industry

From a position of relative obscurity at the Bank of California, Michael Phillips launched a string of major banking innovations including consumer certificates of deposit, simplified checking accounts, and Master Charge, which he played a major role in establishing. How he was able to do this is the result of a "loophole" that makes intrapreneuring in service organizations simpler than intrapreneuring new manufactured products: Because the cost of developing a new service can be relatively low, Michael was able to launch many of his innovations before management found out about them. When they did he was able to show them successes rather than ideas, and thus it was too late for them to object.

In 1966, after leaving a position in the market research department he helped found at the Bank of America, Michael spent four years as director of market research at the Bank of California, then the seventh largest bank in the state. His title suggests that he had a prominent position, but few in the bank believed that marketing was important. However, just because a position is perceived as powerless and unimportant doesn't make it a poor base for intrapreneuring. The bank's senior executives never bothered Michael because it never occurred to them that what he was doing mattered.

As director of market research, Michael wasn't satisfied just to find customer needs and then tell others about them, hoping someone would then develop the new services to fill the needs he had identified. A true intrapreneur, he took responsibility for the entire effort, from beginning to end, working to invent the services *and* to make them happen. To do so he worked with a team in marketing including his boss, Bob Person, and the director of advertising, Bob Jaques.

EXPANDING A JOB DESCRIPTION

The consumer certificate of deposit was typical of Michael's kind of intrapreneuring. He was motivated by a personal ideal: to provide a better savings vehicle for older people. As the head of marketing research, he had assembled groups of older bank customers with substantial savings and asked them to discuss their investment needs. Many of them said they had heard of "certificates of deposit," but they knew very little about CDs except that they were a desirable form of investment, but suitable only for investors more sophisticated than themselves.

Beginning with the typical tasks of his job, Michael had to determine why these customers were putting their money in 4 percent savings accounts instead of 5¼ percent CDs. He discovered from his market research groups that customers were puzzled by the term "certificate," since in most cases the actual certificate or bank-book type record had been replaced by a ledger entry held somewhere in the bowels of the bank. Furthermore, the fact that CDs were sold only in large denominations such as $10,000 intimidated many potential customers, including many who had savings accounts far larger than that.

But Michael did not stop with discovering these facts, as his job description warranted. He went much further in his research. There was, he found out, no legal or operational reason why certificates of deposit could not be offered in smaller denominations; rather, the intimidating certificates were based on a long-standing tradition in commercial banking that Michael abhorred— that dealing with individual customers was unprofitable and somehow beneath the dignity of a proper banker. Michael, on the other hand, saw consumer certificates of deposit as an opportunity to better serve customers and attract substantial deposits by offering them a higher return. His idea was simple: to create and advertise a certificate of deposit in small denominations ($500).

Michael approached Bob Jaques, the advertising director, with his idea. Jaques agreed to help at once because he wanted advertising projects that produced measurable results and provided clear feedback, such as, in this case, dollars of certificates sold. Bob Person also liked the idea, having found his career to be most satisfying when he could champion a creative project. These men formed Michael's basic team, but others in the bank had to be sold on the certificates as well.

The biggest hurdle could have been getting the bank to approve the procedures for processing the new instrument. These procedures had to be highly efficient if the smaller denomination CDs were to be profitable. New streamlined procedures needed to be designed, which could take months or even prove to be "impossible" if the task were given to a skeptical or overworked operations staff. Michael made it easy for the operations staff to buy into his idea by doing most of the work himself and by labeling everything "a temporary procedure to handle the market test." As a result, operations could certainly approve the test with little effort, especially since they reserved the right to redesign the process should the test prove successful.

Next, Michael created instructional language on the certificate that was comprehensible to the layman. When he showed the certificate to one of the bank's younger lawyers, "whom I could identify with and talk to," treating it as something insignificant rather than as something new, he quickly got his wording approved.

He took the certificates to the printer himself. He wrote the instruction sheet for the branches on how to handle the new consumer certificates of deposit during the "market test." With the exception of a few minor changes, which Michael did not resist, all anyone had to do was agree.

The result: In their first quarter, the new certificates brought $40 million in new deposits into the bank.

You would think that the marketing people would have been honored for attracting these new deposits. Yet, Bob Person says, the senior bank officers chided him for his concern with consumer deposits, suggesting instead that he go out and attract customers like Lockheed. The irony was that a few months later Lockheed proved to be insolvent, while the individual customers kept buying the new CDs.

INTRAPRENEURING A NATIONAL SERVICE: MASTER CHARGE

Michael's biggest intrapreneurial venture was one that challenged his political skills perhaps more than his creativity. Back when he was just starting out at the Bank of California, Michael dropped in to visit his counterpart at Wells Fargo. Much to his surprise, he found the marketing people from Crocker and the United California Bank also there. "Whatever you guys are doing, I want to be in on it," he said with a smile. They were reviewing a proposal from

Melvin B. Salveson, a college professor from Los Angeles.

Salveson's proposal was simple: The banks they represented could join to offer a charge card to compete with Bank Americard, then only seven years old. He suggested that the three banks subscribe to a new company he was forming to issue the cards and to process the transactions for the banks. When Michael saw the proposal he exploded. Knowing the bank credit business from his experience at Bank of America, he explained what he thought was wrong with Salveson's plan, including such fundamentals as the omission of service charges, which were the major source of revenue. The other marketing managers were somewhat taken aback by Michael's outburst. "The reason we're not interested in Salveson's proposal isn't that we think he has planned his company badly," they said, "but that we just don't think there is any money in the credit card business."

Every industry has its basic prejudices, and banking's was the belief that all forms of personal credit are unprofitable. Fortunately, Michael knew otherwise. He pointed out that his former employer's Bank Americard had netted a $13 million profit in its sixth year. This fact astounded the other marketers and convinced them of the value of starting their own credit card consortium. In planning subsequent meetings, Michael decided against inviting anyone from his own bank because he didn't think he could convince his superiors to support the idea. The four marketers met a week later with two senior vice presidents and an executive vice president from the larger California banks (excluding Bank of America) and three lawyers.

Michael outlined how to proceed, explaining how the credit card would work, where the income would come from, and how profitable they expected it to be. He had researched what they needed to do to form a company to issue and process the transactions, and the lawyers agreed that, at first glance, the idea was viable.

At the group's request, Michael laid out the next step—hiring a consulting firm to do a detailed design of the system. One of the executives proposed a firm in New Jersey; Michael agreed, and suggested that they request a proposal right away. It was a pattern of behavior Michael would follow throughout the building of a Master Charge team. He would defer to others in everything that wasn't essential to the success of the venture. If someone liked a specific consultant, it was fine if they hired that consultant. It wasn't important to Michael to appear to be in charge; it was important only that the project succeed.

Yet when the proposal from the consultants arrived, it was clear that the firm's knowledge of credit cards, retail merchants, and marketing bank services was limited. Frustrated and angry, Michael reached a private compromise with the firm, while at the same time not causing any rifts in his team. If the consultants limited their efforts to operations research and to designing the machinery and systems for processing the charges, Michael would design the market research and market strategy, allowing them to execute and take credit for it. Everyone's interests were served and the "Interbank" card project, as it was called then, was under way.

Thus finding a way to influence the proceedings indirectly, Michael encouraged executive vice president Bob Dewey, then his boss, to represent the Bank of California in future discussions. Dewey welcomed this opportunity to join with his counterparts from the larger banks. Meanwhile, Michael, keeping a low profile, worked with the research company and the advertising agency on the substantive issues. Within three months of the marketers' first meeting, they had decided on the name "Master Charge" and on the card's design. Two months later, all of the card and slip processing was in place. And just nine months after the first meeting, the organization that was to become Western States Bancard Corporation was incorporated; it had two hundred members and was ready to begin sending out cards to members. Other banks soon flocked to join.

THE INTRAPRENEUR AS POLITICIAN

Part of what made Michael so successful in this and other intrapreneurial ventures was his political skills, stemming perhaps from his experience as San Francisco president of the Young Republicans and his work as a campaign manager for a state assemblyman. Whether by luck or design, he seems to have encountered little resistance in introducing major innovations.

"Didn't you come up against people trying to stop you?" I asked. "No," he replied. "I had lots of ideas I felt the bank wasn't ready for, but I kept those to myself. The only slightly difficult one was Master Charge. I couldn't see how to sell the idea to my management with us as the initiators so I sold it to the other banks first, and then let the camaraderie of bank officers draw us into it." Ironically, most of Michael's innovations were in consumer banking, although he says the chief executive officer was only interested in commercial banking. "But if your CEO didn't care about consumer banking, why was he willing to spend money on it?" I wanted to know. "None of these projects had any cost until much later," Michael explained, "and I never paid for them myself. I always found someone else who benefited and got them to pay. For example, ideas like consumer certificates of deposit and simplified checking were seen as ways to get in deposits, so I let the departments who wanted those deposits pay."

Within his own company, Michael was able to lead such a charmed life in a tough corporate atmosphere in part because he had several sponsors. Among them was Bob Dewey, an older man but old in the best way—he was sensitive and wise.

"Bob didn't always grasp exactly what I was doing or why, but he felt the bank needed vitality and youth. He felt I was honest and knew what I was doing, so he backed me. He had chosen to trust me." I was not surprised to find an extraordinary sponsor behind Michael, because I have never found an intrapreneur without a protector who is willing to suspend his skepticism to see how things work out.

Nonetheless, this was not the whole answer to how an intrapreneur might gain a broad enough base of support to introduce so much change so fast. There was another factor.

While he was at the Bank of California, Michael accepted as an apprentice every trainee that he could get and kept them for as long as he could. In this way he got to know all the incoming people who were destined to become important. Even though Michael stayed at the Bank of California for only four years, some former trainees were already on or above his level by the time he left. As a result, there were managers throughout the bank who had learned his philosophy of marketing.

The third factor for his success as an intrapreneur was his natural inclination to cross turf boundaries. Indeed, Michael had almost a fetish about finding ways to be useful to every department. He was always visiting them and offering to help in whatever way made sense to them. In being helpful he spent long hours with all the department heads and learned how the bank worked.

It wasn't always easy to find a way to help. The trust department saw marketing differently from Michael. "The only thing marketing means to me is nicer chairs in the lobby," said someone from the department. Michael accepted this and asked questions about ways to improve the lobby. It turned out that what the lobby really needed was good paintings of colonial sailing ships to make the kind of old-money people who used the trust department feel more at home. Unable to help in any other way, and dedicated to the principle of serving 100 percent of the departments, Michael wrote a memo recommending an allocation of $25,000 toward decor as a capital item in the trust department budget. The trust department got its paintings and Michael won an enemy over to neutrality.

THE ESSENTIAL SPONSOR

For all his efforts at helpfulness and his basic political skills, Michael still was an irritant at the Bank of California. He survived only because of the constant guidance and protection of Bob Person and the overall umbrella Bob Dewey provided. "Bob Person understood and could explain what I was trying to do in terms other bankers could comprehend," Michael said. Bob Person recalls, "Sometimes it was quite necessary to tone Michael down." When Michael designed the simplified checking plan, later called the "3-2-1 Checking Plan," he wanted to call it "Honest Checking." He came to this name because he believed there was a dishonest motive behind the complexity of the bank's existing checking service charges. It is true that in his market research Michael found that some customers believed that checking-account plans were a conscious attempt to confuse and exploit the ordinary individual customer, but it was highly impolitic to suggest that he believed they were right. This line of reasoning was hardly flattering to the bank's officers, and it would not have been an effective way to introduce the concept of simplified checking to them. Bob talked Michael out of the name by pointing out that only pawn shops and used-car salesmen use the word "honest" in their advertisements or names. By doing so he saved Michael from his own idealism.

Toward the end of his stay at the Bank of California, Bob Person saw his friend Dewey in an internal battle. Bob Person left the bank and bank marketing to go back into operations in another bank. Within three months, without the guidance and protection of his sponsors, Michael was fired.

Bob Person, now head of Bank Consulting Services for Coopers & Lybrand, says that banking is poorer for Michael's departure. Once again financial institutions are struggling with change. "If Michael were still in banking there would be more exciting and imaginative new services."

Where are the intrapreneurs when we need them? Too often

they were fired long before a need is recognized. Michael, on the other hand, has become the spiritual leader of a movement of more than eight hundred small businesses in the San Francisco Bay Area devoted to honesty and openness in business, a policy so successful that less than 10 percent of them have failed since the Briar Patch Network was founded in 1974. He is also happy and prosperous writing books like *The Seven Laws of Money* and *Honest Business.*

And in the end he has proved another point. You can use "Honest" in a title and it sells.

CHAPTER 3

Making the Argument for Intrapreneuring

There is a growing realization that the people who make innovation happen in corporations are very much like entrepreneurs. Academicians like MIT's Ed Roberts, through psychological testing, have discovered a great similarity between intrapreneurs and entrepreneurs. Managers are also noticing the similarity for themselves when intrapreneurs leave their corporations to become successful entrepreneurs.

Although viewing the people who build businesses inside large corporations as cousins to the entrepreneur has in general helped the management of innovation, there have been unfortunate side effects. There are generally held myths about entrepreneurs; when they are carried over into the corporate setting, they prevent clear thinking about intrapreneurs and their relationship to the organization.

You may find that these myths make it hard for people to accept you as an intrapreneur. If the myths were true it would be almost impossible to use entrepreneurial types within the corporation. Fortunately they are not. Here are the myths, together with the facts, which should dispel fears about using entrepreneurial types within the corporation.

Myth #1: The Entrepreneur's Primary Motivation Is a Desire for Wealth

---

Perhaps the most misunderstood aspect of the entrepreneur is his or her relationship to money. This is not surprising, since money has replaced sex as the great taboo of our times.

Popular opinion generally holds that entrepreneurs are driven by greed, that fundamental to their character is a lust for money that drives them to do things that ordinary people would not do. Actually, money is very rarely the primary driving force of successful entrepreneurs. Their attitude toward money is complex and intimate. They do care about it and for it, but it is not the chief love of their lives. As Hallmark Cards' founder J. C. Hall put it, "If a man goes into business with only the idea of making a lot of money, the chances are he won't."° Dick Nadeau echoes this sentiment. "During the building of the ACA, I turned up my nose at a lot of offers for far more money in other companies. What drove me was not the money, but the psychic income of seeing a possibility out there in the market and watching it grow—of watching the people grow with it.

"The ACA was something really new. Du Pont wasn't known in the clinical testing field before and there was great pleasure in seeing it become what it is today."

What drives the entrepreneur is a deep, personal need for achievement, but that need generally becomes wedded to a rather specific vision of what he wants to accomplish. As David McClelland, professor of psychology and chairman of Harvard's Department of Social Relations, stated in the *Harvard Business Review:*

> Somewhat surprisingly, in terms of traditional American business and economic theory, he [the entrepreneur] does not seem to be galvanized into activity by the prospect of profit; it is people with low achievement need who require money incentives to make them work harder. The person with a high need works hard anyway, provided there is an opportunity of achieving something. He is interested in money rewards or profits primarily because of the feedback they give him as to how well he is doing. Money is not the incentive to effort but rather the measure of its success for the real entrepreneur.†

The relationship of the entrepreneur to money is much

° J. C. Hall, quoted with permission of Hallmark, Inc., © 1979.

† David C. McClelland, "Achievement Motivation Can Be Developed," *Harvard Business Review,* Nov.–Dec. 1965, p. 7.

like that of a football player toward yards. Watching a football player, you can see he cares desperately about yards and will go to great efforts to get them. But no one thinks that the football player has a fundamental desire for yards. Rather, yards are how one keeps score on excellence as a football player. So it is with money for the entrepreneur.

For intrapreneurs, a lot of the scorekeeping is done in terms of money made for the corporation rather than personal compensation. One can say, "I created a $10-million new business and feel a great sense of accomplishment." Of course that kind of satisfaction alone wears out. In the end even intrapreneurs need some take-home money and something akin to the freedom entrepreneurs earn when they get capital. As we shall see in Chapter 10, given that the primary purpose of intrapreneurs is not greed, affordable ways to reward them can be devised.

The driving ambition of entrepreneurs and intrapreneurs alike is to realize their visions and be able to say, "I did it." By empowering them to successfully execute their visions, corporations can take a major step toward effective competition with venture capitalists.

Myth #2: Entrepreneurs Are High-Risk Takers

Popular belief portrays the entrepreneur as a daring, devil-may-care risk taker. Such a reckless soul would scarcely fit well in most large organizations regardless of the value of his or her occasional successes. Fortunately, studies by David McClelland and others show successful entrepreneurs avoiding high-risk situations; rather, they seek and enjoy calculated moderate risks. They do choose challenging goals, but they also do everything they can to reduce the risk.

Part of the entrepreneur's strategy for minimizing risk is to find ways to get a head start in the marketplace. Venture capitalists often call this the "unfair advantage"—the reason why the venture is likely to succeed even if things don't go as planned. By "unfair advantage" venture capitalists do not mean something that is illegal, immoral, or unsportsmanlike. They prefer a demonstrably superior patented technology, or a lock on an important distribution channel or the like. They prefer entrepreneurs experienced in the business they intend to start. The "unfair advantage" reduces risk by providing a margin for error. Although that term worries the corporate attorneys, intrapreneurs seek a powerful reason for success even in the face of setbacks.

Another part of the entrepreneurial strategy for reducing risk is anticipating barriers and remaining open to feedback, both positive and negative. Intrapreneurs are not Pollyannas or exaggerated devotees of positive thinking. While they have great confidence they can overcome them, they are aware of and seek information on the risks and problems. Venture capitalists see this fact as a screening device for selecting who to back. Entrepreneurs who cannot see problems or imagine how anything might go wrong are seen as promoters, not as real entrepreneurs.

Entrepreneurs appear to fit the popular swashbuckling image in one regard: They have great confidence in themselves, in their ability to make their ventures work somehow even if things don't happen as they hope.

Chuck House, who defied his chairman to bootleg a product he believed in, put it like this: "It's said that I took great risks, but I never saw them. To me, the risk was in *not* doing it." With typical intrapreneurial self-confidence, Chuck assumed he would keep his job, but he also knew he could always find another if he were fired. The greater risk would have been to court breaking faith with his own convictions by not trying his ideas.

Intrapreneurs dislike uncontrollable risks and do what they can to avoid them. They won't be found at the roulette table. However, because of their self-confidence, they are more willing than most to accept risks that depend directly on their skill; thus the aphorism: If an entrepreneur is betting on a race, the chances are he or she is running in it.

If intrapreneurs were wild risk takers, corporations could

not afford them. Fortunately, true intrapreneurs work diligently to minimize risk within the confines of their basic decision to accomplish challenging but not impossible goals.

Myth #3: The Entrepreneur "Shoots from the Hip" Because He or She Lacks Analytical Skills

If intrapreneurs were totally intuitive in their decision making, it is hard to imagine how they could work within the corporate system. But the fact that intrapreneurs have intuitive skills and a willingness to use them does not imply lack of analytical skills.

"Most people are either intuitive or analytical," says Ned Hermann, formerly the head of training at GE. "But entrepreneurs [and intrapreneurs] are good at both."

Art Fry states, "Making use of and trusting your own insights is where the intrapreneur gets a big jump on things. Where others are making incremental steps, you can jump ahead. You can't always justify it and you certainly can't prove it. At that stage people say 'He's pulling hoaxes,' but actually you are following a higher truth they cannot see." However, having made the intuitive leaps, intrapreneurs sit down and think through their new ideas analytically, extending, consolidating, and testing them.

Were intrapreneurs always only intuitive, they would form a breed apart intolerable to the analytical environment. They complain often about their intuition not being respected, and with some justification. But it is good to remember that intrapreneurs can do the hard analytical stuff too.

Myth #4: Entrepreneurs Are Amoral

Perhaps the most striking similarity of all venture capitalists' descriptions of the entrepreneur is their insistence that honesty and integrity are characteristics of the successful entrepreneur. Some may find this surprising because in the popular mind entrepreneurs are often seen as willing to sacrifice morals for profit. But it is less surprising when you consider that entrepreneurs are generally deeply committed to what they consider to be worthwhile purposes. Their need to achieve produces flexibility with the rules, not a loss of integrity.

Venture capitalists need honest entrepreneurs because they relinquish operating control over their money when they put it in the hands of the entrepreneurs. They have to trust them.

Two weeks before Bill Foster received the financing for Stratus Computers, one of the founders backed out. Fearing Stratus would lose its financial backing, the departing founder kindly made an offer to Bill to keep his resignation quiet and play along for a few more weeks until the deal was closed. Bill thanked him but declined his offer and instead immediately told the venture capitalists he was losing a founder and would understand if they backed out. To his great surprise, they were relieved because they had already detected that something was amiss with the founder who decided to resign. More importantly, his backers now had powerful evidence that they could trust Bill to be honest even when the news wasn't favorable. They made the investment on schedule despite the fact that a key spot was vacant on the venture team. They trusted Bill to fill it.

Honesty and integrity are as important to intrapreneurs as they are to entrepreneurs. You are at least as dependent on the trust of your sponsor as the entrepreneur is dependent on the venture capitalists' trust. When Art Fry of 3M did the early manufacturing runs on his yellow pad project, Post-it Notes, he ran into trouble. It was very difficult to get the product into neat pads and equally difficult to maintain the right level of stickiness. Fry was honest and told his sponsor about the difficulties he was encountering, adding that he was determined to solve the problem. But open as he was to his sponsor, he didn't broadcast his troubles to the entire company. He quickly gathered all the defective samples and burned them lest they fell into the hands of doubting Thomases.

70

Honesty to oneself may be the most important aspect of the intrapreneur's honesty. When you have a problem, you will face it with courage. You are most likely intolerant of delay and tend to take rapid and courageous action to correct problems decisively so they won't occur again.

One venture capitalist described his successful entrepreneurs like this: "They are darned honest with themselves. If there is a problem, they tend to get it out in the open fast and then stick with it until it is solved."[*] Another said of his entrepreneurs: "All are extremely honest with themselves, and will not tolerate untruthfulness or dishonesty from anyone on their team."[†] Since entrepreneurs and intrapreneurs often have to handle dozens of functions that they know little about, this ability to detect malarkey is essential.

Myth #5: Entrepreneurs Are Power-Hungry Empire Builders

Watching entrepreneurs build large organizations with themselves at the helm, it is easy to imagine that they are driven by the need to tell others what to do. But it turns out that the need for power is not an important part of the entrepreneurial motivation. As a young researcher, David McClelland rejected the idea that motivation was irrevocably established in early childhood by deprivation or trauma. He believed motivation could change and people could change—that, for example, people could go from being executives to entrepreneurs and vice versa.

Lying behind motivation, McClelland felt, are the fantasies every person has of what he or she wants to be or do. He began grouping the many different fantasies he found in testing people into archetypes, first into forty kinds and

[*] Richard White, *The Entrepreneur's Manual*, Chilton Book Company, Radnor, Pa., 1977, p. 221. The chapter contains entrepreneurial profiles as seen by three venture capital groups.

[†] Ibid., p. 223.

eventually into three great thrusts, which emerged as the need for power, the need for achievement, and the need for affiliation. In his extensive studies of entrepreneurs, his conclusion was this: Entrepreneurs are not driven by a need for power; instead, their motivation stems from a very high need for achievement.

Entrepreneurs, he found, are not so concerned with the corner offices, large numbers of people to tell what to do, and imposing possessions. They are not satisfied with rising in the hierarchy and having the esteem of their peers. Instead, entrepreneurs (and intrapreneurs) are driven by the need to achieve—to leave their mark by accomplishing things that have never been done before.

People with a strong need for achievement are primarily concerned with setting goals for themselves and achieving them. They have strong internal standards of excellence that challenge them. They want to make unique achievements and find new ways of doing things. They tend to have long-range goals that they work toward systematically. All these qualities match perfectly with the intrapreneurial role.

While achievement-motivated people are very competitive, their focus is on beating their own standards of performance, not on the effect they are having on others. Consider this example. Most long-distance runners are achievement-oriented. In an extreme case, if they decide to run a mile race in 3:52 and they finish fourth in 3:51.9, they are pleased. If they win in 3:52.2, they are unhappy. Making their self-determined goal is more important than winning over others.

The extreme focus on their own performance and their own standards is helpful to intrapreneurs swimming against the stream to start something new. But it also contains the source of intrapreneurs' potential weakness as managers. That weakness comes not in the ability to make good business decisions, which is generally excellent, but in day-to-day people-handling skills.

Achievement-motivated people usually have difficulty as managers of large organizations. They generally set high standards, so high in fact that others rarely meet them. This makes them critical and demanding—not supportive. The need for achievement is often directed toward personal accomplishment, which then makes it hard to let go or to give others credit. Surprisingly, power-driven people are satisfied to achieve things by getting others to do them. As a result they delegate better.

People with a need for power feel strong when others react strongly to them. The power-motivated musician may want to transport people away in bliss, while the gang leader may feel powerful when others fear him. Power people differ as to what effect they want to create, but all want to have a strong emotional impact on others.

The best executives feel good when their influence works to make their people grow and be effective. As long as they feel in control they do not need the constant feedback achievement-motivated people crave. They can live with not knowing how big an effect they are really having.

This need to be influential fits well with the management career path, but a strong need for power can be quite destructive to start-up intrapreneurs because it may lead them to waste time defining their positions in relation to others, thereby provoking conflicts. Intrapreneurs do better to charge off toward the goal, encouraging others to follow.

Venture capitalists have learned to be suspicious of entrepreneurs who want fancy rugs and company cars before they have earned them. They prefer entrepreneurs who frugally select very modest quarters. As one intrapreneur has observed, "The most important innovations seem to happen in buildings with leaky roofs." Achievement-motivated intrapreneurs don't care if they have to sit on orange crates as long as they have the tools to get the job done. Perhaps the leaky roof keeps away those who don't belong.

The myth of the power-motivated entrepreneur turns out to be false—it is, rather, the typical corporate executive who craves power. Quite the reverse of the myth, entrepreneurs and intrapreneurs are less power-motivated than executives, and the fact that they are achievement-motivated instead explains both their strength as business starters and their potential weakness as executives. But as McClelland has shown—if you want to, you can always change. There is no reason why successful intrapreneurs should not become senior executives, or vice versa, if they wish to, but either switch will require a substantial change in basic motivation.

The myths about the entrepreneur suggest to the corporation that intrapreneuring cannot work. With these myths dispelled, your company should be more willing to allow you to begin intrapreneuring.

PROFILE

HULKI ALDIKACTI:
At Home in a Corporate Giant

Intrapreneurship is not a choice; it's the only survival attitude.

Intrapreneuring begins with a vision. Turkish-born Hulki Aldikacti, Chief of Advanced Vehicle Design at Pontiac, had to wait a long time for his vision of an inexpensive, two-seater sports car to be realized. "Hulki had been talking with me about this car for many years," said Ayla, Hulki's wife. The turning point came in the fall of 1978, when Pontiac identified a marketing opportunity for just the kind of car Hulki had in mind. Pontiac's broad market data suggested that a great many young people would buy a car like a Corvette or a Porsche, if it were half the price. Once the need and the potential market had been established, it became possible for Hulki to begin building the car he had been dreaming about. The result of that partnership between intrapreneur and corporation is the revolutionary Fiero.

STEP 1: THE CONCEPT STUDY

Defining the Market Personally

The definition of the two-seater car provided by Pontiac's marketing department was only the starting point for Hulki. To design the car he had to acquire an immediate sense of the customers' needs. To get a picture of the kind of people who would drive the car, Hulki thought of his own children at the University of Michigan, and their friends. He struggled to understand their habits and their values, so different from his own.

Hulki concluded that his prospective customers needed a smart-looking car, one "they didn't have to hide behind a tree when they went to a party." At the same time, the car had to be inexpensive and simple to fix. "Kids can't afford the body shop," he said. He also insisted on adding a plastic body so the car would not rust. However, fiberglass-bodied cars can be expensive to repair after accidents, so Hulki invented a new solution to the high cost of body repair.

"I noticed that the typical family has a $19.95 Sears tool kit," explained Hulki, "so I decided to design a car whose body you could fix with that." And he did. Fiero owners can unscrew a smashed fender themselves and screw on a new one.

Striving to build a car that his children could both love and afford drove Hulki to his biggest triumph. While the public considers the Fiero an exciting and affordable sports car, the automobile industry sees it as a manufacturing breakthrough: figuring out how to get all the screw-on body panels properly aligned in assembly. Hulki and his team had to invent a machine that would simultaneously trim all the places where body parts mount on the frame to insure a panels' perfect alignment—an invention which enabled the Fiero team to leapfrog Japanese quality control.

For an intrapreneur, inventing a new car is not enough; you have to get it built. "I could sit and talk about what will happen in 1995," says Hulki, "but to bring it alive you need a project.

Selling the Idea to Corporate Management

Once Hulki knew precisely the car he wanted to build, he had to sell his idea to management. He had Pontiac management's support because the car fit the need identified by Pontiac marketing; but in the wider world of GM, that support wasn't enough to build a new car. Pontiac had to sell GM corporate product planners on the new vehicle. To sell the Fiero, Hulki and his Pontiac supporters tied it to existing GM corporate goals. Back in 1978 Pete Estes, then president of GM, had wisely decided that GM should be competitive with the imports in fuel economy. Each division was expected to do its part in this effort. Because this was a top corporate priority, Hulki and his Pontiac colleagues positioned the Fiero as a way to improve the fuel efficiency of the Pontiac line.

One has to admire their courage in passing off as sporty a car as the Fiero primarily as a fuel miser for commuters. In fact, it is Detroit's first mass production car with the mid-engine layout found in both race cars and high-performance European supercars such as the Ferrari. The Fiero looks and moves fast. Its radical new body construction may easily revolutionize the way cars are built. And, yes, it is also a small, fuel efficient car suitable for the commuter.

Getting to Yes—A New Approach

To sell corporate product planning on building a Fiero prototype, Pontiac needed detailed information—supporting market data, a preliminary concept design, an estimate of manufacturing costs, and performance specifications. To get approval for the concept design study, Hulki went before GM product planners. When the corporate planners finally said neither yes nor no, Hulki, still undaunted, knew at once what their silence meant: "They didn't say yes or no, so they must have meant yes." He went ahead and prepared the concept study as if permission had been granted.

STEP 2: THE PROTOTYPE

Hulki doesn't believe in going directly from concept studies to a large-scale engineering effort. "It's ridiculous to ask executives to spend billions without showing them what they are spending it on," says Hulki. Instead, he works with a small, elite team to build a prototype of the car itself, even using manufacturing methods as close as possible to the ones that will be used in production. That way he learns what is possible, and can estimate more closely what the real costs will be.

When the concept study was done, the Pontiac Product Planners went back to headquarters with a request for a budget to build a prototype of the Fiero.

Because they didn't have universal head-office support, Pontiac and Hulki chose to create the Fiero on a shoestring budget (by ordinary U.S. new car standards). They also decided to complete it in record time, before such support as there was ran out. Pontiac chief engineer Bob Dorn saw that the Pontiac organization as it then existed was too ponderous for the job and asked Hulki how he thought they should go about building the prototype. Hulki replied, "I'll go outside and set up shop and run it like a small business." His answer should not be surprising. When time and money are in short supply, intrapreneuring is the only answer.

Hulki moved his operation ten miles south, renting space

from one of his vendors, but even at that distance he knew he wasn't safe from well-meaning interference. He told Pontiac general manager Bill Hoglund and his boss, Bob Dorn, "People will come to you with complaints and bitches about me. Don't talk to them without talking to me first. Better yet, send them to see me directly."

To their great credit, Hoglund and Dorn did an exceptional job of protecting Hulki and the Fiero. When someone complained that Hulki hadn't done it by the book, Dorn always said, "Have you seen Hulki about that? No? Then I can't help you. Why don't you go see Hulki yourself? His address is 898 Chicago Road." Most of the critics never showed up; ten miles was just too far to go.

When they did come, Hulki listened. The complaints were on the order of one transmission specialist commenting: "We don't want that kind of shifter at Pontiac." If someone had a better idea, Hulki changed the design, but he always made it clear that it was his choice to do so. He could do this because Bob Dorn never asked him to change something just because someone else in Pontiac didn't like it, or because that wasn't the way things were done at Pontiac. The result was not only a fresh and original design, unburdened by the compromises committees might impose, but also a car finished in record time and with great frugality.

"Without Dorn's support," said Hulki, "the bureaucracy would have eaten us alive. By the book, ordering a pencil can take three weeks—every clerk has rules to follow. But I didn't have to live within the system. Because of our separate location and the freedom we were given, we could just send someone out with petty cash."

Hulki's favorite style of report is written in metal and plastic. On March 10, 1979, six months after starting on the prototype project, Hulki drove the completed Fiero prototype into the Corporate Technical Center to demonstrate the new car to top GM executives. It was an immediate hit as a car and as a method of illustrating a new idea.

"Abstraction is out and demonstration cars are back in," asserted Hulki.

STEP 3: PUTTING THE DESIGN INTO PRODUCTION

The Fiero prototype not only impressed the planners and executives at General Motors, it also fit into their strategies for dealing with a world torn apart by rising oil prices and foreign competition.

Within a month GM told Pontiac to start the long task of putting the Fiero into production. Hulki stayed with his car, heading up the program to produce it. As it happens it was very fortunate he did.

Getting Past No

The Fiero development years were turbulent years for the U.S. automobile industry. All the major companies had losing years and their top managements were looking for ways to reduce the flow of red ink.

Between April 1980 (when the effort to build the production Fiero began) and December 1983, orders went out to stop work on the Fiero three times. Hulki responded with an iron stubbornness that most intrapreneurs must summon at some point in their career. Each time Hulki shielded his people from the order to stop while trying to reverse it.

By the time the third kill order rolled in, the Fiero was not a small, easy-to-hide project. About 225 people working full-time on the project reported directly to Hulki. Another 275 were working on the Fiero in functions such as crash safety. Vendors were working on it, too: About 500 people outside GM were devoted to the Fiero.

Through all this, Hulki encouraged his people to keep working. Finally pushed to the wall, he made an announcement: "You may have heard rumors that the [Fiero] has been killed. Ignore the rumors and keep going."

He took the same approach with vendors. When vendors called because they had been told to stop all work on the Fiero, Hulki told them, "Keep going and we'll straighten it out." The vendors, who also believed in the project, kept on working. Hulki drew his courage from a belief that he wasn't wasting GM's money but rather was using it in the most effective way he knew. "I don't do hobby things," he said, "When I do something, you know it's serious. Time was against us so we couldn't afford to stop. Besides, it is very difficult and very expensive to stop and start again on a very large project—we had to keep going." When intrapreneurs are bold and succeed, they may become heroes. When they bend the rules to save their project and fail, they can be branded as outlaws.

Supporting Controllers

As work on the Fiero continued unofficially, Pontiac controllers couldn't help but know what was going on. Instead of killing the project, they kept talking with the corporate staff to extend Fiero's life. "They could have just dropped the ax on it. Instead they kept analyzing it to find new ways to demonstrate to GM that it was good business financially," says Hulki. By dragging out the financial discussions, Pontiac's controllers bought time, and permitted the project to survive.

Hulki gives credit for this support to GM's policy of having each division's controller work directly for the division general manager, not for corporate. Thus they are part of the organizations they serve. While responsible to corporate for the financial status of their division, they also know all the local facts. "We all know each other as people, not as faceless offices," he said.

Restoring Official Approval

Each time GM reluctantly decided that the company could live without Fiero and that other expenses were even more essential, Hulki got advance notice that the order to stop was on its way. Dorn and Hoglund would tell him, "We're going to get cut again."

In the days of impending shutdown, Hulki spent a lot of time by himself thinking about why the Fiero should be allowed to live. He went for long drives reviewing all the arguments pro and con in his mind, finding better and better ways to refute each reason to stop and to defend Fiero's existence. He spent hours in his workshop carving a piece of wood and thinking. Often he found himself talking to himself out loud, sometimes even when his wife was in the car with him. The purpose of all this solitary work was "to bring them a proposal and an attitude they would accept."

Nor was Hulki alone. Hoglund and Dorn helped him plan ways of getting the stop order reversed. "They were my shield and my protectors," said Hulki. "They believed deeply in this car." Hulki gave them all his own arguments as well so that they would be well prepared when explaining to others the importance of continuing.

Speed

The Fiero Project cut almost two years and many dollars out of the normal timetable for new car development. GM top management considered this system so significant that they are trying to recreate it. As one insider said, "The Fiero experience was a prototype of a better way to new product development at GM. In times of rapid change, and with the challenge of foreign competition, we have to find ways to get cars to market faster." Hulki's success in new product development efficiency holds lessons for many industries.

Memos, Paperwork and Meetings

Hulki's first prescription for speed is "to get rid of all the people who want to do paperwork." There was so little paperwork going on in the original project team that one secretary served twenty-six people. He expects his people to hear what he says the first time, and then take responsibility for their own areas. "My idiosyncracy is this: Don't do things that don't have a purpose," said Hulki. "I can't waste time, and meetings bore me. I only go to meetings when absolutely necessary." If his boss calls a routine meeting, Hulki sends a substitute. He believes that when a meeting is absolutely necessary, it should last about five minutes—just long enough to share decisions that have been made by the people responsible for them.

Cut and Try Prototyping

Few people can see a car—or any other product—as clearly on paper as they can in three dimensional reality. The result of building and designing the car at the same time is two-fold: The process is much faster and it results in simpler, more cost-effective, designs.

Hulki's hobby is sculpture and he approaches engineering with some of the set of a sculptor. He doesn't like refining a design on paper forever when it can be done directly by making three dimensional parts.

To design the fenders for the Fiero prototype, he made rough drawings and then guided the worker in cutting the wood until the shape was right. (It's a sad commentary on auto industry job rules that the sculptor can't shape it himself.) When detailed drawings were needed, they were often made afterwards from the finished part instead of making the part from drawings.

To assemble the Fiero prototype, they first made the major parts. When they had 70 percent of the parts, they began building the car. They had a tool maker, a sheet metal specialist, and a mechanic standing by. As the car was assembled, they could see right away when something was missing, design the part, and build it on the spot.

Teams

One of the great barriers to speed in innovation is slow communication. To avoid that problem, Hulki brought all his people together in a small building away from the noise of bureaucratic interference. Formality slows communication too, so Hulki insisted on direct communication. Only with a small team can members of the group know and trust each other well enough to dispense with formality.

In assembling a team that would communicate well, Hulki included members from all the normal disciplines at GM, but he also included a few people from the areas of purchasing and financial control—areas which are often left out of new product teams. One of Hulki's organizational innovations was to hire a communicator for the team: Tom Kalush. "Tom did everything I didn't want to do," said Hulki. If Hulki bent the rules, jumping over many steps to get to the end result, Tom covered for him. If Hulki was in danger of overspending, Tom said, "Hulki, we'd better hold back for a bit." If Hulki didn't want to go to a meeting, Tom went. When he came back he told Hulki what he had heard, and they would strategize how to keep Fiero going. Almost every intrapreneur needs a "Kalush."

Presourcing

Essential to Hulki's success was his relationship with vendors. He didn't design the Fiero and then let purchasing send out the parts drawings to take bids. He made a purchasing agent part of his team. Together they involved key vendors from the beginning of the design process. The vendors helped design the car to match available materials and manufacturing techniques.

Hulki explains:

> General Motors has got a few percent of the world's technology, but in doing something new you can't close your eyes to all the rest. When you don't know, then go and get people who do and bring them in to influence the design.

Forming such a partnership—called "presourcing"—requires careful selection of key vendors, who had to satisfy three requirements:

1. Possess a unique technology necessary to the project
2. Have the ability to make the parts which were not yet

designed reliably and in quantity
3. Employ people with whom the team could work easily

For new technology, vendors are selected primarily on the basis of process and quality, not price. Although this sounds expensive, quite the reverse is often true. New technology often allows for greater savings than squeezing the last dime out of old technology.

As for problems associated with having a single supplier, Hulki said, "The danger of sole sourcing is a myth. However, forming long-term partnerships with vendors does require care."

Vendors were paid for their costs as they built prototypes, so their profits had to come from the production runs. So, strictly speaking, Pontiac does not owe them a debt, but a moral obligation exists to try to allow them a fair profit if they perform well. If a company's presourcing vendors don't end up doing well, it will become very difficult for the company's intrapreneurs to get the help they need with new technologies.

Imaginative partnerships with vendors have been important in many intrapreneurial successes. Without imaginative use of vendors, there would be no IBM PC, for instance. Presourcing is part of what Norm Macrae is describing when he says "the corporation of the future is a confederation of entrepreneurs." It is a way of combining the flexibility and dedication of small vendors with the large organization needed to produce and distribute on a large scale. This system only works well when there are intrapreneurs like Hulki inside the corporation who can deal with the small entrepreneurial vendors on their own terms.

Hulki believes there is a new industry attitude in Detroit which "will create a new industrial revolution that will make the industrial revolution in England look like a picnic." This new attitude includes new freedom to form imaginative partnerships with vendors. It includes a new cooperation between labor and management. It includes a turning away from abstraction and paperwork, toward concrete actions like demonstration cars. It includes moving away from the essence of bureaucracy, which is tight controls, to the essence of intrapreneurship, which is trust.

Don't count the U.S. auto industry out of innovation or intrapreneurship. Detroit is responding to new challenges faster than we could have hoped. The fact that Hulki prospers in the nation's largest automobile company is yet another proof of the industry's adaptability to a changing world. We will reindustrialize

America because companies like GM have the courage to let their people innovate. When the vast resources of America's intrapreneurs are tapped, we will find our industrial imagination and our ability to execute are second to none.

BOOK II

BECOMING AN INTRAPRENEUR

CHAPTER 4

Why Intrapreneuring Can Be Better Than Entrepreneuring

"I have only so much time in my life and I want to do as much as I can. I can do things faster here as part of 3M, and so I get to do more things," says intrapreneur Art Fry of 3M. Big companies have resources that can make developing a new idea far easier for an intrapreneur than the same task would be for an entrepreneur. For all the bureaucracy and inaction of Detroit, the barriers to building a dream car outside of General Motors proved far greater than John Z. DeLorean anticipated.

If your situation is appropriate, intrapreneuring can be clearly better than entrepreneuring:

If you have a burning vision that is inherently more intrapreneurial than entrepreneurial (if, for instance, your idea offers a way to build onto or improve the company business).

If you want to do new things but your desire to stay with the friendships and security of the corporation is stronger than your desire for a chance at great wealth.

If capital for your idea is easier to come by inside the corporation than outside.

If you want to practice creating a business inside before risking your own funds outside.

If you are dependent on the company name or marketing channels to boost the size or chances of success of your intraprise.

If you need continuing access to the company's proprietary technology to stay competitive.

THE BIG COMPANIES' ADVANTAGES

The competitive advantages companies can provide for their intrapreneurs have been changing. Financial clout and the bigness needed to manufacture cost-effectively have become less important, while access to proprietary information has become more important. Marketing clout, as always, remains strong.

Marketing Clout

When Alfred Chandler studied the consolidation of the early automobile industry, he came to a surprising conclusion. The greatest advantage of bigness was not the traditional economies of scale in manufacturing but rather in marketing, distribution, and service. Marketing clout is often a good reason for intrapreneuring.

Even when the intrapreneur must bypass existing company distribution channels, the *company name counts.* The IBM personal computer was a good machine, but P. D. Estridge and his team could not have grabbed a 23.4 percent market share* two and one half years after introducing the product without the IBM name. The IBM name mesmerized software houses, who dropped everything to write software for the new PC. It calmed corporate buyers, who were made nervous by the proliferation of entrepreneurial offerings. It appealed to dealers, who counted on IBM reliability and continuity. And individual customers liked the name too. It gave them confidence the machine and its architecture would be supported for years to come.

The entrepreneur who is starting up faces the formidable task of convincing customers that he or she will be around to back the product. This costs money. When Procter & Gamble introduces a new product, supermarkets give it space on the

* The Yankee Group, Boston, Mass.

shelves because it's from Procter & Gamble. The entrepreneur with the exact same product would have to advertise more to pull in sales and convince stores to give that product equal treatment.

The economies of scale in marketing and distribution suggest that—to paraphrase Norman Macrae, deputy editor of the London *Economist*—the corporation of the future will be a confederation of intrapreneurs. That confederation may be tied together primarily to gain economies of scale in marketing, distribution, and service, while smaller intrapreneurial units design and manufacture products.

The Technology Base

The second great advantage of the large firm is the technology base. In the 1930s, when Lammot du Pont, then chairman of Du Pont, was asked in an antitrust investigation if he wasn't buying up companies to eliminate competition, he replied that the purpose was quite different, that Du Pont was buying companies in diverse markets to have somewhere to put the results of its research.

Large companies can expect a greater return on fundamental research than small ones because one never knows for sure in which business area the results of research will lead. The larger and more diverse the firm, the greater the chance research results will fit some business the company is in or at least is competent to enter. As a result, large firms can afford to do more fundamental research.

However logical, this theory has run into two problems. First, since few big research-oriented companies have effective systems to support intrapreneuring, they rarely implement more than a tiny fraction of the good opportunities created by new internally developed technology. As a result, the research function itself often falls into some disrepute. Despite many technical breakthroughs, the labs cannot point to enough profitable results from their research to justify the R&D spending. Worse still, when intrapreneurs can't commercialize the breakthroughs inside the company, they leave, taking the new technologies with them. They end up in competitive start-ups that commercialize the new technology before the company that originally paid for its development. This outrages the corporation and again reduces its appetite for research. Empowering its intrapreneurs will restore the economic advantage a large firm should be getting from its technology base.

The large firm that both protects its proprietary technology and encourages intrapreneuring creates a powerful reason for intrapreneuring over entrepreneuring. For boundary-crossing intrapreneurs, a large firm can be a supermarket of advanced technology. In many companies it is possible for technologists to move freely from lab to lab gathering the information needed to produce a new product. Alec Feiner, for example, is one of AT&T's finest technical intrapreneurs. He has learned to get his ideas into production in a system with vast numbers of inventions, few of which are ever produced by AT&T. He is the intrapreneur behind the Ferreed switch, the Horizon® PBX, and System 75. "The intrapreneur has to be an opportunist in the sense of learning how to operate within the system," he says. "You have to put your foot in any door that is cracked open and be quick to grab opportunities to move toward implementation."

In 1959 Alec was working on the idea of distributing the central-office function of the telephone company. In the old system, a pair of wires had to run from the central office out to each phone. The number of wires needed was staggering, and at any time most of them were not in use. Feiner thought, "What if we could build a remote switching system that would serve 100 lines, with only twenty lines going back to the central office?" To build this new remote switching system, he needed a switch with properties that didn't exist.

Part of Feiner's gift is self-confidence, or as he puts it: "a naive belief that the human intellect can overcome all difficulties, that there is always a way to come up with something elegantly simple." His invention consisted of two thin metal "reeds" moved by magnetic coils. The magnetic coils bend the reeds toward each other so they make contact, completing a circuit, or away from each other, opening the switch. The invention was called a "Ferreed" since, in addition to the magnetic reeds, a piece of ferrite was used to give the device its memory.

After getting the idea, Alec's first step was to spend a day making preliminary calculations and convincing himself that the concept was a good one. After putting the idea through his own critical examination for a day or two, he began sharing it with a few close friends at AT&T. The idea began to build momentum and he turned to verifying the economic factors as well as the technical feasibility. "To get things done you have to have breadth," he says. "You can't be decoupled from the realities of the market. Even though development is just a small wheel in a very big machine, you have to know who is going to use your new product, how they will use it and who the competitors are."

Once he had satisfied himself that the device had merit, he set out to build it. He needed a material with properties he had never encountered, a "ferrite with a coercive force of forty oersteds." One of the advantages of being in the Bell System (as it was called before the divestiture) was the access to other minds and other technologies. Alec traveled to another laboratory in Murray Hill where he met with Frank Chegwidden, who had developed just such a material but hadn't yet found a use for it. From there he went to a relay group in the New York West Street Labs, who helped him cut the new material to the exact dimensions and fabricate the first prototype of the Ferreed switch. Within a few weeks from the original idea he had a working prototype.

People You Can Trust

When one intrapreneur left Intel to form his own company, I asked him why he had left and what he missed the most. He finally said he had left because he couldn't get support for his intraprise. His greatest surprise was how supportive the venture capitalists were. Far from just supplying money, they helped him work through all the problems of starting a new venture. Somehow he had assumed that the corporation should be able to supply more support to its people than they could get from outsiders.

For all of his resentment toward Mother Intel for not supporting him in his efforts to innovate, our intrapreneur missed it badly. What he had left behind was people. Inside Intel he had had a vast network of people he trusted, people who could answer questions, people who would do what they said, and people who made things work. He could go to any of them with a problem and he didn't have to worry about confidentiality because they were all part of the Intel family. Information resources are of great value to an intrapreneur, and as an entrepreneur they were gone.

Every large organization makes it its business to know a great deal about the future of the markets it operates in. In addition, as a major factor in those markets, it knows its own plans. Intrapreneurs adding value in and around those markets can gain years of advantage over outside entrepreneurs by access to their company's plans, forecasts, and markets.

It was, for example, highly valuable to Intel's bubble-memory intrapreneurs to know the company's plans for conventional memories. They knew future prices, new technologies, and a great deal about where the memory market was going. No entrepreneurial group could have hoped to find all that out so easily.

The Advantage of Bounded Networks

It may seem at first that independent entrepreneurs should be able to develop a network of resources fully as effective as the network inside a large firm. After all, their networks are unbounded—they can go to the best people in any field in the whole world, while the internal company network is more limited. However, the large firm turns out to have a major advantage precisely because company networks are bounded. They can share proprietary secrets freely with insiders because they know where the boundaries are, while entrepreneurs dealing with other entrepreneurs have no clear boundaries for proprietary information. This shuts down communication.

Because corporations keep their proprietary information highly confidential to prevent it from falling into the hands of competitors, it is extremely difficult for the entrepreneur to have access to state-of-the-art information that Alec Feiner had at AT&T. In a way this is not surprising. In the Information Age more efficient and synergistic use of information may be the primary economy of scale and thus the basic reason for the existence of large firms.

Pilot Plant and Shared-Time Production

When an intrapreneur at 3M wants to make a new product dependent on coatings technology, it is very simple to go to one of 3M's plants and ask them to run a batch for a small transfer cost. The system is set up to do it, and as the product comes on line one always has access to state-of-the-art plants and equipment and to manufacturing people who want it to succeed. According to Art Fry:

> When I want to test a new product there is always some piece of 3M that can make it. It may cost a little more, and I may have to skip it all over the place to get it done, but I can get enough for test market. Then after the tests are in we can design a plant to do it right and the final process will be very efficient.

When Rolf Westgaard, the sales manager for a dry processed microfilm system, intrapreneured a new use for 3M's dry silver process, he put together a bootleg team including the inventor of the process and a good manufacturing expert. They manufactured the product on a shared-time basis in three different plants in two other divisions. This kind of flexibility is very hard to obtain for the entrepreneur without using outside vendors and losing control of the technology.

The intrapreneur in a large firm has a better chance that his idea will be produced in a plant within the company that is operating under capacity and thus eager to try something new. Of course, this advantage, while good in theory, comes to fruition in those few firms that give intrapreneurs the flexibility to cross divisional boundaries freely in search of what they need.

If Toffler and other futurists are right, we are moving away from mass markets and toward products aimed at narrower niches. In this environment it is likely that the practice of allowing intrapreneurs time on manufacturing facilities to produce market-specific products will increase.

Finance

Large firms can of course supply intrapreneurs with financial resources, but increasingly so can venture capital. Once the great advantage only of large firms, financial resources of monumental scale are no longer their province alone. Nonetheless, there are types of ventures where corporate deep pockets are a great advantage to the intrapreneur. These include:

> Types of ventures out of vogue with the venture capitalists but in vogue with the corporation. For example, few venture capitalists are investing in specialty chemicals, but nearly every major chemical company is.

> Acquisitions—corporate intrapreneurs can probably play a bigger game than they can on their own.

> Internal financial plays like General Electric's leasing venture, which created tax write-offs that eliminated GE's income-tax liability.

There are some industries where the economies of scale in production still work against entrepreneuring. No venture-capital syndicate has yet had the steely courage to back an entrepreneur in developing and introducing a new polymer, which might take over a decade to reach breakeven at a cost of from $100 to $600 million.

Intrapreneurs who dream dreams of this size and duration generally must put up with the full brunt of corporate bureaucracy, which understandably seeks to defend itself against hundred-million-dollar blunders. That obstacle course is still the path of least resistance if you must attempt the gargantuan.

In general, corporate financial support as an advantage of intrapreneuring over entrepreneuring has been neutralized by the influx of venture capital. The major advantages now lie in marketing clout, technology, people, and information resources.

THREE ADVANTAGES OF ENTREPRENEURING

Decisiveness

For many entrepreneurs the greatest boon to being out is escaping the indecisiveness of the corporation. Once they have made their initial investment, the courting of which can be agonizing, venture capitalists tend to be dogged supporters. They don't invest "nervous money." Once in, they expect to win.

Sophisticated Investors

One of the great virtues of entrepreneurship is the sophisticated venture capitalist. Competent venture capitalists do more than just supply money. One venture capitalist says his time breaks down like this:

- Selecting investments—15 percent
- Helping out with ventures in which he currently has investments—65 percent

- Public offerings and other selling of successful ventures—
  20 percent

In that 65 percent spent helping companies in his portfolio, the venture capitalist often delivers sophisticated advice on how to manage a start-up that isn't available inside most large firms. In large firms, sponsoring intrapreneurs is rarely a career in itself, so few get as good at advising startups as the full-time venture capitalist.

Ownership

One of the primary advantages of entrepreneuring is ownership. Ownership can, as I have said before, lead to wealth and freedom. Few firms offer intrapreneurial rewards which support either freedoms or lifestyles remotely comparable to the successful entrepreneur. As we shall see in Chapters 10 and 11, this great disparity is unnecessary, but some differences will probably always remain.

THE DECISION TO BECOME AN INTRAPRENEUR

Whether the benefits of entrepreneuring outweigh those of intrapreneuring is your decision. Dick Nadeau tried both and ended up an intrapreneur. "I don't work well in a backyard. I need the corporate environment and resources. I don't think the automatic clinical analyzer could have happened in a garage."

For the right person, intrapreneuring is exhilarating as well as addicting, combining as it does the resources and security of a corporation with the freedom and creativity of the entrepreneur.

PROFILE

RICHIE HERRINK: Selling to Your Own Company

When Richie Herrink was a young man, one of his bosses told him, "Don't ask anyone, just do it. As they come at you, you can back off; but if no one attacks, keep going." Richie's style is typically intrapreneurial, so the advice fitted him well. He is quick to spot an opportunity, quick to capitalize on it, and just as quick to move on when new opportunities knock.

At IBM Richie found his opportunity. What is different about his success story is that his ideas had nothing to do with new products or processes, and in the direct sense, didn't produce revenue for the corporation. What Richie did was to broaden the educational opportunities for 20,000 IBM employees from eighteen divisions in Westchester County, New York; Fairfield County, Connecticut; and Bergen County, New Jersey.

The courses were "paid for" through intracompany transfers to Herrink's Information Systems and Communications Division, and in just one year that division's internal revenue rocketed from $100,000 to over $2 million, with a margin of $700,000.

Richie Herrink and his superior, Bill Weimer, expanded what had traditionally been I. S. & C.'s franchise from a local audience of 1,500 merely by providing what Herrink calls "critical mass." In 1981 each of the eighteen headquarters divisions had its own education department. Separately, the divisions could not generate enough interest to sponsor many employee classes, and no one thought to cooperate interdivisionally. By drawing from all the divisions, Herrink and Weimer could fill classes to overflowing, and they could schedule specialized courses that otherwise would not have been offered at all. On their side were IBM's policies of sponsoring courses, even though they might not be necessary for their employees' day to day work, and of paying for that education through intracompany transfers. Capitalizing on those policies, before Herrick and Weimer were done, they literally grew themselves out of business.

The first course Richie wanted to offer cost $14,000, nearly one-sixth of his entire annual budget. He admits to some initial apprehension—"What if nobody wants to try this course?"—but he went ahead and prepared a flyer which he mailed widely inside IBM's headquarters community. Richie had arranged for a one day seminar by W. Edwards Deming, who had invented Quality Control Circles and is considered the father of Japanese management techniques. Of the 1,400 who applied, Richie could accommodate only 950, at $30 each. Since Deming cost him only $5 a seat, Richie's business was not only growing but had already become profitable.

He was off to a good start, but he needed to grow rapidly to establish a large network of supporters before anyone could complain that his turf was being unfairly invaded. He had already made 950 new friends. He therefore rapidly launched a second major course.

MIT's Sloan School of Management had a course in the management of technology that was very popular at IBM. Richie composed a shorter version of it. The response was enthusiastic, and the course produced almost half a million dollars in internal sales in 1983. Richie kept trying new courses, following his gut feelings, not having time for surveys because they would have tipped off people who might object to his offerings.

Only one or two courses had rocky starts. Shoneberger's "Japanese Manufacturing Techniques" had a high enrollment but did not go over well. Richie took the instructor aside and revamped his outline, shortening the course from three days to two. When they ran it again, it was a smash hit. People asked, "Who is this Richie Herrink coming in like the Marines," but Richie's boss defended him whenever necessary.

For the most part Richie used outsiders to deliver the training he developed. Doing so allowed him to hire people only when training was going on. He did, however, have to use IBM trainers to teach IBM equipment, and his staff grew to six full-time people and two full-time subcontractors.

While he was building his intraprise, both the demands and the satisfactions were great. "When you think in the broad strategic terms of growing a business, you forget that your time is actually spent hung up in the mundane details of rescheduling a class when the instructor gets sick or stuffing envelopes. I did whatever had to be done to get it going, and that takes inordinate energy." He was working 60 to 70 hours a week. (He still hasn't had time to take his accumulated vacation.) After years of immaculate care, his lawn went to pieces, a sure sign of shifting priorities. Nevertheless, Richie loved it. "My wife told me that the period when I was building the business was the happiest I have ever been at work—I believe her."

In many ways Richie's situation was ideal. He had great independence to run his business as he saw fit. He saw his boss, whose office is in Rochester, Minnesota, about once a month. He had complete discretion over a budget of $1 million per year and access to more money when he needed it.

Unfortunately, as is so often the case for intrapreneurs, the thrill of starting a business doesn't last forever. "I am fascinated by the fact that I could walk away from this job tomorrow and it wouldn't bother me," Richie said. The urge to realize his vision and prove something to himself is over. He enjoyed building a business, but finds little satisfaction in operating it once it has reached a stable form.

After two years of fantastic success, the corporate mind caught up with Richie Herrink in two ways: First, his newly expanded division wasn't on the organizational chart. Where did it fit? To whom should it be responsible? This was the first time an internal organization had crossed corporate boundaries and, while only one person from one of the 18 divisions ever complained about territory infringement, the problem remained: I. S. & C. was a division without a slot.

Second, their success did them in—again, partly because of the way corporations work. They had drawn such a large audience, it became increasingly hard to find classroom space. The division whose job it was to provide rental space for IBM's internal needs was spending too much on I. S. & C. Because of corporate limitations, not enough money was available to provide the necessary space. What they needed was a school, owned by IBM and operated by Herrink and Weimer's division. What they did instead was to close down, despite the fact he could reasonably see revenues rising still further, to $4 million in only two more years. It just was not as exciting to double a $2 million revenue as it had been to start the project and watch its early growth.

"When I look back, not many people could have done what I did. It took an unusual blend of skills, fifteen years in and out of education, a feel for what had to be done, a feel for publicity, a feel for what I could get away with, and, most of all, willingness to act on my gut feelings without checking whether I was right or not."

In the end, what may seem like bureaucratic bumbling is probably corporate wisdom. Their original classes may no longer be available, but Herrink is still in business, this time with a clear corporate charter. He and Bill Weimer now head a new division, Technology Management Education, which will be responsible for education companywide. As Richie Herrink put it, "We are answering a higher calling."

CHAPTER 5

Choosing an Idea

Establishing yourself as a successful intrapreneur depends, in part, upon choosing a good idea. That idea must not only be good for the market, but good for the company and good for you. At first, when you are searching for an idea worthy of your commitment, don't pursue one idea at a time. Develop five or ten in parallel until one emerges so strongly that it begins to dominate your thoughts and fantasies. To check out one idea at a time has several disadvantages. First, because you are constantly receiving random information from what you read and from people you talk to, having a number of back-burner ideas gives you a greater likelihood of finding uses for information you pick up. Second, if you are pursuing a single idea by feigning commitment before you feel it, you may paint yourself into a corner. It is very hard to be objective when you are down to your last idea. You may feel so strongly that it has to work that you ignore feedback and plunge on toward certain doom. The time for burning your bridges to prevent retreat comes later, when the idea has pretty clearly demonstrated its feasibility and you are ready to make a significant commitment. Before then you are better off working on a number of ideas to find the best.

SOURCES OF BUSINESS IDEAS

In these times of change, we are floating in a sea of new business opportunities. You may already have ideas that interest you. If so, go directly to page 119, "Choosing an Idea." To find the best ideas to begin intrapreneuring, you should first consider hundreds of possible opportunities. How can you train your mind to find business ideas? The following are ways of discovering business ideas.

Brainstorming

Brainstorming is a technique for generating new ideas. The basic principles are simple:

1. **Assemble a group of people—colleagues or friends—with very different backgrounds, skills, and experiences.**

   Inventions and new business ideas come from putting together known ideas and mechanisms in new ways. By bringing diverse disciplines together, you improve your chances of inventing something others haven't thought of.

2. **Prepare the group for the meeting.**

   Let the participants know what the problem is a few days in advance so their subconsciouses can begin to find solutions. A call or a memo will do.

3. **Don't judge ideas as good or bad during the idea-generation phase.**

   Separate idea creation and idea screening. Insist that your fellow brainstormers playfully accept all ideas in a spirit of fun without getting serious. This is difficult because we have all been trained in our work to be judgmental; it's part of how we demonstrate maturity.

   A new idea is like a butterfly emerging from a cocoon. For the first half hour before its wings unfold, the butterfly is ugly and looks as though it would never fly. Only with time does it develop into a wonder. So it is with an idea, except that the percentage of new ideas that ever unfold successfully is smaller. Nonetheless, it is the silly and weak idea that with one more insight could become a world-beater, while those that seem OK at first often remain ordinary.

4. **Go for volume, not quality, in idea generation.**

   Generate as many ideas as possible in a short period of time. Have everyone write down twenty business ideas in five minutes. Accept silly ones, foolish ones, and mediocre ones as well as an occasional good one. Experience shows that only by playing with lots of ideas do you get to a few good ones. If you try to eliminate the foolish, you are judging and you will get a slow stream of workmanlike but mundane ideas that offer little hope of high potential.

5. **Build on each other's ideas instead of attacking them.**

The virtue of a diverse group is different backgrounds. Someone who knows how ants dig tunnels may have crazy ideas for a new mining machine. It would be easy to just laugh, but in brainstorming the task is to take seemingly silly ideas and try to make them work, seeing what's good about them and then building ways to overcome their weaknesses. This optimistic attitude can easily be labeled unrealistic, but yours will be the last laugh because it is at the core of creativity.

6. **Sort out ideas after the meeting.**

Cluster, ponder, expand, and test your raw idea pile to find a few good ideas.

Even though it is more fun than a cocktail party, you may be reluctant to pull together a group of people and suggest a brainstorming party. Fortunately, the basic principles of brainstorming can be applied to your own idea search without assembling a formal brainstorming group.

Cross-Fertilizing

For some crazy reason, corporations tend to put everyone with like ideas and experiences together. Marketing people end up talking to other marketing people, while somewhere else surface chemists talk only to other surface chemists. As an intrapreneur, you have to get out of this stultifying situation. If you are in marketing, take an engineer to lunch. Better yet, take him or her out to visit customers and then buy a beer and brainstorm ways to apply what you learned together. Visit every lab you can and look over the prototypes and technologies there. Listen to the dreams and visions, and brainstorm ways to make them fit what you know of the market, then keep what you saw in mind the next time you're talking to customers.

If you are an engineer, burst out of your laboratory and meet customers. Offer to help the technical service people as a volunteer. Team up with marketers.

It is also good to remember that all good entrepreneurial ideas aren't external; many, perhaps the majority of intrapreneurial opportunities concern internal services and improvements. Secretaries should consider ways to make an intraprise out of providing better office services or order processing. Manufacturing supervisors can make an intraprise out of increasing quality.

Whether your customers are external or internal, the basic principle is simple: If you want more ideas, expose yourself to more sources of stimulation and let your mind run free. When you glimpse a way to connect a strong need with a new way to satisfy it, you have something worth playing with.

Curiosity

When you are curious about something, check it out. Your curiosity is the leading edge of intuition. When you follow where it leads light-heartedly, the monumental pressures of maintaining the status quo are temporarily forgotten and new ideas can grow. People who are too busy to listen to their curiosity are second-rate innovators; they can make routine product improvements, but the exciting leaps are made by the playfully curious. Ideas without action die and are soon forgotten. When an idea has your attention, even a small step to move it forward keeps it alive.

Current Work

Most projects throw off hundreds of interesting byways. We are trained to ignore them, but for an intrapreneur they are perfect places to begin some bootleg research.

Market Research

Good business ideas happen when you understand the customer. Reports given to engineers by market research departments rarely produce successful new products. The engineers read the words, but the words don't take root in the intuitive part of the mind. To make designs that match customer needs, talk to customers directly. Almost every successful intrapreneur I have ever studied did his or her own market research.

Your Company's Proprietary Technology

One of the most logical places to look for new ideas is by considering what your company can do that no other can do as well. For example, thinking about new uses for the company's proprietary technology can lead to ideas that have an "unfair advantage" and pre-existing support from those who developed the technology.

OPPORTUNITIES FOR INTRAPRENEURING

Consider the following examples of what other intrapreneurs have done and use them to generate analogies in your own industry.

Falling-Off-a-Log Products

Imbedded in the warp and woof of every company are unrecognized opportunities for new products or improvements that follow so easily from what the company already does that they can be called "falling-off-a-log opportunities." These are not entrepreneurial opportunities, because they are dependent on being part of the larger company. They are opportunities to use better what already exists.

At Norton Company's Materials Division, Dick Bratt, with his close-cropped blond hair and reserved manner, appears to be just another member of the technical support staff. But

Dick Bratt in a few months made Norton more money than they would pay him in many lifetimes. Norton's silicon carbide is made in Quebec, crushed there to the size of pebbles, and shipped to Worcester, Massachusetts, where it is pulverized and screened into different-sized abrasive particles. For example, number 40 grit abrasive particles just barely fit through a screen with 40 wires to the inch. Number 120 grit screens, as you may imagine, have very fine holes. Such mundane and dusty details dominate the life of the technical support staffer whose job is to help customers select the right abrasives for their applications and get the performance they need and want.

One thing always bothered Dick: There was a large market in abrasives for wire sawing, but Norton's share was limited due to their high-cost position and limited manufacturing capabilities. Wire saws are used to cut granite blocks. They operate like band saws except that the blades are made of wires twisted together with abrasive particles held in the cracks between the wires. For this use, a mixture of different-sized abrasives particles works better than a single size. Rather than being an advantage, Norton's careful grading produced for this application a product disadvantage, and remixing the carefully separated particles proved too expensive. So Norton let others serve the wire saw market.

Then when he visited the Quebec silicon carbide plant, Dick saw how Norton could profitably expand their wire saw abrasive business. In the Quebec crude crushing process, an undesirable product was formed, material too fine for productive recrushing. These fines, as they are called, contained more impurities than the larger pieces that came from the crystalline centers of the silicon carbide blocks, and were of mixed sizes. Those that didn't blow away in transit arrived in Worcester where, because of their impurities, they slightly degraded the quality of Norton's primary abrasive particle lines.

Dick Bratt reasoned, why not take them out of the process in Quebec and ship them directly to the stone cutters? He gathered a barrel of fines from Quebec and rough-screened them in Worcester to produce a sample wire saw abrasive. He took his sample to a potential customer and came back with a trial order for 200,000 pounds. The order was large enough to justify buying new screens for the Quebec facility to process the fines. With that minor investment a new kind of wire saw abrasives business was expanded.

Dick Bratt, with no significant expense other than packaging, had almost single-handedly created a new business that creates over two million pounds a year of product from what had been treated essentially as waste. But why make a fuss over a million or two in incremental profit? This story is long, dusty, and boring, not at all the kind of thing strategic planners aspire to. It was accomplished by one of the ordinary people, and was treated by the company as a nonevent. Dick Bratt received no significant recognition nor any identifiable reward. Yet we know that it is the sum of many people paying attention and doing something about mundane opportunities that finally adds up to unbeatable efficiency. To paraphrase Everett Dirksen (with a few decimal places loose), a million here and a million there, pretty soon it adds up to real money.

The Japanese know how important the mundane is. They have the great advantage of a philosophy that suggests that all the profundity and significance of the universe is present in every part of it and in every task, no matter how humble. We have no Zen arts of arranging flowers or of pouring tea to perfection. We do not see the honor in the perfection of any task, no matter how humble. In the case of wire grit saws, we did not even see honor in creating a new business that produces more than two million pounds per year for additional profit. Our honors are reserved for the three-piece-suiters who play cleaner games with bigger numbers and handle the real world from a distance with analytical "tongs." If we persist in ignoring the mundane, the Japanese, Taiwanese, Koreans, and others from all over the world will rub our faces in the dust. And it isn't like us. Americans used to be the most unashamedly hands-on people in the world.

Dick Bratt doesn't seem bitter that he barely received a thank you for creating a new business for the Quebec plant. He is from that loyal generation who is thankful for a job, and my questions about recognition and rewards made him uncomfortable.

The opportunity Dick Bratt discovered had existed for about fifty years. Fifty years of failing to sell an extra two million pounds a year adds up. That no one stumbled on the possibility for fifty years means that innovation has been made a very low priority for the people close enough to the situation to see it. Presumably those charged with creating new products know little about fines and wire saws.

We can no longer afford to build organizations which avoid mundane opportunities for innovation while our heads are in the high clouds of strategy. The most important strategy we can employ in the innovation age is to release an army of intrapreneurial Dick Bratts on the world.

As a potential intrapreneur, you will find falling-off-a-log opportunities excellent places to start. Don't expect much in the way of rewards, but use your success to make a reputation for yourself as a *doer*. That reputation is the beginning of the corporate capital you will need for larger projects, and a good way to attract the attention of an influential sponsor.

The lesson for your management is this: Getting at these falling-off-a-log opportunities is easy and has an outrageously high ROI. Management should begin by making it clear that they are looking for individuals to discover and pursue mundane improvements. They should announce it over and over, then back the intrapreneurs who volunteer and make heroes of them when they succeed. Dinners with the division manager, sizable bonuses, freedom to explore new ideas, and personal discretionary budgets for doing so would be a good way to begin. Once heroes are made, more will appear and competition will add spice to the game.

Complementary Products

Complementary products work together with products that already exist. Like falling-off-a-log opportunities, they depend on being part of the corporation and thus are intrapreneurial opportunities, not entrepreneurial.

When transparent Scotch brand tape was first put on the market it was very difficult to use because there was no easy way to get it off the roll. Before there were dispensers, the tape, in a manner familiar to us all, stuck on the roll and had to be picked at to get it started again. At the time, transparent tape was mainly used in stores to wrap packages, and store-keepers were losing their tempers with getting it off the roll.

The solution to this problem didn't come from R&D or product planning, but from a desperate sales manager who took matters into his own hands. John Borden designed an inexpensive dispenser with the now universal feature of a serrated cutting edge and a place for the tape end to stick to be ready for the next user. As 3M put it in *Our Story So Far*, the new dispenser had a very favorable effect on sales; many in 3M feel that without it, Scotch brand cellophane tape might have quickly waned in popularity.*

Complementary products are often good opportunities for intrapreneuring because they generate natural sponsors. Whoever is responsible for the product that an intrapreneur's idea enhances will more than likely want to support the effort.

Defeaturing An Existing Product or Service

Xerox's very successful 2600 copier was a defeatured version of a more expensive copier. Intrapreneurs in the company's East Rochester skunkworks removed the bells and whistles from the fancier version, giving Xerox what they needed to address an important market segment.

---

* *Our Story So Far: Notes from the First 75 Years of 3M Company*, Minnesota Mining and Manufacturing, St. Paul, Mn., 1977, p. 74.

Marketing Products Used Inside

In the early 1960s, two technicians at Du Pont's experimental station bought the rights to the technology for a gas chromatograph developed for internal use. They built a fine little company selling gas chromatographs and in 1962 sold it to Hewlett-Packard and became millionaires. This annoyed Du Pont, which reacted by searching for other internally developed instruments to commercialize, using venture teams. Du Pont intrapreneurs built a number of instrument businesses that are now a significant portion of Du Pont's sales.

MIT's Eric von Hippel has observed that 81 percent of new scientific instruments are first made by users for their own use and later picked up by instrument manufacturers. In many cases those innovations could be developed by the user as an intrapreneurial business, either to keep or to divest profitably once they show promise.*

Internal services taken to the outside make fine opportunities for intrapreneuring. One such case is described by Norman Macrae of the *Economist:*

> A British film studio was going bust, and was likely to close down, because it was grossly underemployed. The studio asked its workers how many would like to stay on running subcontracting firms of their own. The cameramen now operate on subcontract when the film studios are full, but they arrange and shoot TV ads on their own initiative. The carpenters, plasterers, etc., now do outside building work, but with a subcontract to the studio. The chauffeurs who had previously ferried film moguls (when the studio was operating) now run a minicab or chauffeured car hire service, but with a contract with the studio when film

---

* Eric von Hippel, "Users as Innovators," *Technology Review*, January 1978, pp. 30–39.

moguls are using it. By last year all were making more money than in the old days. . . .°

Look at your own firm to find any major internal capacities that could also be used outside.

Training

There is a boom in training intraprises. IBM's Richie Herrink sells his skills exclusively inside. Others, like Judy Klein of Exxon Enterprises' Zilog, have taken educational programs developed inside to markets outside the company.

New Technology Ventures

The first use of a technology is of course a great accomplishment for any intrapreneur, but it is often correspondingly difficult. The early markets for new technologies are generally small, high-priced niche markets that are poorly understood and generally too small at first to justify all the effort that goes into developing the technology. In the end, however, new technologies can create whole new categories of industries. Because of the risks and the long time frame, the introduction of a new technology should be attempted by intrapreneurs with something of a track record to fall back on or by intrapreneurs with very dedicated and powerful sponsors.

Finding Uses for a New Technology

Once a new technology has been created, its exploitation generally demands a series of intrapreneurial acts. Often when a company decides to invest extensively in a new technology, the commitment is felt in R&D, but there is not an equal commitment to commercialization elsewhere in the corporation. This imbalance of effort greatly increases the risk and cost of investing in new technology. People who want to

---

° "Big Business Grows Smaller," c.1980, p. 9. (Unpublished article.)

become intrapreneurs should take note of new technologies or ideas the corporation is backing. If powerful people are backing the technology, the corporation may back a new product based on it as a way to move their technology ahead.

Technically Supported Ventures

Many ventures make more sense as intraprises than new entrepreneurial ventures because they are dependent on the technical support that a large firm can provide. Intel Magnetics is one such case.

In October 1977 Hewlett-Packard decided to discontinue its development of a new form of computer memory called magnetic bubble memories. Three members of the Hewlett-Packard R&D team working on bubble memories approached the venture capitalist, Arthur Rock, who suspected that the opportunity was real, but that it would prove too challenging for an entrepreneurial venture. Following this hunch, he introduced them to Bob Noyce and Gordon Moore, two of the troika that had founded and still governed Intel, one of Rock's more successful earlier investments.

Using the three ex-Hewlett-Packard researchers as a core, Intel formed a bubble memory business that proved Arthur Rock's suspicion that it would be better off as an intrapreneurial business than an entrepreneurial one.

The business benefited from being part of Intel in several significant ways. It was making a new computer memory system that competed with existing memories, many of which were made by Intel. Unlike an entrepreneurial start-up, Intel Magnetics had access to Intel's memory market forecasts and pricing plans for several years in advance. In the rapidly changing memory market, these forecasts were invaluable.

The second major advantage had to do with the strategy Magnetics adopted. After the marketing and engineering staff together visited almost 100 potential customers they developed a strategy quite different from those of their competitors. Others believed that bubble memories would soon be a new and cheaper form of mass memory storage, replacing computer disk storage systems. Intel's projections showed that at least in the short run the costs of traditional memory devices, including disks, would continue to decline faster than that of bubble memories, but that an important niche existed for bubbles in environments too tough for disk memories. Like disks, bubble memories are nonvolatile, meaning that they don't forget when the power is turned off. The customers Intel interviewed wanted a nonvolatile memory for applications like on-board flight computers (disks can't take the turns), industrial controls (vibration and dust destroy disks), and so forth. What was needed, thought people like Stuart Sando, the marketing manager for bubble memories at the time, was a rugged bubble memory system that plugged in in place of the disk. This would require a sophisticated set of custom integrated circuits to go between the bubble memory and microprocessors designed with disk memory in mind; otherwise a whole new microprocessor would be needed that knew how to talk directly to bubble memories.

As it turned out, making the go-between circuits was a monumental task. Intel was one of a handful of companies in 1977 that had enough integrated circuit design capacity to take it on. Had the bubble memory business been on its own it could never have made the go-between circuits and so would have failed, as most of Intel's competition in bubble memories eventually did.

Customer Service, Parts, and Supplies

In the area of increasing efficiency, intrapreneurial opportunities abound.

NBI (the initials stand for "Nothing But Initials") in Boulder, Colorado, makes such good word processing equipment that even IBM considers them a threat, but until recently their record for service on parts and supplies was abominable. How this happened is easy to understand. In this young company, when the shipping department had the choice between getting out a new $50,000 system or filling a $200 order for print wheel and floppy disks, the $50,000 order went and the supplies sat. This haphazard shipping policy made difficulties for NBI's customers. Print wheels they could buy elsewhere, and did. In fact, NBI has estimated that for years 98 percent of their market for replacement print wheels was being served by other vendors. However, in the case of floppy disks, the customer had a real problem. Only NBI preformatted disks would run in an NBI system. Customers understandably grew furious when a $50,000 system was tied up for thirty days for lack of a few dollars' worth of disks.

One of the founders, Jim Mays, who was getting ready to retire as head of NBI's scheduling department, set up a planning group to explore NBI's intrapreneurial opportunities. Although many of the new product ideas his group came up with had appeal, their calculations showed that the highest returns would come from improving what Mays imagined could be an independent supplies business. He foresaw the payoff in two ways. First, the supplies function could generate far more revenue and profit than it had been generating. Second, faster customer service was essential to the base business. If word got around that NBI couldn't back up their wonderful product with service and supplies, sales would suffer.

Jim's plan was to start a supplies division, a separate intrapreneurial business with its own space, warehouse, order processing, manufacturing, shipping, purchasing, and so forth. Jim's team consisted of Ava Allen, from Personnel, and Jim George, who had worked closely with him in inventory control and systems coordination. They were long on efficiency and control, but short on experience in sales and distribution— which didn't bother them because they were going to concentrate fanatically on quality of service, not flashy sales.

They set high standards. The first was twenty-four–hour shipping of almost every order. Then came the ability to answer instantly any question a customer had about his order. Next came first-rate inventory control and purchasing. And last, flexible scheduling of manufacturing (mainly formatting

114

of diskettes—all other supplies were purchased) to meet users' needs.

Jim Mays never worked full time in supplies but was always available to help. Ava and Jim George split the main responsibilities: Ava handled customer contact, order input, office administration, and accounting. Jim handled manufacturing, scheduling, inventory control, purchasing, and shipping. And Jim coordinated the design of a computer system to tie it all together. If a customer called to see where his order was, there was no holding on the line. They would type in the order code and get the reply, "It was shipped by Federal Express at 1:30 this afternoon priority 2 Airbill #742916420." If a rush order came in, the order taker stood up and yelled at scheduling over the partitions. Moments later, the new delivery schedule was in effect.

The supplies division has its own planning, own goals, and own P&L. It makes its own decisions and the service is good. Although exact figures are confidential, it is probably safe to say that after two years of operations sales of the competitive items like printwheels and ribbons have more than quadrupled. Customers' confidence is building as they gradually forget the earlier supplies nightmare.

Having gotten the basics in order, supplies division is branching out into new products. They now have sound covers for printers, furniture, notebooks that hold print wheels with different type faces, and places to store disks. They can make new-product decisions themselves because they are a separate intrapreneurial business and because the boundary between supplies and the main NBI is clear. If it takes a field engineer to install it, supplies stays away, but if the customer can install it himself, supplies may sell it.

In the fall of 1982, after six months of operations, Jim Mays retired from NBI. He brought in a new supplies manager, Les Dace, as a replacement.

His intrapreneurial swan song was a great way to leave behind another legacy, because he turned a problem into profits.

Production Intrapreneuring

Manufacturing departments are excellent places for intrapreneuring because that is where innovation is often lacking. The Japanese manufacturing miracle comes not from always starting with a larger market share, but from a company-wide dedication to find ways, large and small, to make things better and faster.

One company's group of intrapreneurs had a cost reduction business. They simply went on the floor, grabbed a part, and tried to find out how to make it cheaper. Once they had figured out how to reduce the cost, they had to sell the idea to the customer, who was the manufacturing organization. They wrote up their ideas as business plans showing, for example, how buying a new piece of equipment would pay for itself in two years. Their score was simple: Each of them kept track of the savings he or she was responsible for and compared them at the end of the year with their salaries. If there was a large surplus of savings after deducting the costs, they were doing the job. That's intrapreneurial freedom applied to cost reduction.

Production intrapreneuring doesn't have to be a separate job, however. Claude Wilson's experience suggests ways to make intrapreneurs out of workers and their supervisors.

Wilson, the owner of a large tool and die shop in Dayton, Ohio, had finally had it. He decided his employees at City Tool Corporation were depending on him to create a business that kept them employed, but all that the business meant to them was a paycheck. Claude might have ignored this, but his profit margins were being squeezed, so he decided to act. As he walked the floors he saw that the hierarchy had sapped his employees' motivation. Hierarchy was destroying motivation at City Tool, so he decided to destroy the hierarchy. To prepare for the day when he would do so, Claude began explaining to his workers a new system in which they would be in business for themselves. He trained them in accounting, planning, income taxes for partnerships, and the rudiments of small business. When all was ready, Wilson pulled the main power switch and announced that the old City Tool was dead. Those who wished could stay on the new basis. Almost all of them elected to stay.

City Tool continued on as a marketing organization, but the production work was put out for bid to a large number of small partnerships composed of the former employees. The partnerships leased space and equipment from City Tool, but actually ran small businesses on their own.

In addition to sales and marketing, a number of other services were provided centrally. Walter Harvey formed Partners Tool Company, which purchased raw materials for the individual partnerships and gave advice on bids and scheduling machine time.

When the individual production partnerships hired people, they found the burden of paperwork for payroll intolerable, and so a personnel company was formed that charges a small fee to each partnership for the hassle of handling all the paperwork.

The result of this system was to transform the mind set of the former employees. They became masters of their own fates. Not only did average incomes rise substantially, but with their new business perspective many of the partners, like Bill Nolan, became wealthy. The results for Claude Wilson were also good. After five years, during which the tool and die business in general was flat, City Tool's sales had tripled. Overhead was reduced by 40 percent in part by eliminating foremen, supervisors, and managers, who became unnecessary when the workers took responsibility for their own productivity and performance.*

There is no reason why small intrapreneurial production teams cannot work as well as entrepreneurial ones if the

---

* Claude Wilson, Jr., personal communication. He adds a warning from his perspective twenty years later: "Unless there is a continuing learning process going on with the entrepreneurial partners, the system can begin to die out. They become affluent and forget their purpose."

rewards are directly coupled with performance. In addition, intrapreneurial production teams should be allowed to buy and "own" their own equipment out of the profits from their intraprise. Legally, it would still belong to the corporation, but in every other sense it could belong to the employees. An intraprise could not only purchase equipment but could also sell it later internally or externally. By letting people who use them "own" the new manufacturing tools like robots, which are transforming the shop floor, we can eliminate resistance to them. Instead, we will get blue-collar robot jockeys whose pride in their ability to make their machines do the impossible might rival the playful pride of the drop hammer operators in my grandfather's day who could use their multiton drop hammers to crack the crystal of a watch without denting its case.

Blue-Collar "Nichemanship"

Dr. Ruth Davis, former head of compiling of the National Bureau of Standards, sees a big change coming through computer-controlled production. She anticipates "customized production at mass production prices."

As Norman Macrae puts it:

> This is because a computer-controlled system can easily be told, unlike a batch of mere human beings, to make some changes in the 404th item coming down the assembly line. More important it can also be told, without expensive retraining, to make changes in various experimental batches coming down the line.°

This new flexibility is a gold mine to intrapreneurs, who can, at lower costs, make special products for special market niches. To address the diversity of opportunity caused by new customizable but inexpensive production techniques and the

° "The Coming Entrepreneurial Revolution: A Survey," *The Economist,* Dec. 25, 1976, p. 57.

"demassification" of markets described by Alvin Toffler,[*] corporations will need armies of small intrapreneurs using the production capability of the large firm to deftly hit the needs of smaller segments.

CHOOSING AN IDEA

Once you have generated a number of ideas for potential intraprises, you can begin to select one to develop. A good intrapreneurial idea meets three kinds of needs:

- The customer's needs
- The corporation's needs
- The intrapreneur's needs

If any leg of this triangle is missing, the idea won't work.

The Customer's Needs

The best intrapreneurial ideas meet strongly felt customer needs that existing products and services don't meet well. That could be the third floor's need for good typing services or the Ford Motor Company's need for better computer-aided design terminals. When a customer need is strong enough, it becomes a potent weapon for the intrapreneur fighting for the intraprise. When internal political struggles threatened to kill 3M's nonwoven surgical mask intraprise, St. Raphael's Hospital's insistence that they needed those masks cut through the politics. In fact, without a customer, there is no business.

Early in the concept-evaluation stage the intrapreneur should begin talking to potential customers, as much to shape the idea as to evaluate it. In some cases working with customers creates legal problems since it might take a proprietary idea

---

[*] Toffler defines "demassification" as the breakup of mass society, or differentiation. Demassification of production would be short runs or even customized, one-by-one production. Alvin Toffler, *Previews and Premises*, William Morrow, 1983, pp. 14 and 219.

into the public domain. But there are always ways to handle that, whether by secrecy agreements or, as Art Fry did when testing the Post-it idea, by using internal users as models of how outside customers would later respond (see the Intraprise Plan Guidelines in the appendix for more detail on building and evaluating a market plan).

The Corporation's Needs

Probably the quickest things to check when you are considering a new idea are projected margins, proprietary advantage, and fit with corporate strategy.

Projected Margins

A thumbnail comparison of what customers might be willing to pay versus what it might cost to deliver is one of the earliest possible reality tests. It is often easier to guess what the return on investment will be. For this reason intrapreneurs often take an educated guess at the margin on a new idea and compare it with a rule of thumb before doing more complex calculations.

Proprietary Advantage

One way to get at margins is by analyzing proprietary advantage. If the market exists, then your ability to get high margin depends on having a unique advantage. It might be a patent or a trade secret. It might be market position. It could be timing. In general, if there isn't some proprietary advantage, high margins won't last.

Fit with the Corporation's Vision of Itself

Some ideas, no matter how well they fit with what the corporation does well, just don't fit the culture. 3M's failure in nonwoven bra cups is often attributed to poor fit with market needs. Equally important is that 3M just wasn't comfortable working in the manner needed to perfect the product. Bra cups weren't 3M's kind of thing. As an intrapreneur you should avoid trying the impossible.

Sponsor Support

One test of the idea's fit with the corporation's needs is the existence of a high-level sponsor. Ask yourself who could sponsor your idea. All other things being equal, move toward ideas for which there are potential sponsors (see chapter 7 on sponsors).

The Intrapreneur's Needs

When venture capitalists decide to back a project, they are more interested in the skills, experience, and dedication of the entrepreneur than they are in the quality of the idea itself. What this means is that you shouldn't just choose an idea that makes good business sense. Choose one that makes a better intrapreneur out of you.

You can do this in two ways: first, by choosing an idea that fits *what* you are—with your skills and experience; second and more important, by choosing an idea that fits *who* you are—with the deeper things that make you you, what you are striving to become, your deepest values, the people and things you like instinctively, and how you like to spend your time.

Experience in the Business You Will Start

Venture capitalists stress the importance of experience, not just good general experience but experience in relevant industries and types of business. The old idea that management is a general skill is fading, and nowhere faster than in intrapreneuring. When you are groping around while starting something new, it helps to know something about the area you are entering. As Alec Feiner puts it, "You need to be able to get into the customer's boots." If you haven't the knack for that yourself, get someone on your team who does.

Match Your Skills with What Needs to Be Done

As an intrapreneur, you are always stretching your skills and doing things for which you are not yet qualified. Still it is comforting if you have some gift for and experience in the things that you think will be the key competitive factors in the business. When you think about this, consider what kind of help you will need. List the things you think will make or break the idea you are considering. How do your skills bear on them?

Who You Are

In the long run it is probably more important to pick a business you will like than one you are trained for.

The moon monitor engaged Chuck House on several levels. It appealed to the engineer to build something much smaller and lighter than had been done in the past. It allowed him to prove he was right about the strategy he had identified earlier based on the "misuse" by customers of other Hewlett-Packard instruments.

At a deeper level, it allowed him to be part of the space program. He had gone to Cal Tech, and many of his friends were intimately involved in it. The moon monitor gave him a chance to be part of what he considered to be the great adventure of his time.

Living with the Tasks

Different intraprises will require you to spend your day doing different sorts of things.

Though choosing a business whose ends match your deepest drives and fantasies is important, practically speaking you must also choose an intraprise whose means and daily tasks are things you want to do. An intrapreneur has to do all sorts of things, but different ventures require them in very different amounts.

Spend some time thinking about what you enjoy doing. Is it talking, being alone, building, selling, or problem solving? Choose a business you can enjoy on a day to day basis.

Liking the Customer

Your life will be far more pleasant if you like or respect or feel some positive emotion for the people you have to devote your life to pleasing. The more you like your customers, the better your intuition will be about how to serve their needs. When you think about a business idea, think about the customers: Can you enjoy their company and fellowship? Are they worth your time?

Of the three great areas of need that an intrapreneurial business can satisfy, you can research the fit with your own needs most rapidly. Rapidly eliminate ideas that aren't meaningful to you; life is too short for such ideas. Have faith that good ideas will appear that meet the corporation's and the customer's needs as well as your own. If they do not, one of three things is wrong.

1. You haven't been brainstorming enough.
2. You are rejecting ideas that fit your needs because they seem like so much fun you have judged them frivolous.
3. The corporation isn't open to intrapreneuring of any kind.

If you suspect number 1, throw a brainstorming party with some close friends "to help with your intrapreneurial career." If you suspect number 2, purposely pursue the ideas that make you smile even when they seem silly. You may find gold under a rock. If you suspect number 3, audit your corporate environment for intrapreneuring using Book III. If the corporation won't allow intrapreneuring, get a new job elsewhere.

CHECKLIST FOR CHOOSING IDEAS

FIT WITH YOU

Fit with your skills and experience
- Do you believe in the product or service?
- Does the need it fits mean something to you personally?
- Do you like and understand the potential customers?
- Do you have experience in this type of business?
- Do the basic success factors of this business fit your skills?
- Are the tasks of the intraprise ones you could enjoy doing yourself?
- Are the people the intraprise will employ ones you will enjoy working with and supervising?
- Has the idea begun to take over your imagination and spare time?

FIT WITH THE MARKET

- Is there a real customer need?
- Can you get a price that gives you good margins?
- Would customers believe in the product coming from your company?
- Does the product or service you propose produce a clearly perceivable customer benefit which is significantly better than that offered by competing ways to satisfy the same basic need?
- Is there a cost effective way to get the message and the product to the customers?

FIT WITH THE COMPANY

- Is there a reason to believe your company could be very good at the business?
- Does it fit the company culture?
- Can you imagine who might sponsor it?
- Does it look profitable (high margin—low investment)?
- Will it lead to larger markets and growth?

What To Do When Your Idea Is Rejected

Frequently as an intrapreneur you will find that your idea has been rejected. There are a few things you can do:

1. Give up and select a new idea.
2. Listen carefully, understand what is wrong, improve your idea and your presentation, and try again.
3. Find someone else to whom you can present your idea by considering:
   —Who will benefit most if it works and can they be a sponsor?
   —Who are potential customers and will they demand the product?
   —How can you get to the people who really care about intrapreneurial ideas?

CHAPTER 6

PLANNING YOUR INTRAPRISE

The basic job of the intrapreneur is to conceive business visions and turn them into business realities. Vision has two parts. The first is the intuitive discovery of a potential business pattern—involving so-called "right brain" activities. The second part of building a vision is the often tedious yet crucial work of business planning. In business planning, you convert your intuitive vision into an action plan. The two parts of vision cannot be done sequentially. The task alternates rapidly between the creative—thinking up ways the business could unfold—and the analytical—figuring out the concrete implications of the intuitive vision.

Business planning involves documenting as best as you can everything that is important to the business, such as:

- Your destination
- The strategies for getting there
- Where you would like to be at specific times
- The obstacles you may encounter
- The approaches you plan to use in overcoming these obstacles

USES OF A BUSINESS PLAN

Many people think of a business plan as a tool for raising money or getting corporate approvals. Actually its value as a selling tool is a small part of the value of business planning. The benefits of the planning process include training yourself to become more intrapreneurial, screening your ideas, attracting a venture team, building team concensus, as well as getting the money and permission to proceed.

Perhaps the most common mistake made by intrapreneurs

is "hobby horsing"—spending a disproportionate amount of time working on the parts of business formation you excel in while ignoring the parts you don't understand. For example, technical people turned intrapreneur frequently spend 80 percent of their time planning the R&D task while ignoring issues such as how the product will be distributed. The usual result of hobby horsing is business failure. Writing a business plan will ensure that you have considered all the relevant questions. Writing a business plan trains your intrapreneurial vision.

As Hershel Kranitz, vice president of Business Development for NBI, put it: "There is no great secret to making people more entrepreneurial. Just have them write action-oriented business plans."

When you become serious about a business idea, read through the business plan outline in the Appendix with your venture in mind. Don't address any section in detail, just consider your options for dealing with each of the issues. If one area starts to worry you, do a little more work on it.

Do this with several ideas. If you still feel good about an idea after putting it through this test, it is probably worth more careful planning.

Attracting a Team and Building Consensus

When you have an idea and want to attract a team, a brief business plan can be an effective recruiting tool. It is best, however, to keep it brief or at least flexible, or other team members may feel they have been excluded from the planning process.

An outline of the business plan can be used as the agenda for team planning sessions. To help people prepare for this meeting the leader should prepare a brief (three- to twenty-page) preliminary business plan to help everyone think along the same general lines. Then the whole team should make several passes through the business plan outline to amend and develop its sections. If there is a basic flaw in the idea, it should emerge then and either be fixed or at worst convince you to abandon the venture before you make a fool of yourself. If there are irreconciliable differences in the goals or methods of some members of the team, they will emerge before they become a festering wound, and new people can be found who share the vision. You should emerge from these business formation meetings with a common vision expressed, in a written form, such as a business plan on flip charts.

Raising Money and Getting Permission to Proceed

There will come a time in the growth of almost every intraprise when a more formal business plan is finally needed to get approval of funds for the next stage of growth. When that time comes, know who your audience is and what they care about. Your final document must work as a selling tool.

WARNINGS ON BUSINESS PLANS

1. I don't want this book used by management to get product developers to write business plans. Many product developers couldn't, wouldn't, or won't write a business plan, but they are hot-shot developers. If they could or would do all that, they would be entrepreneurs. As it is, they are inventor/intrapreneurs (inventrapreneurs). Adapt the system to them, not vice versa.

2. In most corporations, business plans are used not only to approve budgets and strategies, but also to monitor their progress. Good management is often defined as producing only minimal variations from the plan. A management unaccustomed to innovation will expect you to do *exactly* what you have outlined in your plan, which is not the intrapreneur's job. Rather the early stages of venturing are usually a series of mistakes and surprises which reveal to the resourceful how to succeed.

Therefore, if your management expects you to follow

your plan exactly, you must be very careful what you promise. In the "official" plan you show people, be as brief and as vague as possible, consistent with gaining approval.

You might want to create two versions of the plan—one "official" version that is complete but somewhat vague in its details and another more detailed plan for the intrapreneurial team's eyes only. Although the business plan is generally written to explain the business to those who will decide its fate, its greatest value is in forcing the intrapreneur and his team to clarify and coordinate their thinking.

The plan itself is less important than the thinking and debate that go into it. It may soon become obsolete, but what remains will be a clearer view of the issues and options. As each member of the team is stretched and challenged by the attempt at imagining, predicting, and deciding the future, he develops the mental tools to think more clearly about the business. When changes occur later, after the venture is under way, all the options and debate become the background for what others will call rapid, intuitive decision making. In fact, what happens is that you arrive at barriers you considered, and after only minutes of thought are able to apply a solution imagined long ago in the planning process.

SHARING YOUR PLAN: WHEN AND WITH WHOM

Given the fact that the purposes and uses of intrapreneurial business plans are generally misunderstood in mature corporations, you should not show your plan to people who don't need to see it. Be very careful about who gets a copy of your plan. If possible make the plan confidential so people outside your team get to see it only on a need-to-know basis. You can follow the practice of entrepreneurs, who frequently use numbered copies, insisting that they be returned without having been copied.

As long as you can beg and borrow the resources for a bootleg project, it doesn't make sense to commit to a business plan. Not only is it a better use of your time to continue the learning process, but in all probability, it is premature to commit yourself to a specific plan, because the process of planning may narrow your vision. In the early stages the plan may change daily, and only human intuition is fast enough to keep up with it.

The time for formal business planning is when the pattern gels and there is a basis for orderly growth and meaningful prediction. That time doesn't necessarily correspond to a product development stage such as the point at which you develop a proof-of-concept prototype, or prepare a field test. Instead it occurs when you know that your idea works, that you can make it, what its cost will be, and that customers will buy it at the price you've set. Before you know these things clearly, write plans for your own use but try not to show much more than back-of-the-envelope calculations to people who expect the ultimate results to resemble early plans.

HOW LONG SHOULD YOUR PLAN BE?

There is no one right length for a business plan. The business plans many entrepreneurs write for venture capitalists set imposing standards of diligence. They often run 150 pages in the body with lengthy appendices for marketing, product development, manufacturing, service, quality control, etc.

Yet venture capitalists don't always require detailed plans. Intel was financed on the personal reputation of its founders and a five-page business plan. One venture capitalist, when asked how long a business plan should be, answered, "That depends. Three words are enough if those words are 'Dr. A. Wang.' Anything Wang wants to do, I would gladly back." In spite of these exceptions, the basic practice of the venture-capital community is to finance businesses only after reading a detailed business plan.

Business plans are good for venture capitalists because

they know how to use them. Through the plan, the investor gets to know not only the quality of the ideas but the quality of the entrepreneur's thinking. The plan provides an excellent beginning to the dialogue between the venture capitalist and the entrepreneur. Finally, since it requires enormous quantities of work, it is part of the selection process. Only the serious entrepreneur will finish writing a plan, and venture capitalists won't deal with any others.

Intrapreneurial business plans, like entrepreneurial ones, vary in length. On average, they are far shorter, because in all probability many aspects of the business are already understood by management. Furthermore, in most cases, the intrapreneur is also known to his management and can therefore get away with a less detailed written plan. You will have to be the judge of what's right for your organization. If you are a junior employee or from a technical background you may need to write a very detailed plan to offset management's prejudices about your ability to address business issues. If there are parts you cannot do, get help and strongly consider adding people to your team who understand those issues. Then you can learn by doing.

PRESELLING

By the time an intrapreneurial business plan is formally presented, it has usually been an academic exercise; the decision whether or not to proceed has already been made. Thus the informal preselling of your idea is usually the key to gaining approval. Before anyone in a position to decide the fate of your venture attends a presentation or reads a formal plan, they should already be favorably disposed to your idea. Get on their calendar for a very brief meeting and ask for their advice. Research the answers to their questions and acknowledge their contributions. Once the idea is sold, a brief business plan may be all you need.

INTRAPRISE BUSINESS PLAN OUTLINE

What sections a business plan should contain will depend on the nature of the projected business. Suppose that you are working for an oil company that contracts for all its shipping and that your plan is to buy a ship and fix it up to carry oil to Maine. You won't need a section on manufacturing, but you will need a few sections not included in plans for other kinds of businesses, such as:

> *Acquiring the ship.* Where it is, who owns it now, why it's for sale, what it will cost, what condition it's in, who has inspected it, etc.
>
> *Refurbishing the ship.* Your plans for upgrading the ship, what the work will cost, where it will be done, and how long it will take.
>
> *Operating the ship.* Operations plan, crew, fuel costs, maintenance, etc.
>
> *Government regulations.* Let's say part of the value of your plan is that this is a U.S.-built, U.S.-flag ship and therefore licensed for coastal shipping. How likely is it that regulations will change allowing more efficient Korean-built ships to compete? If that happened, how much would the company lose?

Most business plans will include some version of the following general sections in addition to those specific to the business.

> *Executive Summary.* An overview of the business proposition and the most compelling reasons for its success to whet the appetite of the reader for more information.
>
> *The Product, Service or Process Improvement.* What it is, why it is better than what exists, how far along it is in development, what makes it proprietary or hard to imitate.
>
> *Corporate Fit.* Why this is a good idea for your corporation:

the fit of your venture with existing markets, existing technology base, strategic plans, manufacturing capacity, people resources, and plans for future expansion.

Marketing and Sales Plan. Size and trend of total market, market segments, customer descriptions, market shares, distribution approach, competition, pricing, service requirements, advertising, promotion, sales strategy.

Operations Plan. Requirements for space, equipment, labor, geographic issues, manufacturing facilities, overhead issues, transfer payments.

Summary of Risks. Opportunities, threats, probabilities.

Targets/Milestones. Month-by-month targets.

Financial Statements. Pro-forma projections: orders, shipments, backlog. Direct and indirect costs, cash flow, capital costs, profitability analysis, sensitivity analysis (best and worst case), balance sheet impact.

Managerial Issues. Venture team, organizational form, compensation.

WRITING A BUSINESS PLAN

Let us assume that other options, such as staying in the bootleg phase, have expired. You finally have to write that business plan. Somehow you must come up with all kinds of numbers and information you don't have. What can you do?

Setting Goals

The secret to beginning is to remember that plans follow from goals, not vice versa. This means you begin with a calculated leap of faith—for example, you believe that you can achieve sales of $20 million in four years. Taking that as a goal, you can plan pathways to achieve it. If no plausible pathway can be found, you will have to modify your goals until you can be reasonably certain of achieving them.

The first step of planning is to get a firm vision of where

you would like your intraprise to be in five years. You may find it difficult to imagine so far ahead. Don't let yourself off so easily. Intrapreneurs are visionaries who act on their dreams. Take your dream and imagine it has happened. Live in the future for a while and report what you see of your intraprise.

Having established your five-year goals, imagine what you would like your intraprise to have accomplished in one year. Stretch yourself a bit and write down not only a vision but *measurable* accomplishments. Your goals may follow these lines:

Five-Year Goal. Five years after the project's initial approval we are enjoying $25 million in sales. We have introduced two new products, in addition to the original concept, and there is a fourth product in development. Our new plant, which is only ten minutes from my home, has been in operation for six months and is running smoothly despite leaks in the roof.

One-Year Goal. Only a year after my presentation to management, our product is in test marketing in Duluth (our official projection was to reach this point in eighteen months). The fact that we are half a year ahead of schedule and, more to the point, enjoying sales of $100,000 a month in the test, has pleased management, and there have been hints of better things to come. Our manufacturing costs are $2.15 per unit. Our second product has been approved for development and will use the same production facilities. The total investment so far has been under $425,000. We have solved our basic manufacturing problems and are getting quality out of the pilot plant. Old customers are field-testing the product and suggesting changes. The feedback is so encouraging that our executive vice president has finally become a supporter.

Three-Month Goals. Market research results show that our initial prototype of the instrument embodies desirable features and is perceived as being worth the price we planned. It can perform ten operations per minute and is accurate to within 2 percent. We have spent less than $100,000 since the approval.

Having set goals, relax and consider how far you have come already. List the things you have already accomplished in bringing the intraprise toward reality. Perhaps you have:

Set five-year goals.
Talked with customers for several years; finally figured out what they need.
Built a rough functional prototype.
Drafted a brochure for selling services.
Convinced close colleagues that this will work.
Talked with a large retailer about distribution and with a trade magazine about a possible article.

Consider what information you have gathered. Think about people you have talked to and plans you have made. Consider what you know of the customer and the design of the product or service.

Working with an Events Table

Then, with a firm grasp of where you are and where you want to be, ask yourself how to get moving. List all the things you need on file cards. Lay your cards on a table and move them around until they are in a sensible sequence. For example, you can't print a brochure before you settle on a name for the product. You can't show customers samples before they are made. Figure out when each of these tasks must be completed by moving the cards around. You will begin to get a sense of bottlenecks and critical paths and know where energy has to be focused.

As the pattern of tasks and their sequence begin to gel, insert a time frame into your plan so you can see what you expect to have done at the end of each month for the first year or two, and then by quarters until you reach your five-year goal. If, as you do this, you find that your goals are unrealistically high or low, change them.

Find a large table or other surface at home on which you can leave your cards spread out undisturbed for the entire time it takes to write the plan. Continue to study and add to the cards as you assemble the information for the plan. Ask yourself who will perform each of the tasks on the cards; whose support you will need from outside the intrapreneurial team, and what needs to be done to get such support. Add these tasks to the table. Put down every task necessary to create a fully functioning business. (If you lack table space, I have found Post-it Notes on a wall a good substitute for cards on a table.)

Building a business plan is thus done in several passes by working on each section for a while and then moving on. When a section is complete, add the new tasks you have outlined to the table. This will prevent you from formulating excessively grandiose schemes, simply because too many tasks won't fit on your table. Stick to the basics. As you research and write any of the sections enumerated in the appendix, questions and answers for other sections will emerge. Finally, if you keep at it, a coherent plan will emerge.

PROFILE

ART FRY: Persisting with a Good Idea

> Inventors and intrapreneurs don't get red carpets laid out for them any place because they are always bucking convention. We are trying to do things that are different and trying to do things that people don't really understand yet and you're not sure you understand them yourself.

Art Fry of 3M is the inventor and intrapreneur of Post-it Notes, those ubiquitous little yellow note pads with peelable stickum along the top of the back side. When Art has a vision for a new class of products, he creates it using the tools available to him within the existing system.

Art's brand of intrapreneuring is important. He made use not only of corporate funds but of proprietary corporate technology and existing pilot plants, manufacturing facilities, and marketing channels. Art Fry's access to corporate money and expertise was important to his success—and equally important was strong, loyal sponsorship within 3M. Robert Molenda, Art's immediate superior, was a strong backer throughout the development process, and when Geoff Nicholson, technical director of Art's division, was first introduced to Post-it Notes, he, too, saw real potential in the concept. Nicholson enthusiastically showed Art's brainchild to James Thwaits who, in turn, became a true believer. Thwaits was president of International Operations and Corporate Staff Services. He was in an excellent position to back the project. As he went around 3M's corporate offices passing out sample pads, Thwaits explained the insidious effect the sticky little pages had had on him: "They are just like dope. Once you start using them, you can't stop. But you must try them to understand them." Even given a good dose of venture capital, Art would not have been able to create Post-it Notes outside of the large multifaceted corporate environment.

Art began working on Post-it Notes in 1974 while in church. He had been singing in a choir—two services every Sunday—and would mark the selected hymns from his hymnal with slips of paper. Although these bookmarks worked well for him during the first service, by the second service some of the paper markers would fall out. He decided he needed a marker that would adhere to the page but not damage it when it was pulled off. Taking advantage of a 3M policy that gives technical people 15 percent of their time to work quietly on ideas of their own, Art began work on a prototype peelable hymnal marker.

He decided to use an adhesive that had already been developed in the Central Research Lab by Spence Silver. Samples of the new adhesive had been widely distributed in the company in the hope that someone would find a use for it. There were bottles of the adhesive lying around, so Art made himself some self-sticking hymnal markers.

This apparently foolish use of corporate resources to pursue an idea is typical of successful and creative people. As Art explains, "Most people are really their own stumbling blocks because they don't use the freedom they have." At first that freedom may not be much, but as an intrapreneur becomes successful, he can expect greater access to company resources.

One difficulty in the beginning with a new idea is that it is very hard to describe to others. "At first, when I was struggling to conceptualize the idea, I had a feeling for the market but didn't have words for it. Then, finally, I had words that described the opportunity, but the words were not yet in the common parlance." One could talk of "repositionable notes," but until people could gain some understanding of the product's sensory application— how it would stick and be removable, as well as how it was going to help them in their jobs—they could not get any feeling for the opportunity.

One of the biggest barriers he had to overcome was finding a process to coat this new and difficult adhesive on paper so it behaved properly. Controlling the stickiness proved almost impossible, and Art found himself without much support outside the lab. Manufacturing people thought it would be impossible to produce because it couldn't be controlled.

Yet, where others saw failure, Art envisioned opportunity. The peelable adhesive technology had been applied to make a self-stick bulletin board, but Art at once saw an inherently bigger business in the consumable self-attaching pieces of paper.

"Art is not just an inventor," says Bob Molenda. "He is an innovator. He has a good feel for economics, practicality, and a strong profit motive. He proves things out in his own mind, but he has a strong sense of the end user." One of the great virtues of 3M is the relative ease with which intrapreneurs like Art can get to use the equipment in other divisions to try out their ideas.

"It takes patience to locate all the different kinds of coaters and paper handlers available at 3M and then find out when they have open time," says Art. "It can't be done through formal channels."

"Maybe you know someone in the same cross country ski club or from an earlier job. But whatever the situation," he says, revealing as much about the intrapreneurial character as about 3M, "there is always a way to get on the machine." If the equipment was available only at night, Art worked at night. His dedication is in fact legendary. When he got official permission to use a pilot plant, he worked five consecutive eight-hour shifts, or forty hours, without stopping. "When I came in at the end," says Bob Molenda, "his eyes were glazed. If you asked him a question, instead of his usual instant reply, it took him three seconds of blank silence before he began to speak." But Art kept relentlessly pursuing his goal of a workable process for making Post-it Notes.

As he went through 3M's inventory of production machinery looking for answers, Art was also canvassing the world for suppliers of machinery that might make the product. Eighty percent of those he asked said their equipment couldn't help him. The other 20 percent offered to try but failed. In the end Art was left with a tantalizing idea, but a product that was impossible to manufacture.

Strictly speaking, the way 3M is organized, designing the production process was not Art's job. He was supposed to design the product while process engineering people worked on how to make it. The problem was that manufacturing told him it was impossible, which, using existing 3M technologies, was true. But Art wouldn't accept that. He invented a machine that looked like it might just do the job. Unfortunately, the manufacturing engineering function said the machine he had designed would take six months to build and cost a small fortune. The anguish of that barrier proved too much for Art's somewhat limited political instincts. The next morning when people came to work they found Art's new process up and running. He had built a crude version of the machine overnight in his basement, brought it to work, and installed it. It was working.

THE "18,000 PERCENT" PRODUCTIVITY BOOSTER

Any effort to understand productivity in the Innovation Age must take into account events like Art Fry building in one night what the system estimated would take six months. The dedicated intrapreneur isn't 10 or 20 percent more productive than the system. In this case, using the inferior facilities of his home shop, he produced in one night what would have taken six months, a productivity advantage of more than one hundred eighty to one.

"Art tends to overshadow others with sheer talent," says Bob Molenda. "And although he sometimes upsets a few apple carts, he is a compassionate man who genuinely cares for people."

DOING HIS OWN MARKET RESEARCH

As the manufacturing process began to look solvable, another problem arose. The marketing people did surveys of potential customers and the results were terrible. People said they didn't see the need for paper with a weak stickum on it.

Nearly every technical intrapreneur eventually reaches this impasse. If you survey people about something so new and different they can't imagine how to use it, the result usually comes back that they don't need it. After all, they've gotten along without it for years. But that doesn't mean the rejected product is a bad business idea, only that people have to use it before they know what it's good for. There really hadn't been a piece of paper capable of attaching and detaching by itself before, so people couldn't imagine how to use it. They couldn't comment on whether it filled a need.

To overcome this difficulty Art distributed samples within 3M and asked people to try them out. He gave them samples in several different formats, including tape, labels, and the little yellow note pads, letting them come back for more as soon as they ran out. Geoff Nicholson was distributing samples, too, but he was testing the product among the division's top-level executives. Art kept charts on each person's usage over time. He compared the usage rates with Magic Tape, 3M's biggest office supply seller, and discovered to his surprise that people used the note pads more than they did cellophane tape. Despite the fact that marketing's surveys continued to show that people had no interest, Art observes, "From my own personal experience of people clawing and scratching to get these things and the use rate they had in comparison to Scotch Cellophane Tape, I extrapolated a large market."

Once he was satisfied, he could prove there was a market and he was well on his way to an economical production process. Art began working with a variety of business units to find places for the new family of products he envisioned.

I put together a brochure which showed examples of the products in various forms and it looked good. There's nothing as important as the first impression. If you come up with something that doesn't have the quality you need, looks bad, or doesn't perform right, people are going to give it thumbs down. You may never have the chance to do it again. This brochure had examples, applications, market areas, descriptions. It was typed up and had some pictures and examples on 8-½ by 11 inch paper. As a matter of fact, it was put together into a file folder so that they could immediately have a place to file it with the file name on it and everything, and categories listed under headings, again to make it easy to read as well as easy to keep around so you wouldn't want to throw it away either. . . .

The brochures were sent to every manager in the commercial tape division and times were set up to make presentations to people in the business development units responsible for markets that might use the products. As interest picked up, Art found himself working with a number of project groups; most important of these projects was the one addressing the office market, where Art felt the business would be most significant.

TEST MARKET

3M began selling Post-it Notes in four cities. They launched an advertising campaign, but neglected to include samples. The potential customers simply did not understand what they were being asked to buy. Joe Ramey, general manager of Art's division, had been skeptical at the outset, but despite the promotional setback, had become a strong champion, partly because of the unflagging enthusiasm of Fry and Nicholson. Ramey and Nicholson even took to the streets, calling on prospective buyers, showing them what Art Fry had seen early on: Once you induced people to try them, they were hooked. Jack Wilkins, manager of Office Marketing, also saw that they had been approaching the sales problem from the wrong direction. The campaign had failed to demonstrate the true use of Post-it Notes.

Ramey decided it was time for a different market test. The original campaign was withdrawn, and all efforts were concentrated on Boise, Idaho, where they used heavy advertising and promotional give-aways. The sales were fantastic. Regional, national, and international rollouts followed.

Art says that as an intrapreneur he turns over his baby sooner than he would as an entrepreneur. He is willing to let go of the ball as long as the others don't let it fall. When they do he picks it up again himself.

Intrapreneuring is what you can do as a pioneer these days. An intrapreneur has to be pretty hard-headed and thick-skinned. You've got to let others take credit and just concentrate on getting the idea to happen. And when it does happen, and the product is out there in the marketplace, it is about as close to living forever as you can get.

CHAPTER 7

Identifying Sponsors, the Protectors of New Ideas

Our top executives are never interested in what you've already got on the market. They want to know what's new.

—Daniel J. McDonald, general manager, Occupational Health and Safety Products Division, 3M

Once you have an idea, your next step is to find a sponsor. It is almost impossible to develop and lead a new intracorporate business and at the same time protect your political flanks. For this reason, intrapreneurs almost always need active sponsors. Sponsors ensure that the intraprise gets the required resources, and they also temper the grievances of those who feel threatened by your innovation. In fact, many intrapreneurs have several sponsors: lower level sponsors to take care of the day-to-day support needs of the venture, and higher level sponsors to fend off major strategic attacks that might threaten it.

Understand that a sponsor is different from a mentor, although in some cases the two roles may be held by the same person. A mentor relationship is deeply personal and deals not so much with innovative ways to satisfy customer needs as with ways to align personal needs and corporate life. Mentors are concerned with career strategies as much as with business strategies. The sponsor, however, is involved with technical problems, marketing options, ways to help you present an idea to management, and behind-the-scenes intervention to keep the venture alive.

Bob Person was both sponsor and co-conspirator to intrapreneur Michael Phillips, who introduced a series of innovative banking services. The task of explaining the new ideas to

143

senior management and obtaining funds most often fell to Bob. Even when Michael made his presentations, he was carefully coached. "Bob would teach me to say what I was thinking in terms bankers could understand," said Michael. "He had me rehearse, while he role-played probable management responses, until I learned what I could say and what I couldn't."

Bob Person was even more blunt than Michael in describing their relationship. "Michael was thinking so far ahead, it was a danger to let him go to see a senior vice president. He was so much brighter, he ran circles around them and made them look bad. I had to put a screen around him. I had him sit in an office next to me so I could see what he was up to and protect him."

Michael's need for a sponsor became obvious when Bob left to take a better job. Despite all his prior success, Michael was fired within three months.

Sponsors help keep intrapreneurs in large companies in more ways than just keeping them from being fired. By protecting intrapreneurs from the sense of powerlessness that being in a large organization can engender and by giving them control of the resources they need to realize their visions, sponsors build an environment around intrapreneurs that makes staying worthwhile.

Steve Morton, who runs the very successful frequency domain engineering group at Tektronix, has an enviable record for keeping topflight product developers. In a field where entrepreneurial raids are endemic, the group has kept more than 90 percent of its people over a five-year period. The secret: If one of Steve's intrapreneurs hits a snag, he knows he can consult Steve without losing his freedom to manage.

> I may suggest alternatives, but in the end I let him choose his own way. Then I do whatever has to be done on my end to get that alternative to happen. If we have to go over budget I arrange it.

Steve has a standing policy well known to his managers:

Any purchase order they ask him to sign, he signs.

> I may ask what it is, but in the end, even if I disagree, I'll sign. Their project is their responsibility and they decide. The same applies to travel. If they feel they have to go, I sign it.
>
> I remember once when I was younger, I felt it would be a good idea to go to a trade show in Japan. I couldn't explain clearly why, but my boss signed for it because I said I felt it was a good idea, and I went.
>
> What I saw opened my eyes to some emerging Japanese capabilities which would have had a significant impact on a product we were developing. We redesigned the product to exceed what we projected their next generation would do, and we were glad we had. That outcome would have been hard to predict before I went.

It takes courage to defend that kind of decision making in a corporate culture devoted to quantitative justification. Sponsors temper analytical objectivity with faith and trust. It may seem a risky combination, but remember that trust is a basic tool of the most hard-nosed businessmen the world has ever known: the venture capitalists. It's much cheaper to choose good people and trust them to find their way to success than to stand over them and tell them exactly how to waste money.

The existence of sponsors and protectors is perhaps the most important aspect of the intrapreneurial climate, and fortunately the one most directly under the intrapreneur's control. To find a sponsor, you don't need to restructure the corporation. You need only establish mutual trust with someone in a position to protect you and your idea.

Those who take up the job of sponsorship solve three of the most basic barriers to intrapreneuring: lack of resources, nervous money, and political attacks.

1. **Lack of Resources.**

   Most intrapreneurs can't authorize their own activities, budgets, and personnel. A sponsor who believes in them and their vision can either give or get these approvals.

2. **Nervous Money.**

Entrepreneurs seeking quality investors to fund an independent venture look for people with the courage to let their money work overtime. They refer contemptuously to "nervous money" provided by unprofessional investors who are unsure of their own judgment and run hot and cold on the venture, threatening to remove the funding at every setback. In many corporations, support for an intrapreneurial venture is a hotly contested political issue. The result is to jerk the intrapreneur's attention off making the business work and onto waging the political battle for support.

3. **Political Attacks.**

Good sponsors help detect and head off political attacks. Their support deters those who would attack and their position allows them to defend intraprises at levels where intrapreneurs can't speak for themselves.

The systems and bureaucracies of a corporation generally reject anything new. Staff groups weigh down intrapreneurs with reporting requirements, multiple approvals, safety committees, and other concerns that delay progress and smother initiative. Therefore, a strong sponsor is needed to protect the venture from nitpickers. Sometimes this is done just by letting it be known that the sponsor will have the head of anyone who interferes with the venture. In other cases more devious strategies are required.

John Kenneth Galbraith was one such sponsor when he was a director of the U.S. Strategic Bombing Survey in Germany at the end of World War II. Under his care were a few unruly mavericks whom he could count on to succeed at any task too tough for the military system. Unfortunately, these doers of the impossible had little respect for the system and were always in trouble. Galbraith received stacks of complaints urging him to discipline them.

Galbraith knew that bearing down on them was out of the question, but he had to do something about the avalanche of complaints. He hit upon this solution: Each time he received another complaint he would lift up his desk blotter, slip the complaint underneath, and forget about it. Soon the inevitable follow-up call would come: "Major Stuffed Shirt here, have you done anything about that impertinent So and So?" Galbraith would respond, "Funny you should mention that. I have your memo right in front of me on my desk. Rest assured I am handling it as it should be handled."

After some months of procrastination, the incidents were forgotten. Galbraith threw away the old complaints from the bottom of the pile to make room for the new ones on the top. Polite procrastination is among the best ways to deal with complaints in a bureaucracy. Attempting to explain only makes things worse. Relaying complaints to the offenders is generally useless; intrapreneurs seem to have difficulty with repentance.

Art Fry's boss, Bob Molenda, often found himself facing complaints. When Art built and installed a piece of manufacturing equipment, that he was supposed to wait for others to build, it was a big embarrassment to engineering. According to the rules, they had a right to complain. When people complained, Bob would say something like, "The reality is that it's there and it works. I know it looks awful, but it is too late to do anything about it. That's the price you have to pay for people like Art."

WORKING SPONSORS

Most nearby sponsors do more than protect and fund. They also help the intrapreneur think through and execute his intraprise. Bob Person worked actively with Michael Phillips, bringing out the best ideas and planning their implementation. He also tactfully persuaded Michael to drop obvious losers.

Art Fry worked very closely with Bob Molenda when he was developing Post-it Notes. Although Bob believed in his intrapreneur's vision for a new product line, he had been advised by his superiors to have him work on something else. Instead of killing Art's project, he buried it, which meant hiding it within an existing approved project. For example, when they got a few days in the pilot plant for an approved project, they continued working at night making trial runs of Post-it Notes.

"Every new product has a profit and loss statement, and in the beginning it is negative," says Bob Molenda. "You can't let it run negative too long or let people see too many failures. It is best to keep things hidden for as long as you can, burying the costs in well-established budgets. With Post-it Notes we needed to have an economical process before we showed people the idea. We knew the questions we would be asked, and so we did our homework before we started talking about it."

ONE PERSON'S SPONSOR IS ANOTHER PERSON'S INTRAPRENEUR

The more a sponsor works on a project, the more he or she becomes part of the intrapreneurial team. Above the working sponsors, like Bob Molenda and Bob Person, there is another layer of sponsors who may view the working sponsor as the lead intrapreneur and the Art Frys and Michael Phillipses as the inventor intrapreneurs. Unless it has completely broken out of the system, it is always harder to assign responsibility for intrapreneurial innovation than for an entrepreneurial one. This doesn't really matter. By definition sponsors are generally intrapreneurial in that they take risks to make a vision of something new happen within the company. What exists is the spectrum in Figure 7-1.

Sponsorship Spectrum

Inventor	Intrapreneur	Sponsor	Protector
Understands the new product or service, but not how to make a business of it.	Attention is on business realities; may occasionally forget realities of corporate politics.	Attention is primarily on removing organizational barriers and giving advice to the intrapreneur.	Very high level sponsor who approves and protects, but only occasionally meets with the intrapreneur.

Figure 7-1

FINDING A SPONSOR

"The ideal sponsor is 55 to 60 years old and highly respected by people at the top of the organization," says one canny intrapreneur. He has come to grips with what he will or will not be in the corporation and has no aspirations for climbing higher. Consequently he is motivated not by personal ambition but by a desire to serve the corporation and an admiration for the maverick's way of operating. On the other hand, says our trench-weary intrapreneur, "the worst thing you can have is an ambitious sponsor who suddenly discovers that you have annoyed some important person whose favor he needs to advance." This may be too narrow a definition of a sponsor, but the basic philosophy is sound. Like the intrapreneur, sponsors must have deeper reasons for their commitment to a venture than just a desire to advance, or the commitment cannot be counted on to endure setbacks and opposition.

Bob Molenda is typical. "I'm not very money-motivated," he says. "They pay me well and all my bills get paid. More important to me is getting something new done. I like working with other creative people and helping them to become oriented to our customers' needs."

Outside of work, Bob helps smaller companies become more innovative and has just set up the Midwest Inventors and Innovation Workshop. He continues, "Maybe it's a funny goal, but if I can help people like Art Fry to be more effective, they are better off, 3M is better off, Minnesota is better off, and even the country is better off." As long as such social motivations are stronger than personal ambition, the sponsor can be counted on to try to protect his or her intrapreneurs.

The CEO as Sponsor

Some CEOs become personally involved as sponsors. Al Marzocchi had such a sponsor in the late Harold Boeschenstein, then president of Owens-Corning Fiberglas. Al has invented ways to strengthen fiberglass by bonding it to resins, developed the fiberglass belted tire in conjunction with Armstrong Tire, pioneered new ways to use asphalt, and initiated a host of other successful businesses.

Al's thinking on asphalt was simple: Since it cracks because it is brittle when it is cold, why not convert it to a rubbery compound with stretch? That would make a far better road surface. Having made something that looked good "when playing around in the lab," he immediately wanted to test it in use.

Two options were open to him. The first was to go through regular company channels, trying to convince people that his product idea, which was totally new to the firm, was worth promoting, and that his test on public roads was legal and safe. This would have taken months of hard work. Instead, Al took what in retrospect seems the obvious path: He went to a local patching contractor, explained his idea, and showed him the material. That afternoon the two men went out and patched some cracks. Al watched the patches over the summer, and after some months had passed he was satisfied that his idea was a winner.

"I believe very strongly in the ability of the human mind to observe better than any measurement. When you see it in use, you can interpret what is happening."

What is unusual about this story is that that kind of impulsive testing just isn't done at Owens-Corning Fiberglas. One scientist, who considerably outranked Al, said: "If I just went out and did something like that they would have fired me."

"I guess I'm just a maverick," says Al. "That's just the way I do things. I have to see the product in use to see if it's worth developing."

Al got away with this because he always had the personal support of the president. When he came back to work at Owens-Corning Fiberglas after getting his advanced degree, Harold Boeschenstein came down to his lab and spent the day with him. "I don't know why he took to me," said Al. "I guess he figured I was weird. When I was first with the company, I did a little better job than normal. Somehow he had the feeling I could do something."

When one listens to Al describe himself as weird or talk about "playing around" in the lab, one wonders how he could survive in a corporate environment. But many intrapreneurs are much like Al Marzocchi. They can't flourish in the corporation without sponsors. Without top management support, Al Marzocchi couldn't have proceeded in his informal style, trying out every idea with potential customers when it was still half developed.

Most CEOs do trust a few mavericks and intrapreneurs, but that doesn't alleviate the sponsor shortage. No CEO of a large firm can single-handedly sponsor enough innovators to serve the company's needs. If a CEO wants any volume of innovation, he or she must empower many people to be effective sponsors. Many people must be able to absorb risk, commit the corporation to new courses of action, and make some mistakes without being punished.

In times of great internal turmoil few corporate officers are in positions so secure that they can provide calm and sustained support to intrapreneurs. In more stable and decentralized growing firms there are frequently a number of barons secure enough to afford to sponsor innovation and to beat off any who would attack it.

Former Intrapreneurs as Sponsors

Former intrapreneurs frequently have both the clout and the mind-set to make effective sponsors. For example, John Pearson of 3M's Profab Lab needed to buy a $50,000 machine. In the 1940s this was a lot of money. His sponsor, Dick Drew, who was the intrapreneur of Scotch tape, was a strong supporter of the idea that intrapreneurs should have access to their own tools for research and development. But at the time, 3M had a "restrictive formal engineering organization" fighting to maintain its monopoly on building prototypes. Originally Dick's whole group had gotten around this problem because John had a very complete shop in his basement at home, and many times they built the needed prototypes there. Although this arrangement had worked well for some time and John had acquired a good set of tools, the need for a $50,000 machine made it impossible to continue in his basement. Once John convinced Dick Drew that the machine was really needed, Dick got it for him despite engineering's objections. Because of the sponsor's track record as 3M's foremost intrapreneur, with transparent Scotch tape and masking tape to his credit, he could do the impossible within 3M.

Owners as Sponsors

Owners often see a legitimacy to taking risks that professional managers consider imprudent. They may have time frames extending beyond their own lives to those of their children. Certainly they are not the victims of quarterly profitability panics if the company's balance sheet is sound. Because of the freedom, clout, and long-term stability inherent in their business lives, owners can make excellent sponsors.

Xerox's very successful venture capital arm of the 1970s was spearheaded and sponsored by Abe Zarem, its largest stockholder, who was also an employee. Du Pont's venturing in the 1960s was directly backed by family members who were on the board. They gave such support to former intrapreneur Ed Gee that he could freely sponsor others who were actually doing the innovations.

Corporate Ventures Groups as Sponsors

Corporate ventures groups are organizations which act as greenhouses for internally developed new ventures. These groups seem like the most logical sponsors to would-be intrapreneurs because they presumably have the money, clout, and staying power necessary to help a venture succeed. But, too often this is not the case.

153

It is important to note that intrapreneuring and corporate ventures activities are not synonymous. Corporate ventures groups can be questionable sponsors because they have great difficulty consistently defending their intrapreneurs; usually they themselves are under attack. The attacks come for the following reasons.

Jealousy

When one group is singled out to innovate, everyone else feels slighted and cheated. "Why do they get relief from bureaucratic restraints when I don't?" people ask. The jealousy can be substantially worsened by a CEO who oversupports the ventures group: "These brilliant people are creating the future of our company," says the CEO, insuring that everyone else will hate them, and that the hated "hot shots" fail.

The Danger of Success

Ventures groups that begin to succeed are particularly vulnerable to attack. Success calls for larger investments that come out of other businesses. Success also threatens to put the ventures group leaders ahead of their former peers. One highly successful group found themselves so isolated that for months they could not even get routine supplies from other divisions, which company customers could get delivered on twenty-four hours' notice.

The Spotlight

Putting an idea in new ventures gives it no place to hide. Generally, the new ventures group has no mature profit centers with which to disguise development costs. Consequently, each venture often gets close scrutiny from top managers—which doesn't encourage independent action on the part of the intrapreneur.

One frustrated biotechnology intrapreneur noted, "We spent more than our annual sales in just three weeks on hotel bills for top management visitors. How could anything as insignificant as my little medical business warrant that much senior management attention? In the end, we got so much help, we couldn't get anything done, so I resigned to seek an entrepreneurial career."

The moral? Avoid ventures groups that have to check ideas with all the operating divisions before proceeding. If every division must reject the idea first, two things happen:

- The ideas the venture group gets are usually too far from the businesses the company is familiar with to have a good chance of success.
- More important, ventures get "antisponsors"; the division managers who rejected the idea can't wait to see it fail to prove they were right not to accept it in the first place.

Norm Fast suggests that ventures groups flourish when three conditions are present:

- Prospects for existing businesses don't look good enough, so diversification is necessary.
- There is excess cash to be invested not needed by existing businesses.
- The company is optimistic about its ability to diversify by internal growth.

All three of these factors rarely persist long enough for ventures to come to fruition.

When cash flow shows a downward trend, venture activities are often the first expense to go. On the other hand, if excess cash flow persists, it is often eliminated by acquisitions.

When those traps are avoided and cash flow remains strong, prospects in the existing businesses generally improve to the point where internal venturing efforts are crowded out by investments in existing businesses.*

Illogical though it seems, strong sponsors inside existing businesses often have more staying power and give more freedom of action to the intrapreneurs than to the corporate ventures groups.

---

* Norman D. Fast, "Pitfalls of Corporate Venturing" (March 1981) and "A Visit to the New Venture Graveyard" (March 1979), *Research Management*.

The Clues

Too often new ventures groups become a dumping ground for ideas and people no one knows what to do with. They are far more likely to succeed if they are headed up by a successful intrapreneur who understands how to operate a business start-up.

Corporate ventures groups are most effective as sponsors when they exist in a company where innovation is supported everywhere and the ventures group is just one more place where innovation happens. Jealousies are kept to a minimum and there is a general commitment to innovation even in the new ventures group.

HOW TO ATTRACT A SPONSOR

The surest and most straightforward way to attract a sponsor is to listen to what potential sponsors say. When you hear a wish that strikes a chord in you, figure out how to deliver what the potential sponsor wants. It's an easy way to begin intrapreneuring.

This system works particularly well with former intrapreneurs turned sponsors. Abe Cohen, the Du Pont intrapreneur who launched the $150 million a year Riston® photo resist business, has become director of research for the Photo Products Department. He is currently sponsoring a number of new ventures based on his own inventions. By building business visions around Abe's inventions, the intrapreneurs working with him have almost guaranteed themselves active support. Later they will have learned the ropes enough to push forward ideas wholly of their own creation if they choose.

Hulki Aldikacti is now in a position to sponsor people himself. "I have a few favorite people and I let them do certain things I would not let others do." How does he recognize them? "Through deeds, not words," he says. Also important:

1. **They demonstrate unselfishness.**
    They do what's best for the company, not what's best for themselves.
2. **They have a sense of urgency.**
    They feel a great pressure to get things done rapidly.
3. **They don't have time to get sick.**
    If they do get what others might call an illness, they usually work through it because they are so interested in what they are doing.

Attracting a Sponsor Naturally

Most intrapreneurs don't find their sponsors by a carefully planned approach. Rather, they discover sponsors when the right chemistry occurs. They attract sponsors by behaving according to their natures with integrity and verve.

Every would-be intrapreneur already has some freedom. If you use that to innovate successfully as best as you can, you can attract sponsors. "I'm always looking for someone like Michael Phillips," says Bob Person. "The best thing I have done in business has been finding people like him and turning them loose."

Good sponsors also help their intrapreneurs to get other higher level sponsors. Bob Molenda describes this responsibility: "I strive every minute of every day to push people like Art Fry uphill. When I see Bob Adams [executive vice president of technology] I say, 'Hey Bob, I want you to meet one of the most creative guys in the company.' " Building those bridges pays off when a higher level sponsor is needed later in the development of the idea.

The best sponsors already know their intrapreneurs in another context. The first time Matt Sanders got Allen Michels, the president of Convergent Technologies, and his boss, Bob Garrow, to share his vision for a new portable business tool called the Workslate, "We sat down and I said, 'Look, here is an idea . . . Here's what we can do about it . . . Here is how much I think we can build one for. We really ought to do this.' " They knew Matt well as an engineering manager. They had worked together and knew Matt had good ideas and that he came through on his promises. Once he had explained all that he knew about the project, there was no need for formal salesmanship. As Matt said, "I just had two other partners in the program." Allen Michels knew and trusted Matt and was willing to give him the support he needed. Your most likely sponsors are people you already know.

Good sponsors are not run-of-the-mill executives; they have unusual courage and an unusual desire to see innovation happen. Intrapreneurs will not be discovered by pretending to be one of the crowd, nor will they be accepted if they appear to be firebrands or boasters. Intrapreneurs must reach beyond their assigned duties and accomplish something that creates credibility and a degree of notoriety. Alec Feiner at AT&T, Chuck House of Hewlett-Packard, Al Marzocchi of Owens-Corning Fiberglas, and others like them did it by combining engineering excellence with stubbornness. But any form of excellence will do.

Often a sponsor is attracted from outside the immediate hierarchical relationship. Lew Lehr's development of a $350 million health-care products business at 3M succeeded partly because Lehr secured the sponsorship of Hugh Tierney, head of the company's tape lab, when the project got into trouble.

Tierney had formed a team of three—Lehr and two others—to develop an adhesive surgical drape, which three surgeons in the Cleveland clinic had been working on. After three years the company had spent $125,000 on marketing and advertising the product, but had taken in somewhat less in sales. Tierney received word from one of the executive VPs to kill the project. Lehr and his team had convinced Tierney that the idea was good, so he gave the project one last chance. He told Lehr to make six months' worth of inventory before shutting down. Lehr had also secured the informal sponsorship of William McKnight, the retired company chairman, who was interested in health care. His interest allowed the project a second hearing.

Lehr went out personally to sell that inventory and landed the University of Minnesota Hospital account. The hospital called 3M and its interest played a large part in convincing management to continue making the product.

As the project developed, Lehr's vision grew far beyond the surgical drape business to encompass a whole health-care products business. Health care is a major part of 3M today and partly as a result of the success of his vision, Lehr is now the chairman of 3M.

Sponsors are the basic antidote to the bureaucratic inertia of the corporation and the nearly endless official innovation processes that exist in most large firms.

Innovation depends to a great extent on intuition and insight. In systems driven by the analysis of ideas rather than through the selection of people to trust, intuition is lost and with it the prospect of efficiency in innovation. Sponsors use the time-honored leadership tool of knowing whom to trust and how to trust them. This puts great stress on their ability to judge character, but it is also the only effective way to innovate.

CHECKLIST FOR
CHOOSING A SPONSOR

- Has he or she stood up, been challenged, and proceeded anyway?
- Is he or she willing to be in the center of controversy?
- Does he or she have a deep personal commitment to innovation and innovative people?
- Can you gain his or her respect?
- Does standing behind new things mean more to him or her than another step up the corporate ladder?
- Does he or she know when to fight and when to lose gracefully when it really doesn't matter?
- Does he or she know how decisions are really made in the corporation?
- Does he or she have the respect of other important decision makers and have access to them?

HOW TO BE A SPONSOR

Executives charged with getting innovation to happen need to manage intrapreneurs, which is almost a contradiction in terms. Nonetheless, there are a few rules that make this paradox less complicated.

1. **Clearly express strategic vision.**

    The best way to direct intrapreneurs is to clearly tell them where the company, division, or department is headed and ask them to help. This gives them a chance to align their visions with yours, and at the same time to use their imaginations on how to get there.

2. **Self-selection.**

    Remember that intrapreneurs, like entrepreneurs, are self-selecting. They volunteer, you don't assign them. You can certainly try out your ideas on likely candidates to see if you can stir up a passion for a venture.

3. **Be a colleague, not a boss.**

People with a high need for achievement need someone with whom to discuss their goals and how to achieve them. They don't need an authority figure. Most intrapreneurs, like entrepreneurs, don't think they are going to need much help. Venture capitalists generally spend five to twenty more hours a week on their investments during start-up because entrepreneurs do in fact need someone to help work through many of the problems. Use your greater experience to help an intrapreneur anticipate and avoid obstacles.

4. **Find others to buttress the intrapreneur's weaknesses.**

Often a sponsor sees an intrapreneur's weakness and is dying to intervene. "The best solution is to buttress them with good support people," says 3M chairman Lew Lehr. When an intrapreneur needs a lot of advice, it may be easier to accept from a subordinate than a sponsor.

5. **Frugality and autonomy go together.**

If you grant autonomy it is fair to ask for frugality. Intrapreneurs should use some of their autonomy to find inexpensive ways to get results.

6. **Milestones.**

Intrapreneurs, like entrepreneurs, are good long-term and intermediate goal setters. Work with them on goals and milestones and take an interest in how they are doing relative to their plans. This does not mean grilling them on variations, but it does mean expecting them to meet milestones and congratulating them when they do.

7. **Judge intrapreneurs on results, not methods.**

Intrapreneurs like to do things differently, but they also like results. You must compensate for freedom of method with ruthlessness about results.

8. **Give clear, frequent feedback.**

It is probably an exaggeration to say that the reason intrapreneurs go to market is that it is the only place they can get honest feedback on their ideas, but still there is a grain of truth in that. Intrapreneurs need frequent feedback on how they are doing. They cannot wait for their annual review—they need to know daily or weekly. Don't forget that recognition and strokes are very important to intrapreneurs despite their independent nature.

9. **Expect mistakes.**

Remember that innovation really happens by blundering through to success on the back of one's mistakes.

PROFILE

MATT SANDERS: Dealing with a Setback

In 1982 Convergent Technologies was a two-year-old high-tech company with sales of $96 million. Most companies would have been satisfied with growth as fast as theirs: from zero in 1980 to $13 million in 1981 to $160 million by 1983. Most would have been satisfied with having their intelligent work stations built into office automation systems by RCA, Burroughs, Honeywell, and others. But for Convergent Technologies, it was already time for something new. In early 1982 president Allen Michels, head of engineering Bob Garrow, and Matt Sanders, a senior engineering manager, agreed that it was time to get going on new projects.

"I volunteered to act as a catalyst more than anything else," said Matt. He offered to spend half his time working on a survey of the market and to create a list of new-product options. If he could delegate some of his day-to-day management responsibilities to others, then he would just pull ideas, people, and things together from the rest of the company as they were needed.

His first step was to go out and look for markets. These were the days before the IBM personal computer was available in large volume, and Matt wandered around talking to people in small businesses and offices. He wanted to find out just what they were using their computers for. Matt was not surprised to learn that the business managers and professionals were using their computers to run a software program called Visicalc® for cost estimates, financial projections, and the like, while the clerical and secretarial staffs were using the machines for word processing. What surprised him was that this pattern of use was so consistent. Companies had bought Apples to do a variety of tasks, but once the computers were allocated among the various departments, each computer was used to perform only a single function, usually some kind of repetitive task. When Matt asked managers and small business proprietors whether they would like to accomplish anything else with their machines, almost unanimously they said "No." When he asked if they would like their computers to be linked in a network so they could share information with other people, the typical response was vehement: "I've spent a lot of time and effort getting this machine to a point where I can use it, so don't anyone touch it."

Because of that response, Matt got the idea that there was a market for single purpose personal computers, and that, in particular, Convergent should create a Visicalc® machine that could be used anywhere. "These poor people are in pain," he observed. "They've got to anchor this heavy machine on their desk tops with all these discs and electronics, and deal with questions of how much memory is needed, which software to buy, how to learn it, etc., etc." For the average user, the effort Visicalc® necessitated was greater than need be.

Innovation sometimes starts with research, then bit by bit the concept comes together. But it didn't happen that way for Matt. He began with a lot of generalized thinking from the viewpoint of the customer. "Then all of a sudden," Matt said, "it just slugged me in the head, this clear vision of the product from its inception to sales." He didn't perceive the technical details of the product, but he had a user's sense of it. "When I closed my eyes, I imagined myself using this machine, whatever it was or would be, a year from then. You couldn't clearly focus it, but I could imagine what kinds of things I was doing."

Matt himself had been a frustrated electronics spreadsheet user for a number of years. He had too often found himself either on the wrong side of the country or in a meeting room thinking "Oh God, I gotta do this spreadsheet. If I could only have brought my computer with me." His boss, Bob Garrow, and Allen Michels, the president, felt the need too.

Yet this notion about a portable spreadsheet computer was consuming only a small part of Matt's time. He continued his regular work as an engineering manager. His other main task was to define the next generation of the computer work station that was then Convergent's only business.

MAKING THE COMMITMENT

By May 1982—three months after starting his new product survey—Matt and the others had developed a white paper that described the general state of Convergent's markets and opportunities, one of which was the small portable computer primarily dedicated to doing spreadsheets. "We didn't yet know what it was or what it should do or even quite who would buy one." It seemed likely that their market would be business professionals. They felt that a new set of technologies was converging, one that would allow a very small, easy-to-use machine to be built inexpensively.

To sort out their list of opportunities, Allen Michels, Bob Garrow, and Matt checked into the Pebble Beach Lodge for three days, locked themselves in a room, had meals brought in, and spent the time refining some of the product ideas and reorganizing the company in order to attack them. When they began, Matt didn't realize how important the personal portable business tool had become to him. It was, after all, just one of many ideas to be presented casually to the others. He had, however, put together a "napkin business plan" for the meeting, consisting of an estimate of the size of the target market, how long it would take to get into the marketplace, the basic cost and pricing objectives, an estimate of the money needed to fund the project, and revenue expectations for the next several years.

When they went to Pebble Beach to plan Convergent's future, they didn't know they were going to plan their individual careers as well. By the time all the products on their list were discussed and they had assigned one to each of them, Matt had talked himself out of a job as head of engineering for Convergent's new mainline work station business. He found himself volunteering to take on the portable business tool that soon would be called the Workslate: "It's got to be the most fun. And no one else is going to do it unless I do—I love the product."

Allen Michels, Convergent's president, asked Matt how much of Workslate he wanted to be responsible for—just the engineering or the whole thing? He also wondered whether he should kick Matt out of his office and say, "Good-bye, see you in a year." Matt decided to take on the whole project and asked Allen to commit about $5 million as "venture capital." Matt also formed an informal board of advisors including engineers and managers from the other divisions. Matt was out of his office and on the new job by the following Monday.

A little later, Matt remembers, the doubts began: How was he going to do it? Should he be doing it all or just the engineering? How could he undo what he had committed himself to? How would he find the right people, and the right vendors? What was going to happen, what would it entail, did he have enough money to do it all? He thought to himself, "You know, Matt, you could fail completely." But he also felt the excitement growing, "Here we go again!"

After getting "booted out" of his office, Matt left for Japan on a technology shopping trip. Following that, he wandered around the United States and the rest of the world looking for technology options, talking with potential customers, and allowing his vision of the product to grow and become more concrete. To save money and time, he operated out of an office in his home. Since he was single, there were few distractions.

It was during the period of Matt's travel, research, and reflection, when he was inquiring into what people were doing with Visicalc®, that he made a second conceptual leap. He saw that Visicalc® wasn't really an electronic budget maker. It was a metaphor for expressing business relationships. Rows and columns express relationships. They can usefully contain almost anything that is related in any way: names, quantities, telephone numbers, expense reports, cost estimates, stock portfolios, lists of salespeople, or price lists. It all fits in rows and columns. The discovery of that metaphor was the point at which the idea started to flourish, changing from merely Visicalc-in-a-box to a set of business tools for the individual. As his product idea grew in detail, so did his plans for implementing that product.

BUILDING THE TEAM

Once Matt had his plan ready to go, he rented 3,000 square feet in an old abandoned credit union and set out to find the staff to fill it. In selecting his staff, Matt didn't have the luxury of taking people from Convergent. It was too small and growing too rapidly. Taking even one senior manager (himself) and $5 million away from the business which had grossed $13 million the previous year was scary enough. A raid of Convergent's top talent would have been too much. This decision was doubly fortunate. Many intrapreneurial ventures bog down when a new venture tries to staff itself with people others consider indispensable. Recruiting from the outside thus eliminates a significant barrier, but it is possible only in a growing company and then only when the venture is not based on skills that only exist in the company.

For its mainline work stations, Convergent had mainly been a medium volume systems integrator, buying circuit boards from vendors, and assembling complete machines in small batches. For the Workslate, Matt wanted an automated, high volume assembly line that began with small components and spit out computers. He looked for high-volume manufacturing people at places like Texas Instruments, Kodak, and Polaroid.

Convergent's mainline products were sold to others who

used them as individual work stations for larger computers. Work-slate was to be sold direct to end-users just as it was. This meant Matt needed marketing people who understood selling office machines to business customers.

Matt spent several months in a very strong recruiting effort and got absolutely nowhere. He talked to all the right people. They turned out to be all wrong. He scoured the industry for the team that was organized in his mind, but finally came to the point of saying to himself, "This is a great idea, but you're never going to get it off the ground; you can't find any people to work with you!" He needed a few engineering managers, a marketing director, a sales director, and an operations director. In some cases he originally had specific people in mind, but none of his original choices worked out. The software manager he wanted didn't share his enthusiasm for a small portable machine. "Nothing really interesting can be done with less than a megabyte of memory," he said.

Matt felt depressed after striking out on all his choices but in the end he learned something very important. We are taught to fit the person to the job or at least to find the right person for the job. Matt discovered that the jobs had to be adjusted to fit the people who were available. He had set his heart on a hardware specialist who would have telecommunications experience and a host of other very specific talents. The hardware man he finally hired had absolutely no telecommunications experience, but together they found a software engineering manager who did. He ended up hiring a consultant to work on some of the hardware for the modem and the software engineer kept them on course.

Matt started as a "team" of one, and recruited hardware engineering manager Tod Lynch. As a team of two they recruited a third and the process continued. The new people became part of a collective intelligence, bringing with them their own judgments, contacts, and capabilities. They built the team in a different way than he had planned, but by being flexible, the final result far exceeded Matt's expectations.

LETTING OTHERS ADD TO THE VISION

The Workslate, as it came to be called, had been Matt Sanders's idea from the beginning. After six months, when the technology had been largely assembled and the team was complete, he found himself with a problem he had not foreseen. Workslate was his idea, but if he continued to treat it as his alone, what place would his team have? On the other hand, if he gave his new partners their freedom, Workslate would no longer be his alone. Suddenly he found himself in a new relationship. He had started out as an intrapreneur. Now he was "management," and his team was the collective intrapreneur.

Fortunately, he recognized the path he had to take. He gave the team the freedom they needed to develop the best possible Workslate.

BUILDING WORKSLATES

As the Workslate project grew, new people were added and walls eliminated in the old credit union, expanding the space to 12,000 square feet. When the design was completed, they built a highly automated 100,000 square-foot factory to build Workslates.

The hardest part for Matt of building the factory was learning to deal with the fact that things didn't turn out as planned. A shipment of components that were essential to progress left the supplier's headquarters on schedule but were shipped to Italy instead of California. It took flexibility to see how to use another kind of more immediately available component to keep people working for the ten days needed to recover the parts from Italy.

At times the project almost seemed jinxed. The centerpiece of the new automated factory was a six-foot wide, twenty-five-foot long, 5,000 pound machine from Switzerland. Without it, all the work had to be done by hand, so the team anxiously awaited its arrival by 747 jet.

"We were in our new building and it looked like a gigantic bowling alley without the bodies and machines. I was anxiety-ridden to see the factory look like a factory."

Then, the day the centerpiece was to fly, the 747 developed engine trouble. The carrier offered a flight three weeks later, which was unacceptable; so they located two more 747s that might have been able to deliver it—only to have one back into the other in a fog, taking them both out of service. In the end the carrier found a plane, but as Matt says such chaos can drive you nuts on occasion, especially if you have a tendency toward structure and analytic processes, as many engineers do. Things don't fit neatly in their cubby holes, or turn out as you planned.

"You need direction, certainly. You need excellent planning and scheduling. But you also have to be prepared for, and supportive of, disorder."

In the end, the factory was about a month behind their production schedule, which wasn't bad except that the product was late for the Christmas rush.

THE INDUSTRY WELCOMES WORKSLATE

When finally done, the Workslate, a powerful small computer the size of a piece of letter paper and one-inch thick, was enthusiastically greeted. It appeared on the covers of three major computer magazines, was featured in the American Express Christmas Catalogue and was touted in a mailing sent to a million of E. F. Hutton's clients. A major computer retailing chain was so impressed, they forecast that they would buy everything Matt's team could make.

As they raced to get the capacity ready to meet this burgeoning demand, Matt's team was euphoric. The experts loved their product. Based on this response, Matt's team planned to sell 100,000 units in the first year, a retail value of $90 million. But the experts were wrong.

THE CUSTOMERS CONFOUND THE EXPERTS

As the orders trickled in behind schedule, it occurred to Matt that something was wrong. For some reason, the customers weren't buying Workslate. With the help of experts, the team had grossly underestimated the missionary selling needed to launch a new computer product. They went through the normal phases of letting go of a dream:
- Confusion
- Hurt
- Acceptance

CONFUSION

When the sales didn't come in as planned, the team hunted frantically for what was wrong—so they could fix it.
- Was it the right machine or was something wrong with their offering?
- Were they taking it to the right market, or was there a better way to distribute it?

- Was the timing off?
- Did they need to advertise it to prime the pump?

As the facts became clearer, Matt found himself split in two: "As a leader, I saw a great group that had worked so hard and accomplished so much. I didn't want that to go to waste. As a business guy, I asked, 'Where are we today, how much more do we have to invest to make something of this?' The business guy in me said, 'We better turn this down now.' But the emotional me wanted to go on."

HURT

When Matt first realized that the best thing to do was to shut down, the factory production was just revving up to full speed. Perhaps ironically, the plant turned out to be a fabulous success. It was a testament to all who had worked on it. "You should see the line now," says Matt. "It can spit out thousands of Workslates a week. Some consolation!

"One thing hurts worse than your hurt for yourself and your company: It's the hurt for the other people who have tried as hard as you have. They believed in it and in you and you couldn't make it a success for them. As head of the team, you want the team to be successful. Watching their hurt is harder to take than your own. You ask yourself over and over, 'How can all this good effort have been misdirected?' "

In this period of hurt, Matt struggled with that recurrent question.

"If you lose a sense of why you do all these things, you're in trouble. If you don't see it as a part of your company's business, rather than as essential to your belief in your self-worth, you'll really get in trouble.

"We at Convergent could have made an ego trip out of it and spent $20 million on advertising hoping to solve the problem. But I believe if we had done that, we would be $20 million poorer, and Workslate would still be a failure. We did excellent P.R., and we had trade journal stories. We had the American Express Catalogue and E. F. Hutton. We ran our ads in *Forbes, Business Week,* and *Fortune.* We proved that there wasn't a willing audience, and the risks of finding or creating one were very high."

ACCEPTANCE

When Matt saw that Workslate had become a higher risk proposition than they had bargained for, he thought about all the support the company had given him. He told the other Convergent leaders, "I know the most about this, and it doesn't make sense to me anymore."

The company met the failure with action. They shut down production and stripped Workslate down to a skeleton crew whose main job was to sell off the inventory. All the Workslate people moved to new jobs or other parts of rapidly expanding Convergent Technologies. They wrote off $15 million on the plants. Although one could not say for sure that someone would not buy the business, it seemed that the end had come.

One of the greatest challenges as a business winds down is to maintain your self-esteem. Matt found peace with himself in this way:

"You can't believe that *you* are a failure. Rather, you have to believe *it* was a failure. It's not that you deny responsibility, but in accepting full responsibility you have to look at what you did well as well as the things you did wrong. Then I asked myself, 'Were you negligent? Were you immoral? Were you blindly stupid?' If yes, then you have to think about packing it up—about giving up the leadership role for good. But if you can answer no, then it's time to move forward and make the next thing an even bigger success."

STARTING AGAIN

The company made it relatively easy for Matt to accept the loss. Even the little things counted. He noticed at executive staff planning meetings that everyone was still using the Workslate and telling him they still believed that it was a terrific product. More important, there were no recriminations.

As Matt struggled with this difficult period, Allen Michels began to tap him for a new assignment. He asked if it would be all right to transfer responsibility for the remaining Workslate division to someone whose basic expertise was marketing so that

Matt could again begin building a new business. Matt approved and soon became head of a new division that develops products for AT&T.

CONVERGENT TECHNOLOGIES WINS AT INTRAPRENEURING

For Convergent, the loss of $15 million was bearable. Workslate was just one of three intrapreneurial new product lines begun at the same Pebble Beach meeting. Two of the three are succeeding abundantly, and their profits will dwarf the Workslate losses. The other two are the new work station Convergent called "NGEN" for New Generation, and the Mega frame, a very powerful large computer of the "super mini" class. Convergent sales in 1983 were about $160 million. Analysts predict 1984 sales of around $400 million, about 85 percent of which will come from NGEN and Mega. Clearly intrapreneuring pays at Convergent Technologies, which has gone to bat six times and gotten five hits. As for Matt, since he has been involved with four of the six, his own record is three out of four successes. "What would have crushed me would have been if the things I believe in and the character of the way we try to do business was a failure. If that had been a failure, it would have been awful.

"What gave me the most pleasure in all this was to watch the company and see that it is not going to change its character one iota as a result of a failure. Instead, we say, 'It's working; what's next?' All of the people around me are in this industry because it is exciting. It is risky, but the highs are as high as the lows are low, and that's better than a constant drone."

When I interviewed Matt after it became clear that Workslate was in serious trouble, he gave me a better understanding of how entrepreneurs (and intrapreneurs) treat failure as a learning experience. I expected him to list the things he had done wrong and resolve not to repeat those errors, as one might in a business school case study. I found instead that those negative lessons are a tiny part of what Matt and his company learned.

> We now have a healthy respect for the ante and risks in consumer products, but that doesn't mean we wouldn't do it again—only that we would be more careful. More important to our future, Workslate taught us lessons about high-volume manufacturing. Now there are a hundred people spread throughout the company who know how to set up and operate this kind of manufacturing process. The lessons of Workslate,

both good and bad, are everywhere and that will help us with future products.

Any experience, even a failure, provides new competencies, and thus opportunities to try something new. Failure can be used as a route to growth. Matt continued:

> If you spend all of your time dissecting your mistakes, you'll become paralyzed and never accomplish anything again. It's better to examine the mistakes and failures and then quickly get on with it, knowing the experience will help you be a better business person. The failures tune your senses. It's a tough way to learn, but it works. Since the Workslate, I see myself making better decisions all the time.

CHAPTER 8

The Intrapreneurial Way of Leadership

Seventeen

The very highest [leader] is barely known by men.
Then comes that which they know and love,
Then that which is feared,
Then that which is despised.

He who does not trust enough will not be trusted.

When actions are performed
Without unnecessary speech,
People say, "We did it!"

—Lao Tsu,°

Leadership is an inherent part of the intrapreneur's job; and while not different from other kinds of leadership, intrapreneurial leadership is quite different from management. Simply put, management is the task of those interposed between the leader and the doers of an enterprise. Intrapreneurial leaders generally form a direct link between manager and doer. In fact, even the leader is a doer.

Managers taking on a new assignment inherit a working business—their job is to expand and improve it. Intrapreneurs, on the other hand, must create a new order by selecting from apparently unrelated potential parts to fit the pieces into a new pattern. Because they begin without an established pattern, intrapreneurs face a far broader array of options than do most managers.

To handle such a profusion of opportunity, intrapreneurs must be unusually comfortable making arbitrary choices in the midst of uncertainty. They need a willingness to press on,

° *Tao Te Ching*, Vintage Books, 1972.

true to their own beliefs and regardless of contrary opinion. But the required decisiveness and willingness to stick to their own vision makes them overly dictatorial managers, according to some.

The basic paradox of intrapreneurial leadership is this:

1. There is a strong need for decisive centralized direction-setting in the early phases of a new business. Until the basic directions are clearly defined, there are just too many options for group decision making to work. What is needed is a clear entrepreneurial statement, not a committee-designed compromise.

2. The age of domineering leaders and subservient team members is over. The rest of the team is presumably there for their brains, not their brawn. An important part of their task is not just executing the leader's vision but also questioning, clarifying, and upgrading it. This challenges the centralized leadership model. Successful intrapreneurial leaders resolve this paradox in their ventures, breeding a hybrid of monarchical entrepreneurship and participatory management.

"Consensus leads to mediocrity," says successful Fiero intrapreneur Hulki Aldikacti, bluntly stating what many would-be intrapreneurs are perhaps too polite to say. In a mature business, consensus is the key to high morale and the utilization of the intelligence of all involved. In the early stages of innovation, it often seems that only a firm leader can bring out the strong, simple manifestation of a new idea.

When I asked Aldikacti if he were a "top down" manager, he became impatient. "I got my MBA, too, but I don't think all those generalities do much good. Sometimes I'm a dictator—sometimes I listen. Sometimes I help—sometimes I need help."

Like many intrapreneurs, Hulki tries to give people individual freedom to do their part of the job, but he doesn't tolerate compromise with his vision. In his words you hear no reticence about telling others how he wants things to be: "I set the big picture and frame it. I expect everyone to march in that direction. If they are going in the right direction, I accept their ideas, letting them do it their way."

FREEDOM, DEMOCRACY, AND TRADE-OFFS

Instead of letting people gain control of their work lives by seeking consensus, Hulki Aldikacti, as we saw, does so by allowing them freedom in their own areas. Occasionally, however, good people working on their own parts of a design bump into one another. That happened with the Fiero. To get peak cooling efficiency, the air-conditioner designer needed to put a duct right through the place where the suspension designer wanted to attach the suspension. Neither wanted to give in.

"The people I want on my team are the best in their business," says Hulki. "They don't want to compromise on performance." It's hard for a dedicated suspension person to care about a few percent air conditioner efficiency when the handling of the car is at stake. Likewise a cooling system fanatic can't understand why the A arm can't be moved a few inches to improve the air flow. They either had to widen the car or compromise. "It's my job to make those trade-offs" said Hulki to the two engineers. "You guys are tangling with each other. Let's sit down and discuss the options and before we leave, I'll decide how the trade-offs will be made."

He lets his people make their presentations and usually the right trade-off becomes clear, because he can see the larger picture of the car and the customer.

MAKING OTHERS FEEL GOOD

If, like most intrapreneurs, you are driven by the need to achieve something meaningful, your natural impulse to prove your own worth will have to be tempered. The job of a leader is to make the team members feel good about their own contribution.

You may have a tendency to want to outperform everyone else, for example, by staying up all night to meet an important deadline. Dedication and competitiveness are essential. It's better when the dedication is shared by the group and the competition is addressed to those outside it. Include others in your acts of courage and self-sacrifice, and then make much of their dedication, not your own.

No matter how busy things are, take time to celebrate good news and to congratulate. Most people are not as inner directed as you are. Rituals build cultures. Throw parties and give speeches, post fan mail, and hand out awards to celebrate the group's achievements.

HOW INTRAPRENEURS GET AWAY WITH IT

Conventional modern managers often see intrapreneurs as selfish egotists, more concerned with their own success and power than with their subordinates' welfare. The intrapreneurs demand long, long hours. They may reject the seemingly "good" work of others and insist on showing people exactly how they want it done. The great puzzle to these conventional managers is why some people seem to enjoy working for such egotists—and why they even become intensely loyal to them.

Good intrapreneurial leaders always manage to convey the sense that a project has greater significance than simply a personal ideology. One reason people tolerate them is that successful intrapreneurs are almost never power hungry, even though they may appear to be. They are driven by a need to achieve their objectives, not by a desire to hold power over others. Sensing that they don't love power for its own sake, their people are more willing to let them be directive.*

---

* Jeffrey A. Timmons, Alexander Smollen, and L. M. Dingree, Jr., *New Venture Creation*, Irwin, Homewood, IL, 1977, pp. 77–116.

177

Also, successful intrapreneurs are caught up in a vision which has grown larger than themselves. The vision gives meaning to their lives, and they get others to share the importance of achieving it. If Hulki Aldikacti had bluntly asked the people on the Fiero program to make the sacrifices they ultimately made for him, he would have been laughed at. Instead, he made building an innovative car at Pontiac a goal many could share and sacrifice for—and he asked no one to make greater sacrifices than his own.

FOCUSING ON WHAT YOU ARE BUILDING

One of the keys to Hulki's success in avoiding conflicts between team members comes very naturally to many intrapreneurs. He kept the focus of the discussion on the product and on its effect on the customer, not on personalities. "I don't listen to stories about who did what to whom," said Hulki. "I expect people to solve their own problems—after all, they are competent people. That's why we hired them. All I want to know is, what are our options?"

What Hulki demonstrated over and over by his behavior was: focus on what is best for the car we are all struggling to build. Highly focused management style works best when the team is understaffed and success hangs in the balance. Unsure of the fate of the project, people welcome help instead of fighting for turf.

SHARING THE VISIONARY TASK

One of the most powerful incentives for getting the enthusiastic cooperation of others is allowing them the freedom to help create the new vision. Chuck House did this on the moon monitor project by letting members of his team explore markets that were particularly meaningful to them.

It isn't always easy for the intrapreneur to let others

share the task of building the vision. Matt Sanders describes what happened as his team grew:

> Then we started hiring people, and that's probably the point at which my ego had to take one of two paths— either it was going to get out of the way altogether and let the thing succeed, or it was going to demand that the product be the implementation of my ideas, in which case it probably would have failed completely. We added to the basic idea without radically changing it. It was still a little tough in the beginning, just because it had been my idea for six months.
>
> We added the idea of having data storage via micro-cassette, so the user could store and retrieve lots of work-sheets. From there came the idea of using micro-cassettes for audio dictation as well, then of combining the two so a person could annotate worksheets with audio. Then the idea of putting a modem in it. Then the idea of linking the terminal emulation with the work sheet, allowing the two to communicate. Then the choice to go to a sixteen-line display, based on an understanding of some of the techno-logical opportunities. Then using a lower current chip technology to make it capable of running on batteries. It was a step-wise discovery process based on ideas coagulating and new people coming on to bring their own judgment, skills, and creativity to bear.

The California Compromise

To manage this burgeoning group creativity, Matt used the now nearly traditional methods of Silicon Valley idea manage-ment. He allowed heated and open discussion of any aspect of the project by anyone in it. During this discussion all team members are peers.

"We put all the people who have an interest or impact on a decision in a room, and get it all out on the table. We always find out that we don't have the information we need, and so we all take 'action items' to find out about [something we need to know]. Once the information is known, we generally get consensus."

On some occasions, after they had gathered all the facts they could, the team still couldn't agree. Matt then cast his vote. "In those rare cases where we don't agree, I break the tie. The number of votes doesn't count. In more than one case, I have settled it in favor of one lone dissenting vote."

Part of the California compromise is the process of conflict followed by commitment. Once a decision is made, everyone is to support it enthusiastically.

> The important thing, then, is for everyone to make it work, whatever the decision was. We have no time in this marketplace for indecision. That's worse than anything else. If you make a wrong decision, it's enormously likely that you'll discover it in the process of execution. Indecision, on the other hand, is paralyzing. You go nowhere, achieve nothing, and learn nothing.

REITERATING THE BASIC VISION IN EVERYTHING YOU DO

Matt Sanders described the leader's role of continuous demonstration of the group's objectives:

> Edicts very seldom generate a following. I think the only way of having people understand direction is to be certain that you are always involved in informal chats with somebody about what they are doing. You have to have a constant undercurrent of "here's where I think our business objectives are." We want to be in this kind of marketplace. Let's not think about designing Italian furniture for the next year; we've really got some portable computers to be working on. You don't set those objectives by writing them down on a piece of paper and handing them out to the organization; you get it through human contact and intercourse. With enough human contact, and reiteration of the basic goals, you need few formal controls. Everyone shares a common vision.

Matt Sanders and Hulki Aldikacti have very different styles. Hulki's is more traditional, more "Detroit"; Matt's is more contemporary and "Silicon Valley." But underneath these differences are basic similarities:

- They both set the direction.
- They both give others working on the project freedom and have respect for them.
- They both listen to all comers, but reserve the right to make final decisions.

PHASES OF INTRAPRENEURING

The task of balancing the need to control the vision and the need to let others add to it is made easier by the fact that there are different phases to building an intraprise.

The Solo Phase

Never show fools unfinished work.

—R. Buckminster Fuller

In the beginning, the intrapreneur generally builds the vision alone. There are no delays due to ego battles or differing goals, since all ideas are equally owned by the intrapreneur.

It is a delicate matter to decide when your vision is complete enough to begin sharing it with others. When an idea is unformed and fluid, others' helpful suggestions often feel like assaults. Later, the idea becomes strong enough for you to face suggestions without veering off course. It often helps to write it down before showing it off—both to keep discussion focused on the direction you want in and to establish your authorship. If you allow your ideas to be coopted by others too soon, you will probably lose interest in them, and others, who lack your commitment and understanding, probably won't implement them either.

The Network Phase

Once the basic idea is clear, most intrapreneurs begin sharing it with a few close friends in the company and a few trusted customers. From their reactions they learn more about the strengths and weaknesses of the concept. At this stage, the intrapreneur is not yet leading others into action, just getting feedback and casual help.

It is surprisingly easy to get others to contribute their know-how to your intraprise. To begin with, the fact that you have singled them out as *the* experts is an honor. Intrapreneur Will Lewis, who built General Electric's Job Corps Training business, notes that you can call up almost anyone whose help you need, say you have heard great things about their capabilities, and ask if you can buy them lunch and pick their brain. Few people can resist so easy and flattering a request for help. Having given you advice, they become allies.

The Bootleg Phase

As the network phase proceeds, some people gravitate toward helping with more than kind words and useful facts. Even though no one has yet been officially assigned to the venture, they begin working with you to develop a product or explore the market. This is a crucial stage because several things are happening.

- An informal team is forming around your idea. You are no longer alone.
- Since you have a following, you have the responsibilities of leadership.
- You are working with and testing people who may end up as members of your official team.
- Your idea and leadership skills are being tested—with no

corporate backup. You stand on the merit of your idea and your leadership alone.

- You are probably doing some of the most creative work you will do on the intraprise. A hungry bootleg team, borrowing time wherever it can find it, is usually very productive in simplifying ideas.
- You are creating the microculture of your intraprise. People are learning how to act in your new group.

Your home or a restaurant is a good place to begin working together—any place off-premises where the group can begin to form an identity separate from their normal work roles. When Lee Iacocca set out to create a totally new car for Ford, he did not sit patiently at his desk until the idea for an inexpensive, sporty car called Mustang came to him. He knew the type of car he wanted to build and felt that it would be a roaring success. So Lee put together a group that included people from Design (even though as head of the Ford Division he had no authority to draft people from elsewhere in the company) along with people from the advertising agency (who traditionally were not called in until a project was ready to roll). They met at the Fairlane Motel so they could work without any company interference. Working on the fringes of the system meant the group could present management with a fait accompli. Had the initial work occurred inside Ford's walls, compromise and delay could have ruined it. By stretching the boundaries of acceptable corporate behavior, Lee Iacocca brought his idea to life. Mustang's success is proof that bold techniques work.

When you conduct off-premise bootleg meetings, don't waste people's time. Know what you want to accomplish and be purposeful; set agendas and stick to them. People will appreciate your respect for their time.

The Formal Team Phase

Some businesses can be started by a single smart individual who, as the business grows, acquires an army of underlings to execute his plans. This pattern worked well in the early industrial era. But, increasingly, the businesses that entrepreneurs and intrapreneurs create require accomplishments too complex for one thinker and many doers. The intrapreneur usually needs an intrapreneurial team, each member of which adds to the vision and help to execute it.

Intrapreneurial teams are like the venture teams venture capitalists create. Simply defined, the intrapreneurial team is functionally complete, acts autonomously, and stays together, from development through commercialization and beyond. The team can give the intraprise the breadth of talent necessary to address all the issues and tasks of a complex start-up and to establish the management depth needed for expansion.

RECRUITING THE TEAM

Hulki's Rule:

> If you want a good ball team, you can't let the owner's nephew pitch. You know who is good and who isn't.

Getting people for an intrapreneurial team is one of the fundamental challenges, but there is no right way to find them. Getting good people requires creativity. Matt Sanders decided to recruit his people from outside Convergent Technologies in order not to slow the growth of the existing business. In companies with a less rapid growth rate, the rules require using insiders, even if more appropriate people would be available outside. This means canvassing the organization for projects which will be winding down to find personnel who will soon have time on their hands.

Even knowing that a strong team is an essential ingredient to intrapreneurial success, many intrapreneurs have difficulty forming one. There is no reason it should be easy. As Bill Gore puts it, "Followership is the true test of leadership." The ability to assemble a strong team is a tough but fair test of an intrapreneur and his or her idea, a test that if passed, is highly predictive of marketplace success.

How Teams Are Built

The best teams seem to grow by accident rather than by active planning. The practice of "bootlegging" a new project with volunteers before it is approved provides an ideal environment for growing a team. During the bootlegging phase you ask for help. Some people are drawn to your vision and your leadership style and get things done. Others don't work out. When the time comes to formalize the project, you will have sorted through a fair number of potential team members at a very low cost, both financially and emotionally.

Legitimacy and Leadership

Traditional managers get their authority from above, at least in theory. The hierarchy grants them the right and responsibility to operate some portion of an existing business. Intrapreneurs, however, start without a natural power base. Their source of authority is their vision of what could be and their ability to get others, including potential sponsors and team members, to believe and follow that vision.

"At Gore Associates," says founder Bill Gore, "we have no difficulty finding the leaders: They have people following them." This simple prescription is only possible because Gore Associates strives to avoid propping up managers, and instead allows natural leaders to emerge. The normal trappings of power in organizations are absent. There are no titles because every "employee" is an associate.

The lack of structure at Gore can cause strange things to happen. Bill Gore once became concerned because the Gore Tex division was having difficulties. He knew it needed a strong marketing executive to run it and straighten out the problems, so he hired Peter Gilson from Du Pont. Peter arrived for his first day of work and, as any good corporate citizen would, asked what his title would be. "Associate, of course," said Bill Gore, "same as everyone else." Nonplused,

185

Peter tried again: "But then who shall I say I am?"

"How about 'Peter Gilson,' " replied the enigmatic Gore. "But then how will they know that they are supposed to do what I say?" asked Peter, with some anxiety. "If they don't, you're not the man for the job," said Gore. "But don't worry, there'll be something else for you to do around here."

Then Gore relented from his Zen-like teachings and said, "Why don't you go down and just listen and watch for about six months. Make suggestions when you have a good idea. If my guess is right, within six or eight months everyone will agree you are the right person to lead the group out of its current problems."

And so it was.

Basing a company's entire management structure on the idea that followers create leaders is a radical principle, probably too radical for most companies despite the fact that it produces 40 percent per year growth for Gore Associates. The idea does contain a lesson for intrapreneurs.

What Bill Gore has done is to invert the normal system of a corporation. He has taken the informal network of voluntary associations which exists in every company and turned it into the formal system. The hierarchy still exists, but it has gone underground. As a result, you can clearly see at Gore the environment in which intrapreneurs exist in all companies. Just like a manager at Gore, all intrapreneurs must attract their followers by strength of character and quality of thought. The hierarchy in a firm may or may not prop up inadequate managers, but it can never prop up inadequate intrapreneurs. Intrapreneurs must attract enthusiastic converts to their cause or it perishes.

Choosing the Intrapreneurial Team

As you build your business plan and identify the factors that mean success or failure for your intraprise, you will learn what skills are indispensable. Your major selection task is to find people whose skills complement your own and those of others already on the team. (Use the business-planning appendix as a checklist of tasks to be accomplished.)

Team members should be intrapreneurs in their own right. They, too, must take risks and suffer the indignities of a commitment to a sometimes unpopular cause. Of course, a good team member is not always the same kind of person as the leader. For example, the lead intrapreneur may tend to overwhelm problems by overwork, while a good associate may be an orderly person with less energy who searches for an easier way.

One intrapreneur developed a droll way to find engineers for his intrapreneurial team. He made four lists. First, he went to personnel and got a list of people who were "good engineers, but. . . ." What the "but" was didn't matter, although it often implied some kind of troublemaking. For the second list he went to the model shop and asked the machinists which engineers knew what they were doing in a hands-on way. Third, he went to the parking lot and took down the license plate numbers of all the motorcycles and pick-up trucks, then on to the Department of Motor Vehicles to get a list of their names. Finally, the fourth list consisted of those engineers who skydived, rock climbed, and hang glided.

When one name appeared on two or more lists, he knew he had a serious maverick and a person of courage and thus a good candidate for intrapreneuring.

Promises to Make

As an intrapreneur full of the optimism your role requires, it is very easy to overpromise in the process of recruiting. Not to do so requires discipline. Remember to promise a chance to share in the dirty work and overwork as well as in the glorious results. Promise hardship and times of despair, but remember also to stress the hope of making a real difference. You should also work hard to get corporate commitment to reward your people for success so you can promise that too.

How to Free People Who Want to Join Your Team

One of the most persistent problems in forming an intrapreneurial team is some bosses's resistance to letting people join your intraprise. Another division may fight your attempt to hire their people, and the intrapreneur rarely has clout equal to that of an established organization. This is one time you may need your sponsor.

Freeing people to work in an intrapreneurial team is an issue on which corporations must change: If they want intrapreneurs to succeed, they must let people join intrapreneurial teams. In the Innovation Age, innovators will tell their company where *they feel* they can make the greatest contribution, rather than accepting tasks assigned by others. Impossible though this sounds, the system is already working in companies such as Gore Associates. At Gore, people are hired for good general ability. They're given three months to find a job within the company and a sponsor for that job.

If your company hasn't yet realized this, you will have to be bold and clever to free the people you need. Blocked in all their legitimate attempts, one intrapreneurial team took matters into their own hands. The person they had recruited was so angry with his old boss's refusal to let him join the intrapreneurial team that he decided to quit the company. The next Saturday they went with their new would-be member to his old office. They loaded his desk and things into a van and moved him into their own space. On Monday, they called his boss and said, "He's gone. If you try to get him back he'll quit the company and we'll all look bad. Better just to forget this happened. He can stay on your payroll and be part of your head count on temporary assignment to us." Thinking it over, the old boss agreed. Of course, such bold guerrilla tactics raise the risk of intrapreneuring.

Dealing with the Corporate Immune System

When you start something new, the system naturally resists it. It is almost as if the corporation had an immune system which detects anything that is not part of the status quo and surrounds it. If you are to survive, you will have to lull this immune system into ignoring you. You will have to appear to be part of the corporate self, rather than identified as a foreign body.

Low Visibility

If only we could get these intrapreneurs to keep quiet about their ideas until they have developed a more solid position, they would have a better chance.
—Bob Adams, Vice President of Technology, 3M°

When Art Fry showed his idea to his close friend, boss, and sponsor, Bob Molenda, Bob's reaction was appropriate. "This is a great idea, but let's not tell anyone about it yet." Together, they kept the development of Post-it Notes as quiet as they could, and without official status, until they could demonstrate manufacturability. The fewer people who know about your heroic quest, the fewer will attack it. Only when it is strong will it draw more recruits and supporters than attackers.

One effective way to create low visibility is to cloak the new intraprise in official secrecy. The Lockheed skunkworks that designed many of Lockheed's most successful planes, including the F-104 fighter and the U2 and SR-71 spy planes, gained independence in part because many who might otherwise have interfered lacked the security clearance and need to know to get in.

° Personal interview.

Underpromise and Overdeliver

Rather than promote the wonders of your project, do just the reverse: underpromise and overdeliver. Build slack into all your projections and promise just enough to get to your next stage of funding. This strategy will help you to seem an insignificant threat, ensure your credibility and also give you the opportunity to "discover" greater potential when you need some good news.

Stopping the Impatience Clock

Bob Adams of 3M says, "When people hear about a new idea, a clock begins running in their minds—after a certain length of time they run out of patience if they don't see results."[*] And as Tate Elder, head of new ventures at Allied Corporation, describes it, "In most companies, the clock runs for a roughly fixed time, such as three to five years. When that time is up it doesn't matter whether you were on your original schedule or not." Elder suggests four strategies for dealing with the impatience clock:

1. Keep your ideas quiet. The clock doesn't start until people hear about it. Also, the more they hear about it, the faster the clock runs.
2. If your business has a multiple-product strategy, try to get one of your products out and *profitable* quickly. Even though the business continues to lose money, the existence of a winning product gives hope, resets the clock, and you get more time.
3. Delay calling it a venture until R & D has done all the basic science and you are within striking distance of the market.

[*] Personal interview.

4. When the clock runs out, tighten the belt yourself, starting a new, much more frugal strategy, which may begin the clock anew.*

Location

Choosing a base of operations for your fledgling project will require careful thought. There are several factors, pro and con, that will help you determine whether to locate within the corporate walls, or to operate from a hotel, a restaurant, or the home of a team member.

You should favor operating *within* the corporation to the degree that:

- You need access to the personnel, technology, and equipment it provides.
- You have the freedom to allot the amount of your regular working time necessary to continue your bootleg work.
- You can hide well enough, if necessary, to avoid starting the impatience clock.

You should favor locating *away* from existing facilities to the degree that:

- You need to underline the corporation's wish to have your team proceed autonomously.
- Your project requires a level of secrecy not possible back in the office.
- You want to force the creation of a cross-functional team. Distance makes it harder to draw upon company resources, making it easier to justify a functionally complete team and forcing team members to expand their expertise to fill any gaps.

* Personal interview.

LEADERSHIP IN OUR TIMES

The industrial age created the need for a few leaders to see the pattern for mass production and for many managers and many, many workers to make it all happen. As our economy turns to specialty products and services and as change accelerates, we will need more leaders and fewer managers. Many who expected a comfortable career as managers of the known will find themselves instead exploring the unknown as intrapreneurial leaders.

BOOK III

BUILDING THE INTRAPRENEURIAL ENVIRONMENT

CHAPTER 9

The Freedom Factors: Can Intrapreneuring Happen in Your Company?

In any bureaucracy, there are a lot of freedoms—only they don't tell you about that, you have to find them for yourself.

—Hulki Aldikacti, the Fiero intrapreneur

Before making the commitment to becoming an intrapreneur, you owe it to yourself to take a good look at your organization's environment for intrapreneuring. There are companies and divisions of companies where the outcome is almost certainly heartbreak and disillusionment, regardless of what you do. In others, it will be possible by hook or by crook to get the freedom you need to try your intraprise with a fair chance of success.

Whatever your circumstances, the freedom factors this book discusses are designed to be used in the following ways:

1. To audit your company's environment for innovation— to see how supportive it is.

2. To identify the "hills to die on"—the freedoms so nec- essary that you should stand up for your rights in those areas even if it means risking your ability to continue the intraprise.

3. To give top management guidelines for improving the environment for innovation.

4. To give managers a framework for thinking about their own needs and the tools they can use to create a micro environment for innovation.

5. To give you the tools to argue for these specific freedoms against the powerful rationale of the current systems of overanalysis, overcontrol, and risk avoidance.

In the children's game called "paper, scissors, and stone," two children simultaneously thrust forth a hand in a manner representing either paper (flat hand), scissors (two fingers), or stone (a fist). Stone dulls scissors (i.e., a fist wins over two fingers), paper covers stone, and scissors cut paper.

Long ago, common sense in business was covered by the paper of controls and analytic techniques. The business schools gave powerful justifications to the new apostles of abstraction. Many of today's business tools are used because they sound convincing, not because anyone has proved that they work. They sound convincing because a powerful body of theory has developed to support them. But too often, the theories are half-truths, based on assumptions that squeeze out the imperfections of real life. Unless they are seen in this perspective, many analytical business tools do more harm than good.

The freedom factors of intrapreneuring can serve as scissors that cut away excessive paperwork controls. They are a counterforce to the flawed rationale for eliminating the freedom of intrapreneurs who understand a better way but lack the tools to make management see. The freedom factors are a way of managing, based on looking at the problem from the bottom up, not from the top down. They are derived from considering what the people who actually do the work need in order to get on with their jobs. They are particularly relevant for the people who do the work of innovation and responding to customers. Intrapreneurial management will not replace the now-fashionable analytic method. Rather it should be seen as another piece of the evolving puzzle of how to work together productively and with satisfaction.

The presence or absence of these freedom factors determines how effective intrapreneurs can be in your corporate culture. Sufficient dedication (and a good sponsor) can build a micro climate more supportive of your intrapreneurial career.

Book III is aimed primarily at management, with only occasional asides addressed to the intrapreneur. I have addressed it to management, not only because intrapreneurs need help convincing their managers to support the freedoms they need, but because most managers already know we must find a way to regain the entrepreneurial spirit in large organizations, but may not yet know how to realize that objective.

THE FREEDOM FACTORS

1. **Self-selection.** Intrapreneurs appoint themselves to their role and receive the corporation's blessing for their self-appointed task. Despite this, some corporations foolishly try to appoint people to carry out an innovation.

    Does your company encourage the self-appointed intrapreneur?

2. **No handoffs.** When the innovation process involves switching the people working on an idea—that is "handing off" a developing business or product from a committed intrapreneur to whomever is next in line—often someone not as committed as the originator of a project.

    Does your company provide ways for intrapreneurs to stay with their intraprises?

3. **The doer decides.** Some organizations push decisions up through a multilevel approval process so the doers and the deciders never even meet.

    Are people in your company permitted to do the job in their own way, or are they constantly stopping to explain their actions and ask for permission?

4. **Corporate "slack."** Intrapreneurs need discretionary resources to explore and develop new ideas. Some companies give employees the freedom to use a percentage of their time on projects of their own choosing, and set aside funds to explore new ideas when they occur. Others control resources so tightly that nothing is available for the new and unexpected. The result is nothing new.

    Has your company evolved quick and informal ways to access the resources to try new ideas?

5. **Ending the home-run philosophy.** Today's corporate cultures favor a few well-studied, well-planned attempts to hit a home run. In fact, nobody bats 1000, and it is better to try more times with less careful and expensive preparation for each.

    Has your company developed ways to manage many small and experimental products and businesses?

6. **Tolerance of risk, failure, and mistakes.** Innovation cannot be achieved without risk and mistakes. Even successful innovation generally begins with blunders and false starts.

   Is your system set up to encourage risk taking and to tolerate mistakes?

7. **Patient money.** Innovation takes time, even decades, but the rhythm of corporations is annual planning.

   Can your company decide to try something and stick with the experiment long enough to see if it will work, even when that may take years and several false starts?

8. **Freedom from turfiness.** Because new ideas almost always cross the boundaries of existing patterns of organizations, a jealous tendency to turfiness blocks innovation.

   Are people in your company more concerned with new ideas or with defending their turf?

9. **Cross-functional teams.** Small teams with full responsibility for developing an intraprise solve many of the basic problems of innovation. But some companies resist their formation.

   How easy is it to form functionally complete, autonomous teams in your corporate environment?

10. **Multiple options.** Entrepreneurs live in a multioption universe. If one venture capitalist or supplier can't or won't meet their needs, there are many more to choose from. Intrapreneurs, however, often face single-option situations that may be called internal monopolies. They must have their product made by a certain factory or sold by a specific sales force. Too often these groups lack motivation or are simply wrong for the job and a good idea dies an unnecessary death.

    Do intrapreneurs in your company face internal monopolies or are they free to use the resources of other divisions and outside vendors if they choose?

1. SELF-SELECTION

Some companies paternalistically plan job assignments as if it were a religious act. But intrapreneurs don't fit this mold. They passionately appoint themselves executors of their visions and then find ways to get the corporation to give them the tools to do so.

Self-selection is the first great divide between treating people as mere employees and treating them as intrapreneurs. As more and more people work with their minds, getting them to fully engage that magnificent instrument on behalf of the corporation is the central challenge. The extra commitment of the self-motivated doesn't make just a 10 or 20 percent productivity difference; someone who is fully engaged in his or her chosen work can do in months what routine attendance to a task might not accomplish in years.

The self-appointment process generally begins with bootlegging. Only by working nights and weekends or on time borrowed from approved projects can intrapreneurs build the case for official sanction of their self-appointed tasks. Sometimes, they even pass through periods of outlaw bootlegging—self-determined pursuit of an explicitly forbidden goal.

When Dick Drew, 3M intrapreneur, was selling sandpaper, he noted the difficulty his automotive customers were having painting two-tone cars. They masked off areas with newspaper and library paste. The system was awkward, slow to dry, and potentially dangerous to freshly painted surfaces. After listening to a painter curse when the paint pulled away with the paper, Drew rashly promised to make a tape that would solve his problem. No one appointed him to that improbable task, but his boss let him work on it, since it was for a customer. Neither 3M nor Dick had ever worked on tape before; he was strictly in the sandpaper business. His early attempts all failed and 3M's president, William McKnight, became concerned that 3M's reputation in the automobile industry would be damaged by Drew's frequent failures as he tested them with auto industry customers. McKnight told Drew's boss to take him off tape and put him back on sandpaper.

One of Drew's next assignments was to look at a flexible crepe-paper backing for sandpaper. Drew, still obsessed with solving the problem of painting two-tone cars, saw crepe paper as a potential tape backing for his painters. He took it down to the lab and was in the process of coating it with adhesives when the president happened by and asked what he was up to. What happened next did more than allow Drew to create masking tape: it shaped the culture of 3M.

Drew explained that he was trying to make masking tape. McKnight asked if he knew he had been ordered to stop working on tape and to go back to sandpaper. Drew admitted that he did. McKnight asked him if he knew how to do what he was told. It looked like a black day for innovation at 3M, but Drew explained why he believed the stretch in crepe paper would make the tape peel away, leaving the paint on the car, and how important it was to 3M's customers. McKnight saw the fires of conviction and was wise enough to let him continue.

It turned out that, after the hundreds of failures, the crepe-paper backing worked. Soon, auto companies were ordering masking tape by the carload. 3M had entered the tape business. Once again, self-selection of a task and meritorious disobedience proved essential to innovation. Dick Drew, as we have seen, went on to invent Scotch Brand transparent tape five years later. More importantly, McKnight never forgot the wisdom of allowing dedicated business pioneers to work on the things they believe in.

No one would have faulted Drew if he had given up trying to make masking tape, but he was committed to filling that need, however many false starts it took. That is how innovation happens.

The moral of the story: Management cannot appoint someone an intrapreneur, tell him to become passionately committed to an idea, and then expect success. Managers will do far better if they simply keep a sharp eye out for intrapreneurs who believe passionately in something and then empower some of them to follow their intuitions. In fact, the best candidates have probably already begun without permission.

Even when a senior manager very much wants a specific new business built but cannot lead the charge personally, he had better not rush to appoint someone. He should instead expose potential intrapreneurs to the idea and see who begins building on it and making it his or her own.

It is hard to know why one idea takes root in an intrapreneur's soul and another equally good one does not. Fortunately, we don't have to understand the sources of commitment to use it. Management need only develop the ability to notice and support it.

As an intrapreneur, if you are working on something that doesn't reach down and grab you, you may be better off *not* selecting yourself. If you are cut from intrapreneurial cloth, in time an intraprise will become a larger force in your life, motivating your every fiber and pushing aside many of the self-doubts all humans are prey to.

2. NO HANDOFFS

Innovation is not like a relay race in which an idea can be handed off from runner to runner. Successful innovation looks more like a growing entrepreneurial business. New members join as it grows but most of the core team remains.

Unfortunately, in many large organizations new ideas are handed from group to group during the course of development. It is a natural mistake, when creating organization charts, to break apart the stages of innovation and assign each of them to a separate group. Organizational theorists may imagine, for example, that an idea is formed from the dreams of researchers and is passed on to the more practical people in advanced development, who come up with a prototype that is passed on for design to hard-nosed engineering people, who send drawings to the practical folks in manufacturing, who make it and give it to marketing to sell. Systems of this kind almost never work for two reasons: one, a fact of human nature; the other, a consequence of information theory.

The NIH (Not-Invented-Here) Syndrome

It is human nature to want to work on ideas of one's own choosing. This fact can have positive results: Intrapreneurs become dedicated to an idea, and that commitment is the primary force behind successful innovation. But at each handoff, the committed intrapreneur is left behind and the idea must attract a new champion. The chance that people assigned to work on someone else's idea will learn to love it as their own is very small. The loss of commitment at each handoff produces a high probability that the transplanted idea will be rejected. But this loss of enthusiasm is only part of the problem with handoffs.

Information Loss and the Handoff

Unfortunately, it is impossible for one human being to transfer everything he or she knows about something to another. When an idea is handed off to someone else, most of the information the first intrapreneur has gathered is lost.

One can almost measure this information loss financially. Developing a new product or service costs money and time. So does launching it in the market. During that period the corporation is presumably investing, but few new assets appear on the balance sheet. If the corporation invests half a million dollars in a new product, and has not wasted the money, more than half a million dollars of value exists somewhere in the corporation mostly as some kind of intangible asset.

The implicit assumption made by those who support a handoff product-development process is that the value is resident in the documented progress of the project—that there are drawings, market research reports, and so forth worth close to half a million dollars.

This is not so. Most of the half million dollar asset is in the minds of the people who did the work. The corporation has paid to make them better informed about that specific project in ways that are almost impossible to communicate to others, but that nonetheless form a background for better intuitive decision making. If these people are transferred from the project, that value is lost.

Inventors and Handoffs

One of the major objections to using a single intrapreneurial team to take an idea from development to commercialization and beyond is that many companies have had bad experiences with inventors and researchers as business managers. The inventor need not be the intrapreneur—in fact, these are quite different roles, although a number of famous intrapreneurs are also accomplished inventors. The inventor often seeks satisfaction from the admiration of technical peers, while the intrapreneur measures his or her accomplishments in terms of commercial success and social contribution—ultimately, how much the customer liked or wanted the product.

Frequently the inventor becomes a member of the intrapreneurial team as a technical leader. In other cases, the intrapreneur builds a team that leaves the inventor primarily in the lab, but coming out from time to time to act as a consultant. Sometimes the inventor becomes an intrapreneur. All three systems work, but the leader of an intrapreneurial team must be business-oriented, not dedicated to any functional specialty. Thus the inventor may or may not hand off his or her idea to another intrapreneur, but once an intrapreneur is found, that person and most of the team should ride the new intraprise into the market and through its initial rapid growth. The damage done to innovation by handoffs can be very simply stated: Intrapreneurs cannot exist if their passionate commitment is ignored and their visions given to people who don't understand them. Without intrapreneurs, innovation flounders.

When Should Handoffs Occur?

At 3M, the venture team often goes on to form a new division with the team as its management. That is part of the basic reward for intrapreneuring, and it is the purest extension of intrapreneuring. MIT's Ed Roberts explains that 3M supports its teams by saying to them in effect:

> We are committed to you as a group. You will move forward with your product into the marketplace and benefit from its growth. But we cannot promise to keep you together forever as a new venture team. We will do our best to keep the team going so long as you meet our standard financial measures of performance throughout the life cycle of the product. If you fail, we will give you a backup commitment of job security at the level of job you left to join the venture. We cannot promise any specific job. But if you try hard and work diligently and simply fail, then we will at least guarantee you a backup job.°

Not every intrapreneur wants to remain with his or her business once it is a proven success. Nor does every innovation justify creating a new business. Many new products must sooner or later be reintegrated into an existing business unit. The Fiero, for example, did not become a new division, but only a new product inside the Pontiac division. Chuck House's electronic lens monitor was built into many other Hewlett-Packard products.

Frequently, the reintegration of the new product into the existing structure is done too soon. Once the IBM P.C. group developed the personal computer business in the isolation of an autonomous group in Boca Raton, IBM pulled it back into the main line IBM organization by combining it with other

---

° "New Ventures for Corporate Growth," *Harvard Business Review*, July-Aug. 1980, vol. 58, no. 4, p. 141.

small computers in the new Entry Systems Division. Some observers say that the shock of reentry into the bureaucracy of IBM might slow down personal computer innovation.

It is generally important to keep the team together past market introduction. "The first generation of any new technology rarely produces substantial profits," says Chuck House, director of engineering at Hewlett-Packard. "As soon as your initial product demonstrates the potential, competitors go to work producing a better 'second generation' product. In order to stay ahead, you have to start your second generation well before the first hits the market and start the third before you really know how successful the first product will be." To work that fast you have to keep the team together. Chuck stayed with his monitor team for the first three product generations. Only then did his interests shift.

The Intrapreneurial Slot Machines

The need for continuity of champions doesn't just apply to the intrapreneurial team and its leader. Continuity of sponsors is equally important. One successful intrapreneur explained it like this:

> To win at the slots you have to line up three of a kind; two seven's and a bell isn't good enough. Innovation likewise occurs when there is a fortuitous combination of an idea, an intrapreneur and a sponsor, all of whom match.
>
> You have to keep this combination together long enough for it to pay off. Too often the corporation comes in and moves either intrapreneur or sponsor before the intraprise can bear fruit, in effect jerking the lever on a winning combination before the payoff.

3. THE DOER DECIDES

Intrapreneurs don't like the idea of bosses. They like to believe they are in control of their own destinies, and in a well-run organization, they often are.

Ames Smithers, a *Wall Street Journal* reporter calling in the late 1950s to write an article about the 3M company, interviewed President Buetow. The newsman mentioned at one point that his understanding of 3M would be enhanced considerably if he could see an organization chart.

Buetow changed the subject, almost as though he had not heard. The visitor repeated his request several times. Still no direct response from Buetow.

Finally, in growing exasperation, the reporter interjected, "From your reluctance to talk about or show me an organization chart, may I assume you don't even have one?"

"Oh, we have one all right," Buetow replied, reaching sheepishly into his desk drawer. "But we don't like to wave it around. There are some great people here who might get upset if they found out who their bosses are."[*]

The intrapreneur's job is to create a vision of a new business reality and to make it happen. The primary problem in big organizations, as we have seen, is not blocking the vision but, rather, blocking the action. The solution lies in letting the intrapreneur act.

Probably nothing is more annoying to intrapreneurs than control systems that weren't designed with them in mind. In some cases, control systems are more than annoying; they can keep intrapreneurs from the timely execution of acts that are important to the survival of the intraprise.

At one time when Bernie Loomis, the intrapreneur behind Hot Wheels, Star Wars toys, Strawberry Shortcake dolls and more, was in charge of Kenner Toys Division of General Mills, an important customer, Toys'R'Us, was on the ropes. Suppliers, sensing impending trouble, were starting to put a hold on their credit. Toys'R'Us needed some good news to offset the growing panic. At a meeting of the toy industry credit managers, Bernie announced the much needed good news— General Mills was extending a $5 million line of credit to Toys'R'Us. Although General Mills was aware of Bernie's proposal to extend Toys'R'Us the line of credit, Bernie does not recall receiving an official "OK" to do what he did. What he did have was the confidence and support of his sponsors: Don Swanson, his boss; and Bob Kinney, the CEO; and a track

[*] *Our Story So Far: Notes from the First 75 Years of 3M Company*, Minnesota Mining and Manufacturing Company, St. Paul, Mn., 1977, p. 126.

record with General Mills that allowed him to express his typical intrapreneurial independence. To its great credit, General Mills backed Bernie up and Toys'R'Us survived and flourished.

Bernie recommends this general rule for breaking the rules: "Announce what you are going to do, but don't wait for permission." There probably is no way to be an intrapreneur without having courage.

Multilevel Approvals

Nothing slows innovation more decisively than sitting around and waiting for permission. Many large organizations, hoping to improve fiscal responsibility and control, have placed the authority to approve significant innovative acts many levels above the people who innovate.

As a young consultant, I found that often my job was to help clients prepare a series of presentations, each at a higher level, asking for permission to proceed with an intrapreneurial project. Months would pass between presentations while exalted managers found time in their busy schedules to listen to the plea for funds. But when the presentation was successful, all that happened was that, after the obligatory modification, the request was approved not for action but for presentation at a yet higher level.

The further from direct contact with the hands-on intrapreneur a decision is made, the less understanding will go into it. The ultimate foolishness is a system in which people more than a level apart are not supposed to talk to one another. So the intrapreneur tells his boss who tells his boss's boss and so on until the ultimate decision maker is reached. The result is much like the childhood game of "telephone" wherein the message, after passing from person to person down the line, emerges as nonsense. Not only is all the detailed vision of the concept lost in the multilevel approval process, but the ultimate decision maker has no way to judge the commitment and quality of the intrapreneurial team, which is the most important predictor of success or failure of an intraprise. The solution is whenever possible to avoid multilevel approvals. Let the doer decide.

For those few things that do require higher level approval, what is needed is a direct relationship between doer and approver. If innovation is to proceed rapidly, intrapreneurs must be able to get face-to-face with decision makers. They need rapid access and adequate time to explain the somewhat intuitive rationale that often lies behind high potential ideas.

Approving the routine takes little time, but understanding something really new is very time consuming. It's not just a matter of projecting and adjusting the past. To judge a potential innovation one must grasp a chain of logic so ephemeral that it has eluded the competitors. Most innovations are only obvious afterwards. Practically speaking, top managers don't have the time to hear out all their intrapreneurs—there aren't that many hours in a day. If these decisions are pushed to the top of the organization, presentations will be brief and decision makers will rightly feel they don't know enough to decide. They will call for more study and, hence, more delay. Numerous innovations will only occur if more people, especially at lower levels, are empowered to give the go-ahead.

Freeing the Power of Intuition

A new business is buffeted by surprises. Often there is neither enough time nor enough information to make a rational decision. Thus, the person to make the best decision is the intrapreneur, who has the most information and the most direct experience of the realities of the business. If the corporation doesn't trust the intrapreneur to run the business, it should get a new one, not bypass the judgment of the one they already have.

It will be argued that, though close to the facts, intrapreneurs are not objective. Good intrapreneurs are surprisingly open to feedback and perfectly willing to make changes when something isn't working. That they care deeply about the venture's success is a virtue. Rather than seeing each setback as evidence of a failure, dedicated intrapreneurs begin trying another way. This experimental persistence is how businesses get built.

Ponderous planning systems may be unable to effect changes until next year's budget, but the entrepreneurial competition just does it—now. No matter how strategically wise or strong a boxer is, if he has to call New York to clear each punch during his fight in Las Vegas, he is doomed. Silly though this sounds, many new businesses in large firms face control systems nearly as unworkable. To make intrapreneuring work, intrapreneurs need the power to make decisions and take action.

One intrapreneurial group puts it quite simply as a policy: "If it's my ass and my commitment, I control it." That philosophy has gotten them billions of dollars of new products.

4. CORPORATE "SLACK"

When all corporate resources are committed to what is planned, nothing is left for trying the unplannable. Yet innovation is inherently unplannable. Companies that successfully innovate empower their employees to use corporate resources in ways that cannot always be predicted or justified.

Discretionary Time

The most basic form of corporate slack is the freedom to use a portion of one's time exploring new ideas without knowing where they will lead. Many organizations, including IBM, Tektronix, Ore-Ida, 3M, and Du Pont, permit people to spend 5–15 percent of their time exploring ideas that interest them. When I asked Stephanie Kwolek (then a bench chemist at Du Pont) who approved the research that led to the discovery of the superstrong fiber Kevlar, she said she had. She worked on it without telling her boss—even after she made her first fibers—until she was certain she could make them repeatedly. When asked why she did so she said, "It was my job to spend some of my time exploring new ideas on my own. I didn't need anyone's permission."

Without discretionary time, new ideas remain just that: ideas. And ideas without action die. In their early stages, most new ideas appear unworkable. The creative individual needs time to prove them true or false without showing them to others and being forced to raise expectations that are likely to be dashed.

In addition to his load of official projects, Art Fry keeps four or five very part-time unofficial explorations going at all times. Most of these bootleg ventures go nowhere, but when he finishes a major project something new has always developed to fill the void.

It is easy to publish a policy that allows people some discretionary time to work on their own projects. It is harder to implement that policy if managers are under duress to move the official projects along faster. The concept of planned woolgathering and random exploration time is common for technologists. But every job needs innovation, and innovators need time to think and try new things.

Discretionary Funds

When the products of discretionary time prove interesting, the next step in developing them usually costs real money, not just fiddling around with time and a few inexpensive parts or travel vouchers. This means discretionary funds must be available to continue the increasingly promising exploration. Unfortunately, in an effort to save money, many controllers seek to find and eliminate discretionary funds. The result is not economy; rather it is enormous waste of human energy and cash alike.

Minds that are denied the ability to explore and test are being wasted. At today's salaries that is itself quite expensive. Worse, individuals not trusted to handle money become indifferent to it and, in fact, may even enjoy waste. They pack their budgets full of waste to hide money that can be diverted to useful purposes if the need arises, but which must be spent in any case to preserve the budget line for the next year. They select the safe and expensive way, rather than try something inexpensive and risk failure without backup funds to try again. The resulting brute force solutions not only cost more to develop, but later cost more to produce.

When discretionary funds are scarce, people give up innovating and become resigned or bitter. Rather than beg for funds, the idea makers take their creativity home and become deadwood at work.

It is better to have a few less people, each empowered to act, than to have too many, all of whom sit on their hands waiting for permission to do something. The actions needed are clear:

1.   Increase the proportion of unplanned discretionary funds in every budget. Earmark a portion of them for exploring new ideas.
2.   Push discretionary spending authority down toward and to the people who do the work. Even a few hundred dollars of annual discretionary budget conveys dignity and the right to try things. It will prime the pump for more significant innovations.
3.   Create multiple pots of discretionary monies for intrapreneurs to draw from.

The Ore-Ida fellows program is a good example of how to make multiple-pots discretionary funding work. Every two years Ore-Ida names five fellows, each of whom is given a $50,000 annual budget to fund other employees in the exploration of new ideas. The results have been impressive:

• A new computerized scale system funded by a $15,000 fellows grant has already saved more than $2 million.
• A $10,000 fellows grant supported engineers in developing

a novel heat-recovery system that has already saved $170,000 in one year.

- A researcher had a gut feeling that frozen potato skins would sell but his superiors were unwilling to back him. He got funding from a fellow to move the concept along until it could be approved through other channels.

Bartley N. Wankier was the vegetable-products researcher who believed in frozen potato skins. His superiors had good points to counter his enthusiasm. Ore-Ida had no way to produce the frozen skins in quantity, nor was there proof a market existed. But those kind of reasons just form the starting blocks for the intrapreneur.

Fortunately for Bart and Ore-Ida, one fellow agreed to put up $2,000 to explore ways to get the skin off the potato. With $2,000 and determination he made enough progress to attract conventional product-development funding for a full-time engineer.

Bart's solution went against the Ore-Ida grain, so it needed something special to get it moving. Everyone was used to blanching potatoes with water to remove the skins, but Bart did it the same way you and I do—baking the potatoes first and scooping the potato out of the skin. The only difference is he built a machine to do it fast. With the biggest production hurdle out of the way and successful market tests, Ore-Ida now expects frozen potato skins to be one of the "biggest selling items ever." Without discretionary seed money the idea would have died.*

At Texas Instruments, managers have three distinct funding options for new R&D projects. If their proposal is rejected by the centralized Strategic Planning System because it is not expected to yield acceptable economic gains, intrapreneurs can seek a "wild hare" grant. The wild hare program was instituted by Patrick Haggerty, while he was TI's chairman,

* "Ore-Ida's Crop of Home Grown Entrepreneurs," *Business Week*, June 11, 1984, pp. 154 H and 154 J.

to ensure that good ideas with long-term potential were not systematically turned down. Alternatively, if the project is outside the mainstream of Strategic Planning, managers or engineers can contact one of dozens of individuals who hold "IDEA" grant purse strings and can authorize up to $25,000 for prototype development. The briefness of the one-page application form expresses both a commitment not to become bureaucratically slow and a high level of trust in the people they have hired. It was an IDEA grant that resulted in TI's highly successful Speak-n-Spell® learning aid.*

Gene Frantz was the intrapreneur for the idea he was widely credited for inventing, a low-cost speech synthesizer built on one tiny new chip with a voice quality equal to that of the telephone system. Gene, who stayed with the Speak-n-Spell product for six years before moving on to a new intraprise, credits his boss on the project, Paul Breedlove, as the source of the idea and two others with key technology. When they failed to get funding in the normal Strategic Planning channels, they applied for a "wild hare" grant and were turned down, Gene says, "because we were too wild!" "We never ran out of alternatives for funding," Gene continues; they applied for an IDEA grant and got it. Before they had spent $10,000 of the possible $25,000, Gene and a group of about thirty-five part-time volunteers got to the "proof of concept" phase and could go on normal Texas Instruments development funding. Gene says his role, in addition to designing the printed circuit, was "mother" of the project— he had to go back to the "corporate fathers" every quarter to make a presentation of progress and request the next block of funding.

A company that provides a variety of funding channels encourages the pursuit of alternative approaches, particularly during the early stages of a new idea's development. In fact,

* "Texas Instruments Shows U.S. Business How to Survive the 1980's," *Business Week*, Sept. 18, 1978, pp. 66–92.

no activity should be without discretionary funds.

At Matsushita, the "GE" of Japan, all divisions are allowed to keep 40 percent of their profit for "self-renewal." No portfolio analysis judges a division incapable of innovation.[*]

Total Budget Versus Budget Breakdown

Venture capitalists are tight about total budgets but loose about changes in plan that substitute one expense for another. This same flexibility is necessary for the success of an intrapreneurial venture, and it has been employed in some large corporations with excellent results. For example, when IBM decided to get into the personal computer line, it asked Don Estridge how long it would take and how much it would cost to get into the personal computer market. He reputedly said, "One year and 20 million if you do it my way."

His way included the discretion to create a separate organization well outside the context of IBM's traditional way of doing business. The intraprise was located in Boca Raton, Florida, where IBM's small systems are developed. This gave Estridge the skill base and expertise he needed for his project. The group had simple, straightforward objectives. It had to produce a product that would measure up to IBM's rigorous demands for quality, would be easy to use, and would maintain the company's usual high level of customer satisfaction.

Estridge had almost total discretion about how to spend his project's funding. He had a complete functional team whose members reported to him but who were responsible for their own organizations, such as marketing and manufacturing. He used marketing methods considered "unorthodox" for IBM, selling through retail dealers and third-party retailers as well as through IBM's own marketing organization and Product Centers. In a move unprecedented in IBM, Estridge convinced Armonk to set aside a 70-year-old tradition and let

---

[*] Richard T. Pascale and Anthony G. Athos, *The Art of Japanese Management,* Simon & Schuster, New York, 1981, pp. 56–57.

retailers service a product under IBM warranty. He contracted out much of the hardware development and nearly all the software and brought the personal computer to market in nine months and under budget.

Within a year and a half he had 12 percent of the market share° and was rapidly becoming the dominant vendor of personal computers. The Entry Systems Division Business Unit became a full-fledged IBM division, with Estridge as its president, in August 1983. Its success helped pave the way for IBM's continuing intrapreneurism.

Head Count

Many intrapreneurs find it easier to get money than the people they need. Their current bosses refuse to release people who want to join an intraprise, not only because they are needed now but to keep them in case they are needed later. These problems get worse as companies control expenses by limiting the number of people each division can have instead of just the funds—the most common are the so-called "head count" controls.

Economists know that rationing rarely produces good allocation, and head count restrictions are no exception. They are a powerful force for the status quo because when head counts are frozen, existing activities generally keep their people and new or growing ones do without. If innovation is to happen where head count is tightly controlled, there must be a discretionary head count system to rapidly feed human resources to deserving intrapreneurs.

Informality and Bootlegging

We now know that most corporate innovation begins in an underground economy beneath the scrutiny of the ponderous official systems. The size of this underground economy can be

° The Yankee Group, Boston, Mass.

stupendous. "In the old days we had seventy people working on one hidden project," says an intrapreneur. Another intrapreneur bootlegged $10 million of time and expense money developing a new weapons system. He tested the prototypes using army personnel and equipment. The first news which top management heard of their $10 million investment came when he showed them the test reports. Several billion dollars in sales later, they may have forgiven him.

Management can try to make the official systems of the company as easy to use as the underground, thus obviating the need for sub rosa intrapreneuring. But unless the whole company is built around intrapreneurial teams, like Gore Associates, the official system is unlikely to be sufficiently intrapreneur-friendly. Intrapreneurs are better off in companies that pump discretionary time, money, and head counts into the system and tell managers to tolerate some underground activity. Enough slack to permit the early informal stages of intrapreneuring is an important element in building an environment for innovation.

5. ENDING THE HOME-RUN PHILOSOPHY

Many large organizations approach innovation with huge success as their only goal. Their leaders reason that if a new idea cannot be projected to reach from $50 to $500 million in sales within ten years, it cannot have a significant effect on growth or earnings per share. They forget that several medium successes can equal one large one. Thus, they pursue innovation with criteria like these:

1. The new business must have a projected volume of several hundred million dollars ten years from today.
2. The business must not be risky. It must be based on proven technology and well-understood markets.
3. There must be no significant potential competition in the market (meaning "nobody else has seen this obvious and huge opportunity").

There are very few accurately projectable hundred-million-dollar businesses based on existing technology that no one else has thought of. However, that is not a reason to despair. There is a strategy even for huge corporations that provides a high probability of creating businesses that will have a significant effect on earnings per share.

The highest return will come from starting many initially small intrapreneurial thrusts, each of which has some short-term promise and a variety of future possibilities. Some of these will provide great opportunities for informed, high ROI second- and third-stage investments of major proportions—the very home runs the corporation would love to hit. Others will evolve into smaller but highly profitable businesses, which can be either left alone or sold at a handsome profit. Some will fail, but since little was invested, little will be lost.

The overall returns based upon this strategy will be higher than those from big investments on the first round. A corporation only wants to make big investments in proven concepts where a proprietary position has proven its value in the marketplace. In addition, they will be investing in seasoned intrapreneurial teams who understand those businesses intimately.

Why Big Beginnings Aren't Always Wise

In the early stages of innovation one makes mistakes. The "billion or bust" philosophy tends to generate billion-dollar mistakes. Demand for high volume right away pushes intrapreneurs prematurely into mass markets where profit margins are slim, and margins for error are even slimmer. To complicate this precarious situation, huge adventures put senior management at risk and thus lead to meddling and concern that slow response time and endanger the intrapreneur's ability to run the business. Rather than lowering risk, this excess top management concern increases both the cost and the probability of failure. Worst of all, premature attempts to be big require large capital expenditures that then freeze the venture in its original plans. This prevents the successful pattern of innovation—blundering through to success on a wave of corrected mistakes while small, and then expanding rapidly once the pattern for success is proven.

One of the great difficulties Exxon faced with its office-systems business was that it invested too much too soon. Spending on the early stages was so lavish that intrapreneurs thought they were already a success. They forgot to think small in order to grow big. Eventually they had invested so much that they could only project high ROI by shooting-for-the-moon and promising to beat IBM on its home turf. That, it turned out, was not a low-risk strategy.

Companies that demand projection of the huge before entering a market rarely get in on the ground floor of new industries, and even if they do they rarely find the high-profit segments.

As the business scholar James Utterback explains, multi-million dollar industries often began by serving very small markets:

> The initial uses of major product innovations tend to be in small, often vacant, market niches in which the superiority of the new product, in one or two ways, allows it to command a temporary monopoly, high prices, and high profit margins per unit. For example, ice was first manufactured for refrigeration in the inland South where harvested ice was prohibitively expensive. Mechanical refrigeration was first used on ships for exporting meat and later in food processing plants. Rayon was first produced and used as a uniform filament for incandescent lamps, and only later as a high performance tire cord. Radio telegraphy was first used for ship-to-shore communications and later for broadcast. The jet engine and many other innovations were first used for military purposes. A major product innovation does not initially compete directly with the technology by augmenting it in important ways. A major product innovation may initially be crude, expensive, fragile, and unreliable, and so diffusion starts very slowly while it is constrained by these various problems. For example, ice was costly to

manufacture and early plants were dangerous to run, but it later became an economic replacement for harvested ice even in the North. Rayon was difficult to dye but was uniform and could be produced with high tensile strength. Research and experience with early applications led to ways to dye and weave it into fabrics. Early transistors were expensive and had poor temperature stability and frequency response, but they were light, rugged, and had low power requirements. Thus, they were ideal for missile guidance and for hearing aids. As such problems are overcome, diffusion of an innovation becomes more rapid.[*]

A classic example of creating a new industry using small first steps is the development of 3M's nonwoven business. During World War II, Al Boese and a few other researchers, working on a shoestring budget, were exploring the prospects of making a paper-like product out of the new synthetic fibers that were just then becoming available. They called this new material "nonwovens" for nonwoven cloth.

Their first idea for an application of the new material was in response to a war shortage. A noncorrosive backing was needed for electrical tape, because cloth was hard to get during the war and most paper contained residual sulfuric acid which corrodes electrical wires. They tried to back the tape with the new fiber, but failed to make it work. In the process, however, Boese began to notice some interesting properties of the new synthetic cloth. He found they made good lens wipers. Ordinary cloth tends to leave lint on the lens, but because nonwovens were made with long synthetic fibers, they were lint-free. Having found a use, Al and his friends in the lab made some sample lens wipers and went out to sell them to the Navy and a lens manufacturer. They took a few orders and made the products right in their lab on a little paper-making machine. After they shipped their orders,

[*] James M. Utterback, "The Dynamics of Product and Process Innovation in Industry," in Christopher T. Hill and James M. Utterback eds., *Technological Innovation for a Dynamic Economy*, Pergamon Press, Chelmsford, NY, 1979, pp. 47–48.

221

it was time to send the bills, and then they were stumped: They were finally beyond the capabilities of their lab. So they walked over to the commercial tape division and persuaded a few friends there to do their billings.

For four years they ran their little business out of the lab, with total sales of under $15,000. There just wasn't much need for a better, lint-free lens wiper, and nothing else they tried was very successful.

But Al Boese could not afford to be deterred. As he explained it,

> I am not a college man. A trained technical person always has another place to go, but I wouldn't have had a career at all if I hadn't somehow succeeded. Out of sheer fright I had to get something out in the market.

So with a little more time and money from the company, Al's group continued to explore new uses for their material, determined to make it a commercial success. Finally they began to hit on some products. They had a modest success with nonwoven ribbon that has since evolved into the now familiar shiny package ties. Through Al's perseverance more uses for nonwoven materials were found, until a major new industry for 3M began to grow up. Nonwoven bra cups that didn't succeed became dust masks that did. Combined with abrasives, nonwovens became scouring pads and polishing wheels. Today, nonwovens are used in the untearable envelopes the courier services use and mats to wipe your feet. And finally, forty years after that first effort, we have nonwoven backings for electrical tape.

Looking back, it would have been impossible to forsee all the products based on nonwoven technology that eventually made new businesses and new divisions for 3M. You could imagine many potential applications for the new material, but no single opportunity loomed on the horizon. 3M responded to this ambiguous situation by giving a few flexible and determined people a meager budget and the freedom to pursue the technology through several product failures. The result was a new industry for 3M at very little cost. Starting small does not mean that something cannot evolve into a wide diversity of products and businesses. And if all else fails, it is possible to switch to another small something and begin again.

Small-Scale Intrapreneuring: The MBA of the Future

The broadest business training you could get would be that of an intrapreneur. There you would face the rotating crises of every aspect of business. A new business is small enough for you to see the direct connection between an engineering or service concept decision and a marketing problem, and things happen fast.

By analogy, consider the fact that the best America's Cup skippers were dinghy racing champions before they became cup racers. You can learn far more about sailing by skippering a one-man dinghy than by cranking winches on a fine yacht.

Smaller boats respond faster so you can try more experiments per hour. Since you are in charge, your learning can be guided by your curiosity instead of by someone else's commands. Since your craft is small, it's OK to make mistakes. Hitting the dock with a dinghy is funny, but not with a big, expensive yacht. All of these advantages apply to intrapreneuring. You can learn far more by staying with an intrapreneurial intraprise for five years than by taking several lower level jobs in different functions, each for eighteen months. In the intraprise, regardless of your position, you learn to see the effect of decisions on a whole business and to see the connection of cause and effect.

Even the Japanese, whose products are polished and complete when they reach the United States, are constantly experimenting for an innovation-hungry public at home. A quick walk down the Akihabara Boulevard shows shop windows filled with such a bewildering variety of new products that one begins to doubt the sanity of Japanese manufacturers. Given their success, it is time we became prolific experimenters ourselves.

The Fine-Grain Corporation

Metals can be made stronger and less brittle by reducing the size of the grain structure; the smaller-grained metals respond better to stress. So it is with organizations.

Many companies used to a few very large businesses will have to adapt to what futurist Alvin Toffler calls the demassified society. Gone will be the preponderance of huge volume, undifferentiated commodity products; in their place will be smaller volume specialties aimed at specific needs.

In this environment many large firms will learn to use autonomous intrapreneurial managers not only to start new businesses, but also to maintain numerous profitable, but small, businesses that don't warrant top-management attention.

Intrapreneuring gives companies a way to manage more businesses without tying up top management in supervising them. By finding a way to divide themselves into smaller autonomous units, large corporations can become far more intelligent and responsive. They can match the caring and thoughtfulness about customers that is common in smaller firms. They can give more employees the thrill of calling the shots and controlling their own destinies. But all this is possible only if they learn to be comfortable with a company made up of many self-controlling small business units instead of a few giant ones.

6. TOLERANCE OF RISK, FAILURE, AND MISTAKES

You can't innovate if you don't take risks. In most companies, risk taking is given lip service but hardly honored in practice. I once saw a group of engineers joking about their chairman's latest exhortation encouraging them to take risks. "Do you know what would happen to us if we followed his advice?" said one who laughed so hard he ended up on the floor.

The risk-adverse nature of American business is no laughing matter. Despite our adventurous nature as a people, most companies have become tied up in analytical systems that choke out the risk takers.

Surprisingly, our corporations are often more capable of taking big risks than small ones. They dare to acquire companies for tens and hundreds of millions, but can't risk tens and hundreds of thousands on internal innovation. Partly, this is a result of the way corporations are evaluated by the investment community—they feel free to invest capital but are leery of anything that has to be expensed. More fundamentally, it comes from top managements who trust themselves to manage risk but are reluctant to let anyone else take risks that may come back to them if the risk taker fails.

If a large firm is to be innovative, it must have a way to take many smaller risks, to make many mistakes, and to have many failures. No system of innovation yet designed produces 100 percent success.

Ore-Ida goes out of its way to create an environment in which experimentation is acceptable. "People were getting the idea as we grew that if they failed, they would be criticized," says Ralf Glover, general manager for R&D. "With the fellows program we are saying to people that they don't have to be afraid to fail, that they can just learn things." In fact, Ore-Ida gives all idea champions a certificate, regardless of the outcome of their efforts.* With the certificate Ore-Ida says in effect: "We value your courage and what we have all learned."

Things Don't Turn Out as Planned

Most really good things begin with the unexpected. The truly innovative seek out the surprises not to stamp them out but to understand them. Teflon was discovered when a Du Pont researcher noticed that the pressure in a reaction vessel dropped to zero unexpectedly. Unable to get the resulting

* *Business Week*, op. cit.

solid product out of the reaction vessel, he sawed it open, destroying an expensive piece of equipment. But inside was something worth far more, the substance that became Teflon.

When silver prices began to rise, Du Pont set out to make a photographic film without the normal light sensitive silver emulsion. They began experimenting with light sensitive plastics. After almost a decade they have yet to sell any silverless photographic film, but other businesses emerged. Their new light sensitive plastics are used in printing plates and to make printed circuit boards, two unexpected but profitable businesses.

Failure as a Learning Experience

Intrapreneurs and their managers must remember that even big failures are learning experiences. Most venture capitalists prefer to invest in an entrepreneur who has tried and failed than in someone without experience in venturing. "At HP it is understood that when you try something you will sometimes fail," says Bob Hungate, general manager of the Hewlett-Packard Medical Services Division.

Lew Lehr speaks for 3M:

> As befits a company that was founded on a mistake, we have continued to accept mistakes as a normal part of running a business. . . . Every single one of my colleagues in senior management has backed a few losers along the way. It's important to add, however, that we expect our mistakes to have originality. We can afford almost any mistake *once.**

Marketplace Experimentation

We are somewhat accustomed to experimentation in the laboratory. It is understood that science is a process of trial and error discovery, and that a certain percentage of sales

* Speech at Wharton Entrepreneurial Center, University of Pennsylvania, Philadelphia, April 26, 1979.

devoted to R&D looks good in the annual report, but the basic ideas of science are not extended to business experimentation. Nonetheless, the market, like nature itself, contains many unknowns that can be uncovered only by trial and error. What is needed is an experimental attitude toward exploring business opportunity.

Even in businesses in which major scale-up is needed, such as in the development of a new polymer, getting the product out in a small way may be the best path to take. "Get the new product out in the market however you can," says a Du Pont intrapreneur. "It doesn't matter if it's uneconomically made in a pilot plant or if someone else makes it for you for more than you sell it for. The key is to get the product into the hands of the customers. They will end up telling you what it's good for."

Market research in itself is not enough to fill this need. Market research is notorious for producing false, negative results and rejecting new products that later succeed. Post-it Notes, Chuck House's monitors, and power steering for automobiles were all rejected by customers in the initial market research. Only experimentation will show the right way to present the product to customers or reveal how to turn an innovation into a marketplace success. What is needed, therefore, is not dispassionate market researchers seeking an objective yes or no, but passionate intrapreneurs willing to take risks to find and develop customers for their ideas.

The problem is that in most companies unpredictable marketplace results are seen as a sign of poor management. Unexpected negative results are seen as failure, not as part of a series of experimental actions leading to understanding a new opportunity.

In fact, the experimental approach deserves the name "scientific management" because science is a method for exploring, by hypothesis and trial, new areas as yet uncharted. Instead, the term "scientific management" has come to be associated with techniques that seek to project a riskfree future based on extrapolation of the past. Such a conservative strategy is *unsafe* in turbulent times. It prevents intrapreneurs from finding and testing viable futures and instead focuses on optimizing ideas whose time has passed.

The Failure-Adverse Corporation

Corporations that cannot tolerate failure don't always avoid it. Often they just make bigger failures and learn less from them. Of course, making failure anathema will reduce risk taking and park innovators on the sidelines where they can do no harm. But no matter how hard corporations try to avoid it, things will, on occasion, go wrong. If one can't admit even a small failure, the natural thing to do is to deny that anything is wrong and to try harder to make the old way work. Poker players call this throwing good money after bad and learn to avoid it.

Failure-adverse businesses under attack from new ideas and technologies become ever more brittle in their defense of outdated ways until in the end they exit the business with a colossal blunder. None of the major manufacturers of mechanical calculators, such as Friedan or Monroe, took early advantage of the new electronic technology, and none of them became a major producer of the electronic calculators that replaced their product. Integrated circuits were first developed by industry outsiders like Texas Instruments and Fairchild. For years, conservative IBM refused to build a minicomputer as upstart DEC grew and grew. Everyone in the reproduction business passed over Chester Carlson's invention of Zerography, until the outsider Haloid Corporation took on his process and became Xerox.

As an intrapreneur, you must precondition those around you to failure and mistakes as an everyday part of your job. This means not apologizing at all for your minor mistakes but taking pride in having learned at moderate cost. Never let them think that smooth progress is expected. Go in and say, "Well, boss, I've exceeded my quota this week. I promised you we'd get one good mistake closer to understanding this business, but I've already made three.''

In companies that succeed with innovation and retain innovators, tolerance for mistakes and failure is built deeply into the everyday activities of the corporation.

7. PATIENT MONEY

Sophisticated investors in innovation have the courage and patience to let their investments prove themselves or go bust. They have great contempt for inexperienced investors who rack up losses by nervously giving and then withdrawing support from new businesses.

One excellent and proven intrapreneur bringing a revolutionary and highly practical technology to market confided that despite the fact that his corporation had made major public statements of commitment to his new venture, he got approvals only on a month to month basis. He lives in fear that the political winds will shift and the venture will be cancelled. This is not paranoia; he has watched other large projects grow and begin to fly only to be closed down. Five months later they start up again, run for a year, again fall out of favor, and are closed down, again. Nervous money makes innovation unbearably expensive and inefficient. It dooms the intraprise to such poor performance that it eventually dies.

One great barrier to innovation is not giving it time to reach maturity. In some industries, success takes a long time to achieve. Du Pont began a wave of corporate venture activity in the early 1960s. Using cross-functional teams much like the autonomous intrapreneurial teams of today, Du Pont built large numbers of new businesses. Every department was expected to shelter ventures of their own in addition to those created under the aegis of the corporate development department headed by Edwin Gee (who went on to become chairman of International Paper). By the end of the decade Du Pont's new venture activity was generally deemed a failure. Collectively, the intrapreneurial businesses started in the sixties were not yet large or promising enough by 1970 to justify the investments that had been made. The adventurousness of Du Pont declined drastically as managers and family members were blamed for spectacular fiascos like the artificial leather Corfam®.

As it turned out, some of the 1960s businesses did survive, like the highly profitable Automatic Clinical Analyzer (probably $300 million in sales) and Riston®, Du Pont's system for making printed circuit boards photographically. The rewards just took longer than expected.

By 1982, the magnitude of success sounded a far more positive note. An internal study, described to me by several retired insiders, traced the history of about seventy of the sixties ventures. Together, by 1982, they accounted for half of Du Pont's profits and half of its cash flow. Du Pont had done a very good job of innovating. Nor were these new, highly profitable businesses capital-intensive; they used less than one-third of Du Pont's total assets to produce over half the profit. The result was so startling that the studies were repeated in greater detail for two of the nine departments with similar findings. Innovation works, but you have to give it time.

The pace of innovation in the chemical industry is slow. Another internal study was conducted of forty successful new product lines, each of which had produced at least 1 percent of Du Pont's bottom line. The study showed that from the moment of lab bench demonstration it took an average of nine years to reach full-scale commercial application, twelve years to break even, and seventeen years until the new product line first contributed its 1 percent. Few companies have this kind of patience.

Du Pont has had patience in the past because the family controlling it made decisions for the long run. They thought not only of their own lifetimes but of what Du Pont would be for their children. Not many professional managers can afford such a perspective.

Fortunately, creating new businesses doesn't have to take

as long as it did at Du Pont. The principles of intrapreneuring are the principles of more rapid innovation. Few industries have as many barriers to moving rapidly as the chemical industry. For example, in the electronics industry significant new products such as Shugart's three-and-a-half-inch disk are often created in a year. New services can be launched even faster. The Bank of California's consumer certificates of deposit and corporate cash flow training were each launched within a few months of their inception. Nevertheless, most innovations take more time and patience than most corporations are willing to grant them.

Slowing Down the Corporate Dance

As we learn more about intrapreneuring we can greatly speed up the pace of innovation. But the rhythm of corporate life still clashes with the rhythm of innovation. The dance up the corporate ladder requires frequent lateral movements to gain experience and promotions to maintain the pace. Fast-track managers don't stay in one job long enough to make and observe fundamental changes. They find themselves forced to assume the posture of appearing good rather than accumulating the wisdom necessary for the company's long-term interests. The problems they create are left for others to handle.

Clearly this system of frequent job changes works against most kinds of innovation. Too often, the manager who encourages intrapreneurs leaves before their work comes to fruition. He bears the cost, but others, if they carry through, reap the benefit. The result is that in most companies innovation is not rewarded, and the fast-track manager learns to invest in solutions that can make him a hero faster than backing fundamental innovation.

Slowing down the job-transfer dance is one of the most direct ways to improve innovation in large firms. As we eliminate layers of middle management, people will need fewer steps to reach the top so there will be more time to spend in each of them. Fewer but bigger promotions will be the rule.

In addition, there are other steps corporations can take to create a better time frame:

1. Reward people for taking the steps that lead to innovation, not just for the final results.
2. Make a manager's rewards dependent on what happens in an area well after he or she has moved on.

The Time-After Reward

The CEO who encourages innovation generally does more to increase earnings under his successor than during his own term. If we want to encourage innovation it makes more sense to pay him a bonus for the time after he is CEO than for earnings per share during his tenure. A CEO looking forward to substantial extra retirement earnings will continue to look ahead right up to and past his last day on the job.

The time-after reward principle can be more generally applied to all managers to encourage innovation. Kollmorgen uses a version of time-after rewards to encourage growth. Because a Kollmorgen division, by policy, must divide in half when it reaches 200 employees, it was feared that managers might slow growth, preferring to be the manager of a 200-person division, rather than the manager of one of the 101-person sections left after division. Now, for five years after the split, general managers receive bonuses not only for their half, but also for the performance of the part that split away, as if they were still managers of the whole.

Who Should Consider the Long Run

Conventional wisdom states that planners and senior managers should consider the long run. But as one moves down the hierarchy, the focus of employees should be on shorter and shorter time frames until we reach hourly workers who think hourly thoughts. This idea makes almost no sense in the Information Age, wherein nearly everyone is called upon to think and decide. If we want responsible employees at all levels we want all of them thinking of the good of the company in the long run. For example, the practical advantages of quality appear only in the long run when customers make their next buying decisions. If we want employees to be involved and to make good decisions, even about acts as trivial as properly tightening a nut, we need to have them thinking of the consequences of today's acts well into the future. In an effective organization it turns out that everyone thinks about both long- and short-run consequences.

One key to spreading long-term thinking throughout a company is the intrapreneurial team. All the members of a team can buy into the team's objectives and future because the group, if left intact, has continuity and will face the consequences, good and bad, of its actions.

Ownership

As we saw, owners tend to weigh the long run more strongly than do professional managers. Part of this is due to the security of ownership and capital. Capital may be seen as a quantitative measure of the ability to invest value now in hope of future return. People with adequate capital can afford to play for long-run returns because they have the capital to last until the long run comes. Few professional managers have that security. Instead, if the cost of innovation makes numbers falter in the short run, managers fear losing their commands and someone else getting the credit for their farsighted investment.

What is needed to give employees something like the farsightedness of owners is something akin to ownership and capital. A tiny share of the company based on the percentage of contribution is not enough because their role in shaping the company as a whole may be too small. What is needed is the ability to earn a more localized form of ownership and something akin to capital that funds freedom, security, and long-term perspective. Intracapital, as discussed in Chapter 11, will help employees to think more like owners. As employees earn substantial amounts of intracapital, the company will become better able to act in its own long-range interests.

Sponsors and Time Frame

Currently the most available form of patient money in most corporations is a strong and committed sponsor. This situation is like that of an innovation in the period before capitalism was in full swing. What an innovator needed was a friend in high places, a patron. So it is in most corporations, but this system is limited. Sponsors can retire or be transferred, so the empowerment doesn't last. In addition to intracapital we need to dignify the sponsor-intrapreneur relationship so events like reorganizations and transfers don't separate sponsor and intrapreneur. The relationship needs more formal recognition and should be maintained by the sponsor even if he or she is transferred, and perhaps on a consulting basis even if he or she retires. This policy, of having sponsors continue on after retirement, would have several positive effects. It would produce a wave of innovation as senior executives sought to get something good going that would give them a role and extra income during their retirement. If after retirement they still had a network of influence inside the corporation, it would give the intraprises continuity of sponsorship and the sponsors something worthwhile and rewarding to do.

Intrapreneuring can work only if something is done to align the rhythm of the corporation and the time needed for innovation. Intrapreneuring can greatly speed up innovation, but even intrapreneurs require more patient support than they generally receive.

8. FREEDOM FROM TURFINESS

Instead of addressing the challenges posed by the competition, many executives see their greatest challenge in beating their peers in the race to the top. This leads to an obsession with turf. Nothing suffers more in a turf-obsessed corporation than innovation. When the titans struggle for position, even today's results take second place and the future becomes irrelevant. An effective organization must therefore focus the competition on performance and contribution, not on politics.

New ways of doing things more often than not cross the existing boundaries of the way things are done. And in organizations with ongoing turf battles, intrapreneurs must negotiate three types of turf boundaries: (1) boundaries between different business units such as the Plastics Division and the Medical Products Division; (2) boundaries between functions such as marketing, manufacturing, and R&D; and (3) boundaries between levels in the hierarchy, such as corporate staff and divisional management, or headquarters and field. Whenever there are organizational boundaries—which are inevitable—the potential for turfiness exists. But it doesn't have to manifest itself if the people involved value innovation more than politics.

Boundary Crossing with Ease

3M's profab lab never seemed to behave the way a lab should. They manufactured and sold small quantities of products in order to establish new markets. Then they transferred the business to operating divisions and created a number of new basic "technology genes," each of which spawned multiple divisions.

John Pearson, one of the first three profab employees, retired as Vice President of Development in 1982. As a young man working with Dick Drew (the inventor of Scotch tape), he faced a problem he couldn't solve. At the time, 3M had a unique system to minimize the effect of boundaries between technical people in different divisions. Every Saturday, after writing up their patent logs for the week, they took turns visiting each others' labs to see what was going on.

The Saturday after discovering he had a problem he couldn't solve, John rushed over to Howard Brinker's lab. Unfortunately Howard was facing a crisis of his own so he said, "I'll give you some starting ideas, but I don't have the time to do it for you. What I can do is help you set up apparatus in my lab, look over your shoulder, and steer you." For weeks John came in nights and weekends and worked in Brinker's resin lab until the problem was solved.

"We had territorial boundaries in terms of actual floor space," John said. "I can remember saying, 'Hey, your files have shifted over onto my side of the line,' but there were no intellectual boundaries."

3M was a community of friends, John explained, because management never played one group against another. The emphasis was on results, but when the results came in it was "We did it," not "I did it." Everyone knew who was responsible but the emphasis was on the group.

Ending Internal Comparisons

One of the surest ways to prevent free and easy boundary crossing is to compare people in the performance review process. One has only to say to a general manager of adhesives, "Why can't you be more like the guy running sandpaper?" to remind the adhesives manager of all the times he helped sandpaper without worrying about who got credit. Once the invidious comparison is made, the invidious game begins. The solution is to compare people with their counterparts outside the company, not with others inside it. This places the focus on the real competition of the corporation.

Win/Win vs. Win/Lose

The need for internal comparisons comes from the conceptual framework of a fixed pie to be divided—the idea that there are only so many positions and so much money, so some must win and some must lose. In fact there is no limit to the number of good jobs or money available. All one needs is the time and the intrapreneurs to create new businesses to run and new profits to divide. This is the self-reliant philosophy of abundance—if everyone is productive, everyone can win. Too often, the rituals of companies, such as the salary review, lean on the old win/lose fixed-pie philosophy to explain decisions. Better to lengthen people's time horizon and urge them to demonstrate their resourcefulness.

Functional Turf

As organizations grow large, functions such as marketing research and manufacturing become territories whose denizens develop loyalty to the function rather than to the purposes of the corporation as a whole. Perhaps this happens because the corporation becomes too large and abstract to focus people's tribal impulse. Perhaps it is the result of people's need for status, as when scientists belittle those who don't understand their technical language or when marketers bolster one another's egos with talk about the narrowness of "technicians."

Whatever the reasons, functional snobbery and struggles between functions exist in most corporations. The existence of turf battles poses great dangers and difficulties for the intrapreneur whose job is to span and integrate all disciplines in order to do something new. When there are turf struggles, each functional empire rejects the ideas of the others and offers instead its own. Each has the NIH syndrome: if it was "not invented here," it's not a good idea.

If ideas must be worked on and approved by several different functional areas, this causes problems because the

237

intrapreneur cannot be from all of them at once and so perforce is an outsider in most of the places where he or she must seek approval. The struggles that ensue often reduce innovation to a crawl.

Intrapreneurial Continuity vs. Lateral Job Hopping

One strategy many companies use to break down turf boundaries is to transfer people across the boundaries, giving them a feel for what it is like on the other side. Thus engineering managers take turns in marketing and so forth. The system works poorly because it involves too little continuity and thus produces only superficial understanding.

A far better idea is to allow people to travel with their ideas across all the functions. Take for example researchers who travel with their ideas through the strange lands of engineering, design, manufacturing, and marketing. Even if they are untutored in marketing, the researchers have the most intimate knowledge of the products to which the marketing wisdom of others is being applied. They can contribute their vision of the products' virtues, and they can observe the consequences of their earlier decisions and so gain wisdom from their stint in marketing.

Intrapreneuring and building small cross-functional teams, which travel with the new idea from development to profit, are perhaps the most powerful ways of breaking down barriers between functions. When the group that has responsibility for all aspects of a new idea is small, loyalties form around making the new idea work, not around functional turf.

Intrapreneurs should fight boundary barriers by networking with others who have more interest in problem solving than in politics. And managements wishing to encourage boundary crossing should begin by rewarding it. But easy cooperation of the kind needed for innovation comes only with security.

The Secure Turf Principle

Paradoxically, to prevent turf battles one doesn't have to prevent turf building; one has to allow people to build solid ownership of, at least, a small kingdom, and then encourage them to move out from that secure base in a spirit of generosity and cooperation. In times of insecurity, which can be caused by a management that judges harshly or reorganizes and moves people around frequently, people cling to whatever insecure ground they have. People who have no doubt that their base will be there when they return are more likely to be adventurous.

The secure-turf principle works best when the secure turfs consist of tangible territories. Make the plant manager secure that he controls and will control his plant without preventing people in other plants from making similar products. Make a marketing group secure in controlling a distribution channel or a brand name without preventing others from bringing similar products to market through other channels, or other brands. Giving groups broad charters and the right to keep others out will lead to endless unproductive political battles. Let secure turfs be places from which people can say yes to their own visions, rather than sources of the power to say no to others who pass nearby.

9. CROSS-FUNCTIONAL TEAMS

Why will corporations come to rely increasingly on intrapreneurial teams? Because small, functionally complete teams solve the problems of bigness in innovation. Since whenever a new idea begins, it encounters resistance from other functional areas, each idea needs the support of all functions before it can be a success. It does no good to design a product that manufacturing will not make, or make one that marketing is reluctant to sell.

When all the skills needed to launch a new product are brought together in one small, functionally complete intrapreneurial team, three things happen:

1. **The intrapreneurial team forms its identity around the new business rather than around a single functional discipline.**

    As a result, ideas easily cross the boundaries between specialists. Since marketing is in reality just Harry and engineering is just Joe, and since they see each other as friends in the same boat, it is easy for them to pull together to keep their intraprise moving.

2. **The intrapreneurial team maintains consistent focus on the needs of the intraprise.**

    When a large functional organization like marketing, engineering, or finance has many responsibilities, new ideas often take second place to crises in the existing business. As a result, new businesses get inconsistent support from a number of people who have other, more important responsibilities. Intrapreneurial teams, on the other hand, focus the responsibility for creating a new intraprise on a few full-time people, thereby guaranteeing that on every day someone is thinking about it from the point of view of each functional discipline. The result of this is more consistent efforts and better continuity of thought.

3. **The cross-functional team solves problems holistically.**

    Developing a new business requires adaptability. When a problem arises, this often means considering hundreds of possible solutions, each of which has ramifications in every functional area. Practically speaking, all the possibilities can be considered only when all the people involved are together in location and spirit.

Speed

One of the most consistent observations about intrapreneuring is the superior speed of autonomous, functionally complete venture teams in creating new businesses.

Shugart, Xerox's disk manufacturing unit, was being beaten to market by smaller, more entrepreneurial companies. Its employees were leaving to join those faster moving firms. President Bayer responded by devoting a complete intrapreneurial team to each new product.

> By providing each team with its own engineering, marketing, manufacturing and financial resources, Bayer aimed to cut at least a year out of the normal product-development cycle, and to stem the flow of employees to outside start-ups. "It all gets down to how quickly you can get decisions made and effected," explains Thomas R. Farrett, marketing manager for the 22 man Shugart team that developed the 3½ inch "micro floppy" disk drive.
>
> His team succeeded in cutting the development time from more than a year to four months. It also had prototypes of its new products in customers' hands for evaluation in just nine months—the fastest new product introduction that Shugart has accomplished since 1976.*

A major cause of 3M's record of maintaining innovation year after year comes from its use of intrapreneurial teams, which it calls business development units. Ed Roberts, MIT's new ventures expert, describes 3M teams: "At the early stage of developing a product, 3M tries to recruit individuals from marketing, the technical area, finance, and manufacturing to come together as a team, each member of which is committed to the further development and movement of this particular product into the market."†

* "A Memory Maker that Refuses to Be Forgotten," *Business Week*, Feb. 6, 1984, p. 70a.

† Ed Roberts, "New Ventures for Corporate Growth," *Harvard Business Review*, July/Aug. 1980, Vol. 58, No. 4, pp. 140–141.

Du Pont was an early pioneer in using small cross functional teams to develop new products and businesses. The company drifted away from this concept, but as development times grew unacceptably long, Du Pont has once again begun experimenting with the team system it helped pioneer. In one case, Du Pont had worked for five years to develop a new test for its clinical analyzers without success. As an experiment, the recalcitrant test was turned over to a functionally complete venture team. Marketing worked closely with the technical people to simplify the task. The new test will be on the market less than a year after the team's formation.

The Characteristics of an Intrapreneurial Team

An intrapreneurial team is not the same as a project team or task force. There are specific characteristics that make it an intrapreneurial team:

- Functional completeness
- Continuity of personnel
- Reporting through a single leader
- Freedom to do it their way
- Recruited, not appointed

Functional Completeness

Intrapreneuring means taking responsibility for seeing that all the things needed to make a business reality out of an idea happen. In practice, this generally means the team is built of people from a variety of functional disciplines so that the team has expertise in every aspect of its task.

The fact that the intrapreneurial team is functionally complete, however, does not necessarily mean that it has people who have extensive backgrounds in each area. In many cases, the members of a specialized team may learn to perform functions for which they lack training; frequently, engineers learn to do market research, or marketers learn to do financial controls, in order to accomplish all aspects of the innovation task. Addressing all problems, not the breadth of training, is what makes a functionally complete team.

To make matters even more complex, there are intrapreneurial teams that don't themselves *do* every task necessary to create a new product or a new business. Just as an entrepreneurial start-up often subcontracts manufacturing to a job shop and uses manufacturers' representatives or distributors to sell the product, intrapreneurial teams may farm out pieces of their intraprise to existing manufacturing facilities or sales forces. The key to functional completeness is that they take responsibility for all aspects of making it happen, even when others perform those tasks.

Continuity of Personnel

Handoffs are the bane of intrapreneurial teams. (See "No Handoffs," page 202.) Growing with the business is typically the most effective reward available for intrapreneurial teams.

Reporting Through a Single Leader

The team can be autonomous only if it reports through a single leader. Otherwise, it must serve the needs not only of the intraprise but also of the other organizations to which team members report.

"Matrix teams," made up on an ad hoc basis from members from the different functional organizations, have some of the advantages of a functionally complete team, but they are still not as effective as an autonomous intrapreneurial team. They are appropriate for some activities but frequently lack the commitment and the focused dedication needed in today's competitive environment.

The problem with matrix teams concerns mixed loyalties. Employees tend to be loyal to the people who write their reviews and decide their salaries. When each functional organization sends a representative to the new business project, that person tends to come as an ambassador, representing the concerns of his functional area, rather than as a member of the team. Meetings resemble the UN's efforts to achieve world peace more closely than a tightly knit team moving rapidly toward a common goal.

The formal reporting structure is not the key issue; rather, it is a question of whence the individual draws his or her support. Team members on loan can work out nicely as long as the team leaders determine their performance, rather than having them evaluated by the organization that loaned them. Charismatic leaders can overcome almost any organizational pattern by generating loyalty to a higher purpose.

Freedom to Do It Their Way

In an intrapreneurial team, the planners are the doers. There are no managers whose job it is to tell others what to do—everyone pitches in and gets the job done. If there are people calling the shots from above who don't show up full-time and get their hands dirty, it is a *puppet team,* not an intrapreneurial team.

Recruited, Not Appointed

One of the keys to a successful intrapreneurial team is a sense of ownership of the intraprise, a sense on the part of the team that they own the problems and the joys of creating the business.

To make their teams more effective, 3M does not *assign* people to such activities; the team members are recruited, says Ed Roberts,

> This makes a very big difference in results. In most companies, a marketing person assigned to evaluate a technical person's idea can get off the hook most easily by saying that the idea is poor and by pointing out all of its deficiencies, its inadequate justification, and its lack of a market. Given

the usual incentive systems, why should the marketing person share the risk? But instead of assigning him or her to evaluate the idea, 3M approaches Marketing and says, "Is anyone here interested in working on this?"

Here is a good instant test of a new product idea. If no one in the organization wants to join the new team, the idea behind it may not be very good. More important, whoever says, "I want in," becomes a partner, not a subordinate. He or she shares both in the risk and in the commitment and enthusiasm that go along with it. Team members are not likely to say, "This cannot be produced. It can never break even. It will never sell." They are involved as a team because they want to be, and they have a lot invested in making the idea work.[*]

The Members of the Intrapreneurial Team

The members of the team are, by definition, intrapreneurs themselves. They, too, take personal risks to turn a vision of something new into a reality. Therefore, reward systems for teams should distribute rewards in a ratio resembling the one used by venture capitalists. There the lead entrepreneur receives the largest share, but all the key team members become significant shareholders in the enterprise. Similarly, when an intraprise fails, the lead intrapreneur is not the only one whose career may be set back. Each team member must accept part of the responsibility proportionally.

How a company treats its intrapreneurial teams provides perhaps the best measure of its receptivity to innovation. A firm that truly believes in the possibilities of new concepts will spread rewards and attribute blame fairly. More importantly, it will not stunt the growth of intrapreneurship by applying too heavy a hand to those who have chosen to stand behind the good idea whose time has not yet come.

[*] "New Ventures for Corporate Growth," op. cit., p. 141.

10. MULTIPLE OPTIONS

Given the odds against people welcoming new ideas, allowing the intrapreneur to select from all the possible ways to get each job done—from marketing to sales—makes a great deal of sense. An intrapreneur may be better served by an outside designer, for instance, than by being required to use an inside design specialist, and he or she should have the flexibility to make that choice. This is exactly what happened with the IBM personal computer and why it proceeded so rapidly and successfully: Within a generous budget, Don Estridge had the freedom to choose from a variety of IBM resources or from outside vendors, depending on who could get the job done best and most quickly.

Multiple-Option Manufacturing

The cooperation that intrapreneurs receive from 3M manufacturing plants is unusual. When Rolf Westgaard was the sales manager for a dry-process microfilm business at 3M, he became excited by the idea of extending the basic technology into a new business—making convenient photographic copies of information on computer screens. He saw a ready market in the then-new medical imaging devices such as ultra sound and CAT scans. While continuing his work as a sales manager, he and others, like David Morgan, the dry silver process inventor, began a bootleg project to develop and market the new product. It is not surprising that he got the full support of the lab that invented the dry-process film for his new idea—after all, inventors love to see their ideas used—but the support he got from manufacturing is more noteworthy.

When I asked him how he talked a plant in another division into making experimental quantities of the new product for customer tests, he looked at me strangely. Finally, I got him to understand that in some companies turf barriers, even within a division, make getting access to manufacturing facilities for experimental runs very difficult.

3M plants are cooperative not just because the culture supports intrapreneurs but also because of the nature of the control system. Rolf explained how the system worked: "The plants are profit centers and anything they can sell to me absorbs overhead they would otherwise have to allocate to their main products. More importantly, anyone can go to any plant to get his product produced, and there were many 3M plants capable of doing my coating job. All of them wanted the business that would come if it worked out as a significant product line. They knew that the easy time to develop relations with a customer is in the beginning."

In all, 3M's system of plant sharing includes: (1) multiple competing facilities (each a profit center); (2) easy divisional boundary crossing; (3) a simple system for cross-divisional transfer payments; (4) a culture that honors innovation; and (5) intrapreneurial teams that include process design people as well as marketing and product design specialists to complement the manufacturing talent connected with the plant. The fact that 3M intrapreneurs have many options for manufacturing makes the system responsive to new ideas.

Component Options

Many companies end up with divisions that manufacture components used by other divisions. Frequently, these in-house component-manufacturing businesses begin because no one outside will supply exactly what is needed. The facility, once established, is then protected. The rationale becomes this: Better to keep the facility busy by forcing other business units to pay above-market prices for some components than to let them buy cheaper parts outside and then have to charge even higher prices for the remaining output of the components division in order to offset the cost of running the plant far below capacity. Given a monopoly inside, and no opportunity to sell components to other companies, many components divisions become complacent and uncompetitive over time.

A number of companies, noticing this vicious cycle, have decided that, rather than continue to burden the customer divisions with overpriced components, they will make the components producing units either compete or exit the business. Tektronix, for example, has put its components divisions on notice that they will soon be expected to compete for other divisions' business and to show a profit. In return, they will also be allowed to broaden their market by selling outside.

When NCR reorganized itself as a large number of autonomous divisions, many of the units were components manufacturers selling to other parts of NCR. No effort was made to make one unit buy from another if outside sources had better or cheaper products. This has led to some unusual situations. Don Coleman's Data Entry Systems Division is broken into thirteen business units. One components unit shared a building with another unit which happened to be its major customer. Under the old system, the customer had to buy those components from that neighbor. After the reorganization, the internal supplier was beaten out by an outside vendor. "They [the members of the business unit] have taken it well," says manager Don Coleman. "Instead of complaining and trying to get me to put pressure on their former customer [to buy from them], they are determined to get the business back on merit alone. That's exactly what we hoped would happen."

In general, the results for NCR of this new, freer multiple-option system have been spectacular: 50 percent of the Data Entry Systems Division sales come from products introduced within the last year, and a wonderful change has come over the component business units. Whereas before their real "customer" was the corporate decision makers who "bought" their arguments for monopoly status, now they understand that their survival depends on serving the businesses that buy their products. They have rapidly become more courteous, cut costs, improved quality, and speeded delivery. Once again, they are an asset to innovation at NCR, not an anchor.

The Vendor/Customer Relationship

The vendor/customer relationship brings out the best in people while hierarchical relationships encourage less competent behavior. Taken from the viewpoint of transactional analysis, the explanation is obvious: vendor/customer relationships are conducted between two adults on an equal footing—each can walk away if he or she doesn't like the deal. Boss/subordinate relationships have overtones of parent and child, and bring out manipulativeness and dependency, not competition to perform.

Whenever we can move from the politically controlled, monopoly decision making of a hierarchical system to the voluntary relationships of free choice, the chances are good that better decisions will be made.

The plunge into the internal and external free markets is a tonic to many business units, but to some the shock may produce "cardiac arrest." There is a way to approach competitive reality more gradually, namely, to give the components manufacturer something like a small subsidy or to erect a small "tariff" wall against outside vendors. One can then, each year, lower the subsidy or tariff until the components group is standing on its own. By this system, senior management can make it clear exactly how much they prefer internal purchases over external by setting a number such as a 20 percent subsidy. Having established that subsidy, the decision on the cost effectiveness of internal manufacture can be made locally by the people involved.

Multiple Options in Sales

Frequently, intrapreneurial teams fight with management over who should sell the product. Intrapreneurs usually believe no one can sell the product as well as they—the dedicated people who love it. They often believe the main sales force will ignore the new product in favor of selling more of the lines they know well. Frequently, they are right.

One veteran intrapreneur, with over a billion dollars of successful intraprises behind him, has observed that 95 percent of the time it is best for the venture team to have its own dedicated sales force, at least in the beginning. "That's the only way to get the rapid feedback from customers that the intrapreneurial team needs." Never having seen a true innovation succeed without its own sales force, he would abandon an intraprise if he was forced to sell through another force.

The Intel bubble memory project found another, effective, if inefficient, solution to this problem. The bubble memory venture was allowed to have its own marketing people but had to use the Intel sales force. Stuart Sando, head of bubble memory marketing, saw that the missionary selling effort needed to get bubble memories going was too much to ask of an established sales force. He also knew he couldn't change the official responsibility for sales, so he learned to live with it. He filled the bubble memory marketing staff with people who spent most of their time warming up major prospects, both with and without people from the official sales force present. For closing a deal, however, an Intel salesperson who was sympathetic to the new business was brought in and given credit for the sale. Because the marketing department had done all the missionary work, the sympathetic sales people got an excellent return on their time. They became more and more enthusiastic about bubble memories. The bubble memory marketing people urged them to give speeches at sales meetings about their successes and to teach others how to sell bubble memories. It took patience on the part of Stuart Sando and his team, but bubble memories were sold without ruffling any feathers. In 1983, bubble memory sales reached $50 million.

It isn't always the right decision to use a dedicated sales force, but a good general policy is to let the intrapreneur—

who generally cares primarily about the success of the intra-prise—decide. Ideally, the company will have several sales forces competing to handle new products, so they will be very receptive to intrapreneurs when the initial missionary phase is over.

Performance Shoot-Outs

IBM tolerates competing design projects. They have found that several smaller design teams competing outperform one giant one, both in the cost-effectiveness of the final design and in the time needed to produce it. To settle the issue of which design becomes the next generation computer, they have performance shoot-outs in which each team shows off the performance, manufacturing cost, and adaptability of its designs. The best design, rather than the designer with the best connections, frequently wins.

Unfortunately, this is not always so elsewhere. One intra-preneurial team, whose skunkworks had already designed products worth more than $4 billion in sales, found its latest prototype rejected in favor of an inferior design. "But what if this division were a small company and you owned it, then which machine would you chose?" the frustrated intrapreneur asked the decision maker. "Why yours, of course—no contest. But the reality is that this baby here, for all its flaws, was designed by the mainline engineering group. They have the clout—you and your cost-effectiveness don't." The real winners in situations like this are the Japanese, who, faced with less than the best American intrapreneurs had to offer, are currently trouncing the inferior mainline machine.

Humans are inherently competitive. It is better to focus that competition on performance than on political struggle.

Redundancy and Efficiency

The strongest argument against multiple options is that smaller units cannot be as efficient as large ones. In practice, this is rarely true, because the costs of monopoly generally far outweigh the costs of redundancy, particularly in the area of innovation.

Letting Intrapreneurs Do Their Own Purchasing

Purchasing is one of the internal corporate services intrapreneurs would often prefer to do without. The reason for this is that the fastest way to develop a new product is with the help of vendors. This requires a very direct and trusting communication system linking customer and vendor. Talking to vendors through a purchasing agent who demands documentation of every change greatly slows down the development problem.

When Brian Ehlers was developing the Apple Graphics Tablet, he needed the close support and help of his vendors. Apple was so young that no purchasing function even tried to come between him and his vendors. Summa Graphics, his major vendor, knocked themselves out to meet Brian's needs, making over twenty-five free prototypes before they created what Brian wanted. They were willing to do that because Brian and Apple treated them so well. When they came to call, Brian himself would meet them at once, without any waiting room or intermediaries; and their conversation dealt mainly with joint problem solving, not price. In the long run, not only did Summa solve Apple's problems, but Apple solved Summa's as well: As a favor, Apple engineers redesigned one of the Summa Graphics circuits, thereby improving the product they sold to all their customers.

The helpful, informal relationship with vendors worked to get a significant product to market in under a year with only one full-time Apple person and several internal helpers.

Later, when more formal systems were in place, Brian found it took as long to make a minor upgrade to the product to meet new FCC specifications as it had taken to create the whole product a few years earlier.

Of course, the friendly and informal relations with vendors that Brian used to get to market fast do have a price. To cover the graphic tablet, Brian had found a clear plastic sheeting that stood up to the stylus writing on the tablet. His "specification" for that material was mainly an agreement with the manufacturers not to change it. When Apple's internal purchasing department took over they wrote up a specification, put it out for bids, and bought from another lower priced manufacturer. Unfortunately, the new material was too soft and scratched in use. Thousands of tablets had to be remanufactured. Fortunately, the flaw was discovered before the tablets were on the market.

The moral of this story is simple. In rapidly moving fields, it is worth putting up with intrapreneurs who use Brian's informal methods of purchasing to get new products to market faster. Later, if the product proves successful enough to make reducing the cost worthwhile, then the work necessary to write an airtight specification can be done.

Easing the Tyranny of Staff Services

The original rationale for corporate staff groups was that as corporations divisionalized it was too expensive to replicate specialized services in each business unit. It would be cheaper to locate services like personnel, legal, and accounting at the corporate level.

Originally, staff organizations were supposed to serve line organizations, but many have gone from suggesting to telling. While in major matters divisions have, in many cases, learned to fight back, most staff groups can still dominate intrapreneurs. In over 100 interviews of managers at six multinational companies, Drexel and Lawler of the University of Southern California found the most frequently mentioned barrier to innovation was the interference of corporate staffs. The worst situation they found was that in some companies innovators not only had to seek approval from many different types of staffs, from legal to planning, but, to make matters worse, each area of staff had a multilevel approval process beginning at the divisional level and ending at the corporate level.[*]

One company in the instrument business established an industrial design group to allow the company to have high-quality designers that no individual project could afford full-time. Over time, however, the designers came to see themselves not as a service to the teams bringing forward new products but as policemen whose job was to prevent products from going out whose appearance didn't meet their standards of excellence. As there were no checks and balances on their aesthetic arrogance, they insisted on changes in everything from the type fonts on the panel to screw size, switch design, and cabinet-fabrication techniques. These changes introduced major delays in new-product introductions while adding little to customer satisfaction.

Several years ago, Dayton Hudson, a major, highly innovative retailing conglomerate, took a bold step toward eliminating internal monopolies. Dayton Hudson made most of its corporate staff groups into profit centers that had to sell their services to the divisions. In areas like personnel, advertising, site location, and legal, the divisions had the choice of using the corporate staffs, outside vendors, or building their own capability. Suddenly, stripped of their monopoly status, the staffs became highly customer-oriented, and began serving the divisions better than they had before. In some cases, the rationale for centralization was weak. For example, most of the divisions hired corporate personnel staff to create their own personnel departments. One design group left the company en masse and formed an independent design company

[*] Edward E. Lawler III and John A. Drexler, Jr., *The Corporate Entrepreneur,* Center for Effective Organizations, Graduate School of Business Administration, University of Southern California, Los Angeles, 1980.

that now serves many stores owned by Dayton Hudson. Others, for whom the efficiency of scale argument is true, remain as profitable units in their corporate location.

Allowing intrapreneurial teams and divisions to use outside services or perform staff functions themselves is a radical but effective system for eliminating corporate fat and speeding the innovation process. In the case of legal services, the corporation may wish to retain some assurances that the overall corporate needs for legal security are met. For this reason they may prefer not to let divisions use outside law firms. In a situation like this, the corporation can still end the legal services monopoly by setting up competing internal legal groups, each of which is charged with protecting the corporation but each of which must also compete for the business of divisions and intrapreneurial teams needing legal advice and approvals.

How Kollmorgen Teams Played Their Options

When Kollmorgen, Inc. was divided into small intrapreneurial product teams, each team was given the right to perform all aspects of their business themselves or to buy services from the divisional staff. Many of these little profit and loss centers were so small that they occupied only part of a building. Their territorial boundaries were delineated by lines painted on the floor. It didn't make sense to distribute the building maintenance responsibility among five separate tenants, CEO Swiggett explained:

> If a function is not critical to success in serving the customer or meeting the cost bogey, we usually leave it centralized. That's why maintenance of the buildings is usually a function of the division, not the product line. Frequently, we have a divisional shipping function, because scheduling trucks is rarely a crucial factor and there is just one shipping dock in the building.

How different this philosophy is from most control systems, which seek to centralize decisions about important matters while unimportant ones are moved to the periphery. Most Kollmorgen product lines let the division worry about payroll and cash management, because these functions don't have to be customized to serve their clients. On the other hand, most product teams want to do their own cost analysis and collect their own receivables. Since they are being judged on return on assets employed, they want the control needed to keep receivables down, so as to keep their working capital employed low.

The lessons learned by making the use of staff service, components manufacturing, or engineering organizations voluntary are quite generalizable. Monopolies breed stagnation and a distant attitude toward customers. The focus of monopolistic systems shifts toward internal political struggles, beside which customers and intrapreneurs alike become secondary considerations. Soon, the system has all the dynamic urge to explore risky new options of the average utility or government bureau.

The solution: Whenever possible, let voluntary and multiple options flourish. Whenever possible, let decisions be made by voluntary vendor/customer relationships, not by a political process. Encourage redundancy and internal competition as long as it is performance-based.

PROFILE

BRIAN EHLERS: A Classic Intrapreneur

If there ever was an archetypal intrapreneur, that person is Brian Ehlers. He has spent his working life pursuing visions others lacked the imagination to see, building two successful businesses as a result, and is now running his own small business while continuing as a marketing manager at Apple Computer.

During his early twenties Brian began his career at Control Data and then switched to Hewlett-Packard, where he was involved in the creation of a graphics tablet—an electronic notebook that reproduces anything drawn on a special tablet directly onto a computer screen. In time, Apple convinced Brian to bring his graphics tablet expertise to the company, then still a small firm with fewer than seventy-five employees. However, when he arrived Brian discovered a great need at Apple for other software, so he was put to work writing programs for a year before he could begin working on a graphics tablet in his spare time.

Brian had no official help, although he managed to borrow expertise when he needed it. He designed the system, wrote programs to make it work, specified the interfaces that would connect the various components, did some preliminary market research, and talked to potential customers. Then he arrived at the point where he needed real help. He found two Apple engineers who were interested enough to spend a bit of their time building prototypes for the project. In the morning Brian would tell them the type of interface he needed. They would have it designed and built by late afternoon, and Brian would spend the evening testing it in order to report his findings the following morning. Had they used formal channels, the work these three produced in a few days might have taken months.

This extraordinary cooperation and generosity was typical of Apple in those days. But with everyone working overtime on projects that had official sanction, experiments like Brian's could not use very much of anyone else's time, so Brian went outside the company for assistance. He found various vendors, saw what they had to offer, discussed his project's needs, and worked with them to develop what he needed. At one time or another, Brian had about fifteen outside vendors working on the various components of the tablet. As soon as he had something to show, Brian moved into marketing. Less than a year after he began working on the graphics tablet, Brian Ehlers was taking prototypes to electronics shows, preparing brochures, and writing advertising copy. At the age of twenty-seven he had completed a project, put it on the market almost single-handedly, and watched it sell at the rate of $4–$5 million a year. Apple's investment was paid off in the first year.

Brian stayed involved with the tablet peripherally, but he had another project in mind.

As he saw it, businesses could never fully utilize the graphics tablet until they had a way to transfer their picture from the CRT to paper. Apple already had a color printer in mind for their Lisa computer, which was not due on the market for some time. With Lisa on the way, Brian's different printer idea was not entirely welcome at Apple. Those who were counting on Lisa's high-tech scanning printer felt that Brian's plotter was redundant. Because of this opposition, Brian could not get his plotter built by Apple's peripherals division, even though they were ready and willing to take it on. So once again he developed and manufactured it outside. The plotter was a success. Informed sources place sales at somewhere between $10 and $20 million a year—not bad for a product Apple's sales department told Brian would not sell.

Why do intrapreneurs routinely face opposition inside their companies? Brian had struggled with a problem typical of intrapreneurs. He was too much a maverick and was too outspoken. Thus, after two successes of some magnitude, he was still on the outside, not invited to work on the highly graphic Lisa project, even after clearly demonstrating his aptitude in graphics.

Brian is good at getting along with people. Witness his success in dealing with the outside vendors who supplied so many of his components. Despite the fact that much of his work was done outside Apple, the success of the project depended upon Apple's approval. Apple did, after all, pay his salary and it was Apple's name that was going on his finished products. Probably because of this, Brian's project seemed to contradict management's view of priorities. They were trying to run a growing company, which had already achieved amazing success, in an orderly fashion. Brian's main interest was in his own projects. This is what makes him such a good intrapreneur. And this is the source of friction between Brian and his superiors.

An intrapreneur has to be more interested in the success of

his ideas than in making friends and keeping the peace. As such, Brian is not overly sensitive to opposition. But he is not unaware of his troubles. "I don't walk away from a fight," he said. "But sometimes in a corporation you need to. Some time ago I decided I didn't care about getting a management position. Good people need good management. That means spending time with them individually, hand-holding. . . . But I would rather work on the project. I'm not a good delegator. I don't have the patience to delegate; when I see someone doing something I could do faster, I have to get in there and do it myself."

Despite the opposition he finds at Apple, Brian is still there because, although his personality is questioned, his judgment is valued. Out of his intraprise he has started his own small software company, which he runs nights and weekends, distributing programs Apple doesn't want to sell but that still have an audience. He is in marketing, which is not a bad spot for intrapreneurs, who seem to have an intuitive sense of the services, skills, and products that people need.

CHAPTER 10

Rewards Along the Intrapreneurial Career Path

In 1976 Bill Foster left Hewlett-Packard to go to Data General. In 1979 he left Data General to form his own company. Wanting to build a culture like Hewlett-Packard's in his new company, he decided to seek his other founders there. He made a shopping list of thirty of the people at Hewlett-Packard he considered to be the best, and flew to California to talk with them. How many were still at Hewlett-Packard? Only two. Twenty-eight had left to start or join small entrepreneurial firms.

When companies as good as Hewlett-Packard start losing their best people, it is time to rethink how corporations reward their innovators.*

Imagine building a $10 million intraprise for your company. Where would you go from there, and how could your company adequately reward you?

A team of entrepreneurs who built such a business might each be worth more than $1 to $5 million when the venture went public. With their financial freedom they could start a new business or become small-time venture capitalists. But intrapreneurs with similar accomplishments inside a large firm seldom earn anything close to a million dollars, and they enjoy far less freedom. They also earn less than their managerial counterparts who simply manage larger, more mature business units in the corporation.

Prevailing standards of fairness suggest that since managers generally supervise more people than intrapreneurs do, and

---

* Personal interview. Stratus Computers, Bill Foster's new company, went public in August, 1983. On March 31,1984, the company's market value was 192 million dollars.

since their units of the business currently generate more profit, they indeed should be paid more. Never mind that managers have not created the source of that profit but merely inherited it. Never mind the extraordinary effort and creativity needed to build a new business. And never mind the risks that intrapreneurs face if it should fail.

But corporations are beginning to mind the disparity in rewards, given the rapid growth of venture capital and an increasing interest in innovative skills on the part of head-hunters. "The challenge of the eighties is to keep your key people," points out Alan Shugart of Seagate Technology, a new computer disk drive company.* Rewards that worked five years ago are no longer adequate for intrapreneurs.

Most firms haven't yet devised a system of rewards for their highly innovative people, and their present systems fail for many reasons:

1. Traditional rewards for success don't match the risks of innovating or intrapreneuring.
2. The basic reward of most companies is promotion, which doesn't work well for most intrapreneurs.
3. The career path of successful intrapreneurs doesn't lead to the one thing they really need to do their jobs: freedom to use their intuition, take risks, and invest the company's money in building new businesses and launching new products and services.

Consider the possible career outcomes for innovators compared to their more conservative peers. The situation often looks like that diagrammed in Figure 10–1. In most companies, even when the intrapreneur succeeds his or her career progress falls behind that of the manager who keeps out of trouble. In Lawler and Drexel's eye-opening study of 100 employees in six multinational corporations, they discovered just how widespread was the opinion that successful risk

---

* "A Memory Maker that Refuses to Be Forgotten," *Business Week*, Feb. 6, 1984, p. 71A.

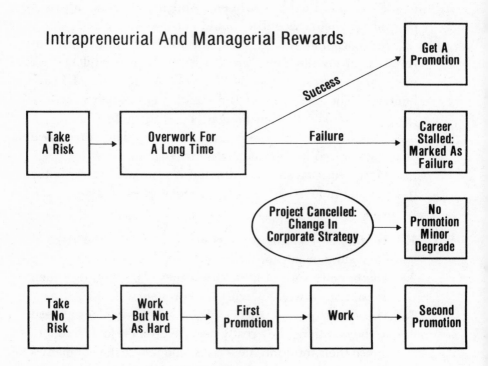

Intrapreneurial And Managerial Rewards

Figure 10-1

taking is inadequately rewarded and failure overpunished. Most of the managers reported that their companies' reward systems "encourage behavior that is safe and conservative." Many managers reported making decisions that would maintain the status quo rather than trying possibly more effective ways of doing things. Why? Because from a risk-benefit perspective it was in their best interest not to try.[*]

A single failure in a failure-averse corporation can mark someone as a loser and stall his career. If that talented "loser" is foolish enough to remain in that corporation, being marked as a failure might cost him or her an average of $25,000 a year for, say, forty years, or $1 million over a working lifetime. Few entrepreneurs risk more in their start-ups. Not surprisingly, there is a dearth of intrapreneurs in failure-averse corporations.

If intrapreneurs paid much attention to the risk-reward ratio, they probably wouldn't venture. Fortunately, because of self-confidence and nonmonetary goals, they add up the risks and rewards differently. As General Mills intrapreneur Bernie Loomis puts it, the one secret of success for an intrapreneur is "to go to work every day willing to lose your job." Intrapreneurs don't fear losing their jobs because other issues are generally more important to them. Ayla Aldikacti, Hulki's wife, saw the risks of bucking the system this way: "There were a lot of layoffs and a lot of insecurity in the auto industry. A lot of people didn't take any risks. We had a chance of being fired, but that didn't mean anything to us. We believed in the Fiero, and we had to follow through."

But the fact that intrapreneurs are optimistic doesn't relieve corporations of responsibility to give rewards that balance risks and acknowledge extraordinary contributions. Not only is this fair, it is necessary to make innovation happen in today's new entrepreneurial environment.

[*] Edward E. Lawler III and John A. Drexel, Jr., *The Corporate Entrepreneur*, Center for Effective Organizations, Graduate School of Business Administration, University of Southern California, 1980.

Of course, companies can reduce the risk of intrapreneuring by being careful not to punish mistakes made by innovators. But the risk cannot be reduced past zero. After that corporations must seek the positive by offering better rewards to right the imbalance.

REWARDING THE INTRAPRENEUR

Recognition

It is surprising how strongly some intrapreneurs feel about recognition. One experienced intrapreneur wept when telling me about the time the president of the company came to visit his little group to thank them for creating a new business.

While the power of recognition as a reward at first seems strange, it makes sense when one sees recognition not as simply a gesture to make the intrapreneur feel good, but as a source of empowerment.

Ken Olsen, chairman of Digital Equipment, was sitting in on a staff meeting in which a frustrated manager was describing how his own project had become completely entangled in red tape. Olsen asked questions, found the project promising, and mused aloud about such a good idea finding so little support. The result, according to the manager: "Suddenly the barriers to my project came down. What normally might have taken a year or more to complete became a six-month project." Intrapreneurs know recognition is an important tool for moving their visions into reality, and so it is valued highly not because they are other-directed but because they grow tired of being weighed down by the defenders of the status quo.

Multiple Credits

Part of the difficulty in assigning credit comes from not separating out different kinds of contributions, each of which was essential to the innovation's success. For the same innovation it is appropriate to recognize

- A few who made the key inventions
- The intrapreneur who drove the business into being by unremitting dedication
- The members of the intrapreneurial team who dared to join early on
- The sponsors who put their reputations on the line to protect and secure funding for it
- The network of people who supported it from positions throughout the company
- The entire business team, so everyone involved can feel recognized

Top management must learn that recognizing one kind of contribution doesn't make less of the others. For example, recognizing a sponsor doesn't dilute the credit of the intrapreneur, nor does recognizing someone else as the inventor. Each has an honor all its own.

For all its importance, recognition cannot be used alone to motivate innovation; intrapreneurs have too many options in today's world. They expect more and deserve more. Recognizing that, most corporations turn their thoughts to promotion.

Promotion

For a variety of reasons, even companies that go out of their way to reward intrapreneurs encounter difficulties because the most straightforward corporate reward—promotion—often backfires. Promotion to broadened responsibilities is the fundamental corporate reward. The other rewards of the corporation—status, discretionary authority, and so forth—are generally coupled with promotions. Therefore, when promotions are not appropriate, it is often difficult to find an alternate reward.

Intrapreneurs have difficulty with promotion as a reward for two basic reasons. First, they are too ornery and independent to be considered for positions that match their level of contribution. Second, even if promoted, their interests and temperaments are usually unsuited to either managing large established businesses or to senior staff positions. Intrapreneurs need the freedom to create new businesses, not broader responsibilities for managing old ideas.

Frequently, intrapreneurs show a kind of disdain for the system. To do their job they break the rules, and they are proud of it. Sometimes they get away with it, as when Chuck House decided to build the moon monitor despite a direct order by Dave Packard to kill the project, or the time Bernie Loomis gave the nearly bankrupt Toys'R'Us a $5 million line of credit he had no right to extend. Breaking all the rules may get new products out the door and make money for the corporation, but it doesn't guarantee promotion, even when the business is successful.

Successful corporate careers are built at least in part on understanding the power structure and doing what the powers want done. This requires caution, tact, and subordination of the urgings of business needs to political wisdom. As one successful intrapreneur put it, "People with business acumen make good intrapreneurs, but people with political savvy get ahead."

Intrapreneurs tend to have their attention not on internal politics but on the market and the technology. If they have a strong vision of an emerging business, they go for it, regardless of the barriers. Their obliviousness to politics not only gives ammunition to their enemies but also colors the opinions of those who wish them well. "He is honest and unbelievably energetic, but his judgment is questionable," said one senior manager, discussing a talented intrapreneur. This particular ex-Marine-turned-intrapreneur was fearless and honest to the point of political suicide, which one might call questionable judgment. On the more positive side, he was gifted in understanding market opportunity and pursuing it. His record: He is almost solely responsible for several important new businesses, but others are given credit for them.

The Intrapreneur as Manager

In the start-up, the intrapreneur's ability to get others to do things his way allows a coherent venture to get off the ground. He does this not just by giving orders but by constant reiteration of the goals and objectives of the venture, and by working closely and flexibly with others to solve problems.

Once the basic pattern for connecting technology and market in a workable business is discovered and defined, different kinds of problems arise that call for different kinds of skills. In its growth phase, the business requires a far less direct and creative management style. On the contrary, it may require rigid rules and regulations to give quick clues for behavior to the torrent of new people joining the group. At this point intrapreneurs separate themselves into two groups.

Classic intrapreneurs: Great start-up people who love building a business from the ground up. They are so dedicated to their visions that they have difficulties with delegation.

Managerial intrapreneurs: Able to turn the corner from being creative with things to being creative with people. Learn to enjoy empowering others and letting them make their own mistakes.

Managerial intrapreneurs often go far in large companies. Lew Lehr, the intrapreneur of 3M's new business in medical products like surgical drapes and tapes, has gone on to become chairman. Jack Welch, who with Rubin Gutoff spearheaded GE's entry into engineering plastics, is now CEO of GE.

As intrapreneurial ventures grow, a small percentage of intrapreneurs become more interested in getting peak performance out of their teams than in making every decision right.

They take on the challenge of empowering and developing others, and lay down the need for personal brilliance.

To do this leaders must transform themselves into managerial intrapreneurs. They must shift from envisioning new products or services to envisioning new ways to make more effective use of people.

There is probably no better training for top management than managing a small, rapidly growing business within a large organization. It is an opportunity to make many small mistakes, which is the best way to learn, while at the same time learning exactly how the culture of the large organization functions.

In the entrepreneurial world, only about 5 percent of the entrepreneurs who start companies can turn the corner from start-up entrepreneur to managerial entrepreneur. Many businesses tend to peak at about 100 to 200 employees, which reflects the limit of the classic entrepreneurial management style. Beyond that point, one person can no longer understand everything that happens in the business.

The growth transition is probably easier for intrapreneurs than for entrepreneurs. Not only are all the rewards pushing in the direction of a managerial style, but the system guides intrapreneurs into their new roles as managers.

At first, Lew Lehr was very disappointed when he was promoted away from intrapreneurial health care, a business he had formed at 3M. But his activities as the new head of the tape group taught him a new way of thinking. He served on committees that helped him recognize a world greater than his focused interests as an intrapreneur. Buttressed by good supporting people whose advice he respected, he learned the skills of a less direct management style.

That some intrapreneurs succeed in advancing in management is encouraging, but in many cases it may not constitute the best use of their talents. As Arthur Rock, one of the great venture capitalists, whose credits include the backing of Intel, has said, "Good managers are a dime a dozen; the really hard thing to find is an entrepreneur." Intrapreneurs, like entrepreneurs, may have greater value in that role than as managers.

Consider the old saw: How can we stop the progress of science? Take all great scientists and make them chairmen of their departments. How can we stop innovation? Take all intrapreneurs and promote them to nonintrapreneurial roles.

More fundamentally, the rewards given a few managerial intrapreneurs are cold comfort to the much larger number of classic intrapreneurs who provide the valuable service of leading start-ups but who are ill-suited to managing large or mature businesses.

Thus we need to find ways to reward intrapreneurs who remain intrapreneurs whether or not they have the capability to turn themselves into managers and reap the traditional benefits of promotion.

A CAREER PATH FOR THE CLASSIC INTRAPRENEUR

Classic intrapreneurs reach their limits when they can no longer deal directly with everyone in their intraprise. They are generally uncomfortable with hierarchy. As the organization becomes larger and more hierarchical, they ignore the chain of command and make changes in anything they see "wrong" at any level of the organization. As their ventures grow, however, the tasks of management change and many intrapreneurs find themselves ill-suited emotionally to the demands of managing a large business. They have difficulty when the task shifts from doing it themselves or in a small group to supervising others. "I don't have the patience to delegate," says intrapreneur Brian Ehlers. "When I see someone doing something I could do faster, I have to get in there and do it myself."

More fundamentally, Brian doesn't find supervising others—regardless of how well they are doing—as satisfying as doing it himself. As the manager of an engineering team, his involvement with the tasks of his subordinates limited his effectiveness. As an intrapreneur, he is almost unbeatable.

The tragedy of promoting intrapreneurs to the managerial

levels of large businesses is that they are then undone by the very character traits that made them great. As intrapreneurs they succeeded because they could not be deterred from realizing their visions. They could act on new ideas when others were paralyzed, because of deep faith in their own intuition. While others struggled with the paperwork of asking for permission, they succeeded because of a predisposition to do things themselves.

One can only admire such courage, determination, vision, and willingness to take on any task, no matter how humble or great. These same virtues, however, limit the growth of the classic intrapreneurs' intraprises. Determination to realize their visions regardless of obstacles, which was so admirable during start-up, can easily become interference with subordinates' efforts to do their jobs in their own ways. Faith in their own intuition may cause intrapreneurs to substitute their snap judgments for decisions others made on the basis of weeks of investigation. To make matters worse, they are often "right" about these business decisions, but their style of interference keeps others from growing, learning, and being right in their own way.

When the group is small and everyone has access to the intrapreneur, they manage his or her weaknesses. Everyone feels he or she can influence the vision of the intrapreneur, who, though perhaps something of a difficult genius, has integrated their ideas into the overall group goals.

As the group grows, the informal feedback systems break down and the group needs managers as well as leadership. The crisis that ensues can have several outcomes. The leader can hand over operating control to a manager and maintain the leadership role. This frequently happens with technologists who continue as leaders of product development but turn over administrative management and marketing to others.

In another common outcome of intrapreneurial success, the corporation promotes the intrapreneur to a much larger scope of responsibility—running a major, mature business. Now a real watershed is reached—either the intrapreneur learns very rapidly to delegate and manage in a bureaucratic framework or he or she becomes a liability. The intrapreneur's natural bent is to bring order out of chaos. The management of a mature business generally requires the optimization of an existing order. The intrapreneur may find this a stifling task and begin tearing the "cash cow" apart to find out why it isn't growing and changing. In all probability that isn't what senior management had in mind, and the intrapreneur is removed.

Frequently the next step is a staff job. Some intrapreneurs, because of their great business acumen, are natural strategists. But the inactivity of making recommendations that are acted on partially and slowly rankles the action-oriented intrapreneur. The staff position at best provides a cooling-off period. Then the intrapreneur needs another business to build.

The natural intrapreneurial career path consists of a series of start-ups (Figure 10-2). If we examine this path in the way corporations normally judge career growth, namely, by the number of people supervised, it doesn't seem to lead toward progressively higher levels of success.

Some people have suggested that the technical contributor systems that are becoming popular will work for intrapreneurs. The intrapreneurial career path is not at all like that of the individual technical contributor because intrapreneurs are not individual contributors. They are managers of a special kind, namely, start-up managers. Nor is the intrapreneurial career path like that of the professional manager, which involves promotion to steadily higher levels of management. There is, in fact, no provision for career intrapreneurs in most organizations.

Bonuses

One proposed remedy is substantial bonuses for intrapreneurs in lieu of promotion. There is no reason why intrapreneuring should not be at least as rewarding as managing, given that it is a rarer talent. But as companies understand the need for

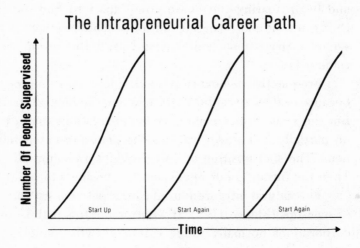

Figure 10-2

rewards other than promotion, the usual next step is to try unusual compensation, often in the form of bonuses.

"Let us avoid promoting intrapreneurs to their level of incompetence," the thinking goes. "Let them go on starting businesses for the corporation, and let us reward them with substantial stock options and bonuses for each start up."

This career path of intrapreneurial recycling (Figure 10-3), in which each start-up venture is rewarded with an increased bonus, makes more sense than promoting the classic intrapreneur to a managerial role. But several problems arise.

First, it misses the fact that the intrapreneur needs freedom to act, as much as he or she needs more pay, so rewards based on pay alone will fail to give the intrapreneur what he or she needs to be effective.

Second, a Catch-22 occurs when intrapreneurs have capital and suddenly the external environment may become more supportive than the internal one. One intrapreneur described the situation this way:

> After building a $30 million business for the company, I found myself putting together a series of overhead slides to beg for permission to spend $10,000 exploring a new idea. Meanwhile, I had a quarter of a million in stock from exercising my options. Given that, I could do it so easily in my garage, there just seemed no point in putting up with the bullshit any longer. When I then began exploring the idea with venture capitalists, I discovered that a man with a track record of having started a $30 million business inside and quarter of a million ready to invest would have no difficulty raising $10 million with a good team and a decent plan. By not telling me "Go for it" inside, they virtually forced me to leave.

To prevent sudden influxes of cash from forcing people to leave, payments of bonuses and stock options should be spread over time. One lump sum paid when the venture reaches its major milestone puts a lot of hot discretionary cash in the intrapreneur's pocket. One quarter of that amount paid out each year for four years, but only if he or she remains

273

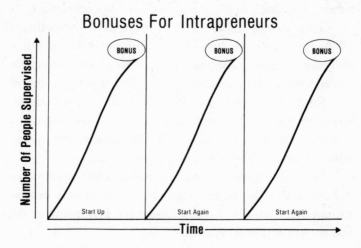

Figure 10-3

in the company, gives breathing space for the intrapreneur to start something new within. Once reinvolved, there is a good chance he or she will stay. But there is no bonus system that will work to keep good intrapreneurs that is not accompanied by an increased freedom to act.

Financial Discretion

Perhaps the most tangible form of business freedom is the power to spend money on new ideas without having to ask for permission. Managers get bigger budgets and, implicitly or explicitly, bigger "slush funds" as their responsibilities increase. Entrepreneurs measure success in capital, which can be viewed as the right to spend society's resources on expanding a business or starting a new one.

But most intrapreneurs don't earn comparable freedoms. Given that the basic motivation of the intrapreneur is the drive to realize a vision in his or her own way, failing to provide the freedom to do so is a fundamental failing in reward systems. Intrapreneurs should be able to build up "freedom credit" on the basis of past successes—that is, something akin to the capital that entrepreneurs earn. The next chapter addresses rewards of this kind.

CHAPTER 11

Intracapital: Freedom as a Reward

Progress on the intrapreneurial career path is not measured in promotions that lead to the pinnacles of corporate power. The most fundamental measure of progress for the intrapreneur is the increasing freedom to use corporate resources to build new businesses for the corporation.

As we have seen, the entrepreneur gains the kind of freedom intrapreneurs need by accumulating capital. Capital is a measurable form of freedom to take risks and build a strong business. It carries the entrepreneur through the ups and downs of starting a new venture. But what would be the functional equivalent in the corporate setting of individually owning capital? The answer is intracapital.

Intracapital is a timeless discretionary budget. It is earned by the intrapreneur and used to fund the creation of new intraprises and innovation for the corporation.

- *Discretionary budgets.* A discretionary budget is similar to the capital an entrepreneur can earn: Both external and internal discretionary budgets provide general purpose funds that can be used without having to ask others for permission. They empower the holder to act rapidly on the basis of hunches and best guesses. Managers have discretionary budgets to cope with surprises and change. Intrapreneurs, especially, need them because surprises and change are their natural environment.

- *A timeless discretionary budget.* Intracapital is like a bank account: It is there until it is used. Normal budgets are just the reverse. Whatever is unused vanishes at the end of the year, but if you use them up they are generally replenished. Clearly this second system doesn't encourage self-determined frugality. But more important, it doesn't give predictability.

Discretionary budgets, in fact, fluctuate. In good times, money is available, but in tough times, discretionary budgets are the first to go. The timeless endurance and predictability of intracapital is an important step toward long-term rational decision making about innovation.

The capitalist free market system provides funds to individuals who make profits which are then used for two very different purposes: (1) improved personal life style and (2) the freedom to try out new business ideas. Intracapital differs from capital in that it clearly separates those two uses. It gives the intrapreneur freedom to build new intraprises for the corporation, but it cannot be used to put a new wing on the house or to buy a Ferrari. Intracapital does fit the two most important needs of the intrapreneur with regard to money: It gives them a way to keep score with money, and it provides them with a tangible claim on the resources needed to turn their visions into businesses.

INTRACAPITAL AS A REWARD

Intracapital is an unusual reward system. Not only is it a powerful motivator, but it can actually have a negative cost. It is a powerful motivator because it gives intrapreneurs what they crave—the freedom to make their ideas happen. It has a negative cost, because there is every reason to believe it will be spent more carefully and effectively than money that is just a small part of a senior manager's budget. Despite the fact that many don't want to manage routine operations, most successful intrapreneurs have unusually sharp business judgment, particularly when it comes to new ideas.

Frugality and Ownership

For intrapreneurs, intracapital means freedom. As long as they have it, they call the shots in their careers. If they exhaust it without creating a new source of profit for the company, they are back to being ordinary employees. Then they have to do others' bidding for a living. Rather than suffer that fate, intrapreneurs will go to great lengths to make their intracapital pay off.

They will consider each investment they make as carefully as if the money were their own—which, in a large sense, it is. If there is a cheaper but equally effective way to do something, ordinary corporate citizens may prefer the more expensive and elegant route; after all, it's not their money. Let's say there is a way to reduce risk by doing some research into a new field over the weekend; the intrapreneur on salary may go home, but not the one whose freedom is at stake. Intracapital, because it is a kind of freedom renewable only on the basis of more success, grabs deep and motivates the individual to greater care and frugality. No system of budgetary reviews and approval by seniors could be half as tight as spending "one's own" irreplaceable freedom.

Betting on Winners

When intracapital is earned, the corporation is putting money in the hands of a proven innovator. Venture capitalists have observed that choosing a good entrepreneurial team is the most important factor in getting a good return on new ventures. They want people who have started businesses before.

Intracapital not only places funds in the hands of proven innovators, but it retains those winners who might otherwise use their records as intrapreneurs to become entrepreneurs. Companies that don't retain and empower their intrapreneurs will end up betting only on first time intrapreneurs. Not only is experience useful, but without track records it is very difficult to gauge talent. For these reasons, money set aside as intracapital is likely to be the most cost-effective investment in innovation a company can make.

The intracapital system thus gives the corporation two benefits for the price of one. It is a cost-effective reward that

278

partially bypasses the jealousies that plague other efforts to compensate innovators, and it is an effective investment in the future.

More Than a Reward, A Guarantee of Freedom

Effective as it is as a reward, and cost-effective as it is as a means of investing in innovation, intracapital can be seen most fundamentally as a principle of freedom. In economic life, capital is a powerful form of freedom. It is:

- The right to choose one's own vision to pursue. Without capital to pursue it, one is not free simply to choose to act, one has to beg for permission.
- The right to make mistakes. Without capital, one is fully accountable to others for one's mistakes. With it, one is accountable only to oneself.
- The right to invest today's assets in the future—the right to think ahead.
- The right to benefit from one's own diligence—to pursue happiness as an adult owner—not as a dependent child. Existing forms of corporate structure have only a few parents and many dependent children.

SOURCES OF INTRACAPITAL

Formal intracapital systems are new, but its functional equivalents are found everywhere that innovation is working. Intrapreneurs gain the equivalent of intracapital by having a strong reputation and hence sponsors who will approve whatever they want to do. Others "own" the cash cow they are managing and use its profits to fund new ideas.

Bernie Loomis, the intrapreneur of Star Wars toys, Care Bears, and Strawberry Shortcake dolls, first earned the functional equivalent of capital in General Mills by turning around the Kenner Toy Division. When he was hired to head it, the division was losing $550,000 per year. Two years later, it was earning several million dollars and, as the following story illustrates, Bernie Loomis had earned the right to make his own mistakes.

One day in 1977, Cliff Whitehill, the chief corporate attorney of General Mills, called Bob Kinney, then CEO. The attorney was quite upset, just having gotten off the line with an angry member of the Securities and Exchange Commission. The day before, *The New York Times* had printed a story saying that the largest toy company in the world had acquired the rights to make a line of toys based on the movie *Star Wars*. Mattel's stock shot up four points, but Mattel issued a report denying that they had made the purchase. The SEC wanted to know if the buyer was General Mills and set the public record straight to prevent "insider trading" of General Mills stock. The problem was that neither Bob Kinney nor the chief corporate attorney had a clue whether their company had made this important purchase.

Now I imagine that, like most CEOs, Bob Kinney doesn't appreciate surprise calls from the SEC. It would have made sense to get angry at whomever had caused the situation, but Bob had a gift for dealing with intrapreneurs. "Let's give Bernie a call," he said. Bernie, of course, was Bernie Loomis, then the highly intrapreneurial president of the Kenner Toy Division. When he found out what was going on, Bernie did not apologize; in fact, his comeback demonstrated a rather lighthearted relationship with his corporate sponsor. He explained that he had not acquired the national or international rights, allowing the suspense to build, but he did admit to having acquired the *galactic* rights. In fact, without checking with corporate, he had signed a deal obligating General Mills to make minimum royalty payments of $500,000 a year. And so it was that *The New York Times* reported the General Mills acquisition.

General Mills stock shot up two points, and Star Wars toys became the toy soldiers for a generation of American boys and girls, selling $100 million a year or more from 1978 through 1984.

After hearing this story from Bob Kinney, I was a bit

puzzled. Here was the CEO of a large and successful company telling a story about how to manage innovation and growth in which he was all but boasting that neither he nor the corporate attorney had even heard about an acquisition that attracted SEC notice and has produced $100 million a year ever since.

Bob Kinney, seeing that I didn't quite understand yet, told another story to clarify his message. He had flown to Chicago to see a premarket showing of a new line of dolls taken from the American Greetings Cards scratch-and-sniff Strawberry Shortcake series. The new line consisted of small dolls that smelled like strawberry shortcake, blueberry pie, and so forth, according to their names.

Riding back to the airport and somewhat disturbed, Bob Kinney turned to Loomis and said, "Bernie, I've been through a lot with you and I've always backed you up in whatever you wanted to do, but this is the worst idea you have ever had. Not only will it never sell, but I have to tell you I believe it is in questionable taste." There was an awful silence, but then he leaned back in the taxi seat and said, "But then again I'm just an old Gloucester fisherman who happens to be chairman of General Mills, and you are Bernie Loomis, president of Kenner Toys; good luck, Bernie." The Strawberry Shortcake line went on to become another $100 million product line because Bob Kinney placed faith in his proven people above his faith in his own intuition about the value of a business concept.

Bernie Loomis's situation at Kenner demonstrates two of the most common sources of intracapital. He had the strong sponsorship of Bob Kinney, of his immediate boss, Don Swanson, and of others who believed in him. He was also the manager of a profitable business in a decentralized company, which gave him a bubbling spring of income that was under his control. His "ownership" of that division was strong because it was losing money when he took it over and he made it into one of the largest U.S. toy companies. Management didn't want to disturb his winning streak, so they let him run it his way.

When he was at Kenner, Bernie Loomis clearly had

something intangible that functioned as an intracapital budget. If he wanted to launch a product he did so, and the funds were available. In part that intracapital was there because his sponsors, like Bob Kinney and Don Swanson, understood his need for freedom. But that sponsorship alone was not enough; having the cash cow of Kenner Toys in his care gave him a source of funds and a place to put his intrapreneuring. Few intrapreneurs have so supportive a situation.

Like many other intrapreneurs, Bernie got in trouble when he was promoted to a more administrative job. Over his repeated protests, he was appointed group vice president for toys. The results pleased neither Bernie nor General Mills. Quite predictably, rather than sitting back and watching as a good group vice president does in a decentralized company, Bernie got involved in things.

The real problem is that Bernie is an intrapreneur, not an administrator. As a group vice president he no longer had the intracapital or the charter to try new ideas, and everyone was unhappy.

In most companies they would have fired him or let him quit. But for some reason General Mills was smarter: they gave him back his intracapital and a way to earn more. When the end of Bernie's time as a group vice president of toys was at hand, his boss and sponsor, Don Swanson, explained to him that it wasn't working. Bernie's skills were probably greatest in the area of product development. Swanson suggested, and Bernie agreed, that a solution might be more along the lines of the earlier "Jeep" deal.

The Jeep deal was a kind of intracapital that Bernie had invented earlier for a key innovator, Joe "Jeep" Kuhn. After his success with Hot Wheels°, Bernie was hired as president of Kenner Toys. His new associates at Kenner watched to see how the new hotshot would deal with Jeep, then the reigning genius inventor of Kenner. Some people thought Jeep wasn't easy to get along with. The others waited for the confrontation

° Registered trademark of Mattel Toys, Inc.

and put money on Jeep's being gone within three months. Sure enough, before the three months were up Jeep tried to quit. He explained that his wife was tired of living in Cincinnati and wanted to move to New York. "OK," said Bernie, "you can move to New York, but you don't have to quit." Bernie explained his idea to the puzzled Jeep. They would set up a research facility in New York whose sole employee would be Jeep. He would go to New York and design new toys. Bernie would send money, but within two years Jeep would send back designs that made it all worthwhile. To measure its success, "Design East," Jeep's new office, would be "paid" 5 percent of the sales of any toys Jeep invented. If Design East was "making money," Jeep could do whatever he wanted. It was an inventor's dream.

Within two years Kenner launched Stretch Armstrong, a jelly-filled doll invented by Jeep that stretched and slowly recoiled in a way that fascinates children. Fifty percent of Stretch Armstrong sales guaranteed the budget of Design East, and Jeep had something like intracapital.

Bernie took the deal and built up a twenty-two–man marketing and design operation whose multimillion dollar annual royalty income provided more discretionary funds than they could spend. In 1982 they turned back to the corporation over half their income as "profit," a good measure of the surplus funds they have to explore new ideas. Said Don Swanson of Bernie, "Product development and merchandising are in Bernie's blood. He didn't enjoy the group level, he needs to work hands-on. He's doing an excellent job at Marketing and Design."

Don Swanson and Bernie had every reason to be proud, because they solved a problem almost everyone else has failed at: what to do with the intrapreneur who has been promoted beyond the level he can enjoy and at which he can produce well. Their answer was one form of intracapital. But this particular form may be better suited to an inventor than to an intrapreneur. Despite his successes, Bernie found the opportunity to be as effectively intrapreneurial as he had been diminishing. Unable to start a new intraprise to launch his newest product, Bernie left Kenner in May 1984 and moved on to Glad, a free-lance toy design company.

Intracapital comes in other forms as well. Art Fry of 3M's Post-it Notes struggled to get support for his crazy ideas. He had to hide them and work on them at night. Now he is recognized by the company and has been made a member of the Carlton Society—3M's innovation hall of fame—and has built a good record of new products. Although no one reports to him, he has good access to resources. "Before he had to fight for resources, but now we are trying to push them on him," says 3M's vice president of technology, Bob Adams. Art notices his abundant resources, saying that because of his reputation, others want to work on his ideas. Without his recruiting anyone, there is always someone around to help.

WHERE IS INTRACAPITAL STORED?

A person or a group with formal intracapital keeps it as an account that is really the equivalent of an ordinary bank account. "Checks" can be written on that account in the form of purchase orders that are preauthorized if adequate intracapital exists to cover them. Intracapital accounts can be located at either the corporate or divisional level. The accounting department, of course, has the responsibility to be sure that funds are not being diverted for noncorporate purposes but otherwise has no say in how they are used.

TOUGH QUESTIONS

What if the corporation lets an intrapreneur create a new product or business and then takes it from him? Does the intrapreneur have something akin to "ownership rights" to what has been created with his or her "own" intracapital? To explain my answer to this question I will first look more generally at the issue of ownership to provide a context for considering options.

It is not a coincidence that property rights occupied so much of the thinking of our forefathers in drafting the Constitution and are the subject of a large portion of the law. The rights of individual ownership free from the whims of a powerful central authority are fundamental freedoms. Our primary freedoms are the freedom to think, the freedom to communicate, and the freedom to act. Freedom to act, to which the other two must eventually lead, is, in reality, generally permitted by ownership.

Ownership is basically the right to say what happens with something. If I own a ball I can take it with me and use it as I please, as long as I do not violate the law. I am not free to throw it through a neighbor's window, but I am free to throw it through my own.

If an intrapreneur uses his or her intracapital to buy a new milling machine and the corporation decides the machine would be better off deployed elsewhere, they have several options:

1. Take the milling machine and justify doing so by telling the intrapreneur he was wrong to buy it so they are going to find a better home for it. Losing his intracapital should teach him a lesson. Because the concept of intraownership is weak, such totalitarian tactics are all too common. Bitterness, demoralization, and an urge for revenge will result from this kind of management.
2. Decide that preserving the idea of intraownership is more important than achieving what seems to them to be better equipment allocation. If they really need a milling machine in another location, they can buy one.
3. If the need is desperate, offer to "buy" the machine, returning the intracapital the intrapreneur invested in it. The transfer price can be negotiated on the basis of free choice by both parties, or in an emergency the corporation can commandeer the equipment and pay for it a flat price,

as governments occasionally do through eminent domain. They can also "rent" the machine from the intrapreneur and return it when a new one arrives.

If we want to encourage intrapreneurs, number two is clearly the best choice. It took centuries for individuals to win private property rights from the rulers. It will take time for intrapreneurs to establish the boundaries of ownership rights within the corporation. We already accept the desk and tool box as "owned" for the duration of employment; the rest is a question of degree.

If the intrapreneur creates a good business and the corporation wants to take it over by integrating it with an existing division, the company has a similar set of choices. If the intracapital system is to work, they must pay the intrapreneur in intracapital for his or her intraownership share, and probably give a significant bonus for the appreciation of the assets entrusted to him or her.

If intrapreneurs have intracapital, what role is left for corporate management? The formation of intracapital marks the beginning of a transformation in the role of corporate management. They cease to act as rulers and instead become governors whose task is to create an environment in which manager-intrapreneurs can have freedom while still being guided by an "invisible hand" to make the decisions that foster the growth and profitability of the corporation. This is a far more interesting and challenging role than that of making a few acquisitions, doing a reorganization, and approving decisions better made by managers closer to the action.

In addition to creating and shaping the internal marketplace, corporate management must put out a clear vision of what the corporation is and what it is struggling to become. The role of leaders is to create within the company a vision of what the company is and of what it means to be a member of the group. Sharing in the vision, members can overcome pettiness and work together toward common goals without draconian systems of control.

Once the vision is clear, the corporation can shape the internal environment so people are motivated to become a part of it. Top management need not worry that it has less control over any project as long as it offers freedom to those who use capital profitably.

Of course there will always be experiments, but these may be seen as a method of gathering the practical kind of data needed to formulate the next strategy. If a maverick intraprise begins succeeding wildly, leaders should not bemoan the confusion; rather, they should look to it for clues about the kinds of things the company is good at and should be doing routinely.

INTRACAPITAL AND A FREE INTRAPRISE SYSTEM

Intrapreneurs achieve their goals by stepping on others' toes. In fact, that is part of their function.

The role of the entrepreneur, as the great economist Schumpeter points out, is to innovate, and innovation is an act of creative destruction. New and better ways of doing things diminish old ways or make them obsolete. In large organizations some of those diminished will be inside the organization, and they will resent the intrapreneur. Intrapreneurs' weaknesses as managers, their turf-challenging role, and their lack of any permanent turf of their own can combine to ensure that a political process for distributing rewards and discretion over corporate funds will not favor intrapreneurs unless they have good friends in very high places.

The political weakness of the intrapreneur becomes less important if politics is less important in shaping corporate decisions. Intracapital and the free intraprise system are a way of controlling corporate decisions about innovation. Combined, they place the emphasis on performance, not politics. When a company has many successful intrapreneurs with substantial intracapital, they will have the clout to try their ideas and retain their freedom of judgment even if there are senior managers who don't like them or their ideas. The organization will begin to support and air a greater diversity of opinion and thus become smarter about its environment. It is just as true inside the corporation as out: The security of individual ownership is an important part of creating a free culture.

REWARDING OTHERS FOR GIVING INFORMAL INTRACAPITAL

The most common form of intracapital is the informal one— the consistent support of a strong sponsor. It is important to reward not only the intrapreneur but also the sponsor.

Sponsors

Sponsorship can be time-consuming, may require the expenditure of political capital, and can carry with it substantial risk. Sponsors need to be rewarded strongly when the intraprises that they support succeed. It seems reasonable that they should receive both bonuses and intracapital along with the intrapreneurial team. Sponsors who develop good track records, as well as older intrapreneurs, are reasonable candidates for a sort of internal venture-capital role. They can use their intracapital to sponsor financially as well as to give other less tangible kinds of support.

General Managers

Many corporations have done good thinking about how to get their general managers to support innovation. At 3M, for example, to get a favorable review and good bonus, division managers must do more than meet bottom-line objectives; they must take measures that contribute to innovation. A 3M general manager must be able to demonstrate that 25 percent of his or her product line is not more than five years old. Of course, this might produce some trivial "new products" that are really minor variations on existing ones, but it does keep the general manager looking for new things and helps clearly establish corporate values.

General managers should be able to show that ideas that were developed in his or her division, but that didn't fit, have been successfully transplanted into other divisions. He or she must also be able to demonstrate that other ideas, originating outside that division, have been adopted and developed. These two rules help keep innovations alive and fight the not-invented-here syndrome, in which adopted ideas or products suffer extreme neglect.

At GE, general managers have such responsibilities to innovators in their divisions. If the division cannot use an idea that might fit somewhere else, the general manager is required to help find it a new home.

There are numerous ways of getting general managers to sponsor and welcome intrapreneurs. The most obvious, making innovation in all its aspects a part of their job descriptions and appraisals, should not be overlooked.

FORMAL INTRACAPITAL SYSTEM

A formal intracapital system has the following elements:

1. The intrapreneurs take some risk along with the corporation.
2. There is an agreed-upon method of measuring success and profitability.
3. The profits of the intrapreneurial venture are allocated in an agreed-upon manner which includes, for the successful intrapreneur, provision for an increasing ability to act autonomously.
4. Certain likely contingencies must be dealt with in advance.
5. Earned rewards and earned autonomy must not be trifled with.

1. To Enter Into the New System of Reward, the Intrapreneur Must Take Some Personal Risk. This may involve, at the least, "sweat-equity" in the form of working on the project nights and weekends, or it may involve more tangible risk such as agreeing to forego salary increases until bonuses are earned. In extreme cases it may involve a base salary reduction in view of a generous and well-defined bonus plan. Tektronics, for example, asks key intrapreneurs to take a 20 percent pay cut to buy into their reward package.

Asking the intrapreneurs to take a risk has several functions and rationales:

(a) It mirrors the successful pattern of the venture capital industry. They ask entrepreneurs to take a personal risk because it both tests and increases commitment. If the idea isn't worth a second mortgage and asking relatives for loans to the entrepreneur, venture capitalists wonder if they should invest. Once those funds are committed it becomes very tough for the entrepreneurs to walk away when the going gets tough.

(b) It aids in the self-selection process. Intrapreneurs, like entrepreneurs, are self-selecting and the corporation's job in sorting them out becomes far easier with a clear-cut test of commitment.

(c) The introduction of risk at the beginning will later form a partial justification to other employees when and if the intrapreneur receives unusual rewards. It is not a singling out for special merit, rather it is a reward for risks taken and privations suffered on a path they chose not to take. No comparison of merit or contribution is thus implied.

(d) The acceptance of formal risk-taking by the organization is a consideration which binds the organization to the execution of the implied contract.

Innovation suffers in most large organizations because they have short attention spans. They have great difficulty persisting with new ventures long enough to prove them either success or failure. Management personnel rotations and changes in strategy or financial conditions wipe out old intentions, and with them the seedlings of future growth. In accepting a contribution of risk from an employee, the corporation then owes that employee the chance to win or lose based on whether or not he can achieve what he promised. If large organizations can find ways to support new ventures and products which continue to show the promise which led to their original funding, ROI on innovation will increase radically. Accepting a defined risk reward "contract" with innovators is one method of extending organizational persistence in innovation. The implied contract also binds the organization to the agreed-upon rewards in the case of success.

2. There Must Be an Agreed-Upon Method of Measuring the Success and Profitability of the Intrapreneur's Endeavor. If it is a new functionally complete business, entirely independent of all existing corporate facilities and services, then measuring profitability is just a matter of setting a suitably low charge for corporate overhead and corporate capital allocated to the enterprise. More likely the intrapreneur will use the services of other parts of the organization and may even have internal customers. For example, the intrapreneur who designed a new product may wish to use existing sales forces or manufacturing facilities. In this case the intrapreneurial enterprise can remain a profit center by paying appropriate transfer payments. Care must be taken not to overload these transfer payments with overhead. It is in the corporate interest to innovate, but new products can rarely stand overheads appropriate to large volume runs and high levels of automation. In case of doubt, it is often useful to compare internal pricing with bids from outside vendors. If internal services are noncompetitive, but both innovation and use of those services are deemed to be in the corporate interest, perhaps the corporation should pay the difference and allow the new business to grow, providing the price paid is still above the actual incremental cost.

There is also the possibility that the new venture may primarily or even exclusively serve internal customers. It may manufacture intermediate components used by several divisions, provide better maintenance on machinery, operate a word processing center more efficiently or even provide internal consulting. Inasmuch as these services, either by their nature or by economies of scale, must be internal monopolies, pricing is difficult. If they can compete with internal and external services, pricing is easier. In computing costs for these intrapreneurial ventures it is wise to remember that to the degree that they become self-managing, they reduce the burden on central management and so they and their customers are entitled to favorable treatment on overhead charges.

In many cases it will be useful to set up a board or even to use outsiders skilled in the task to resolve disputes about ways of calculating the profit of intraprises.

3. Profits from the Intrapreneurial Venture Must Be Allocated in an Agreed-upon Manner. There are three basic places to which the profits may be allocated: (a) the general fund of the corporation; (b) personal bonuses for employers in the enterprise; and (c) intracapital earmarked for reinvestment by either the intraprise as a whole or the individuals in it.

In the long run organizations invest to get a return, and category a, the general fund of the corporation, will probably reap the lions' share of any profit. At the same time the start up and early growth phases generally require continuing investment. For this reason it is unreasonable to expect a return to the general fund during this period.

A typical division in the long run might be:

General fund of the corporation	60 percent
Personal bonuses and profit sharing (within the enterprise— replaces corporate profit sharing)	10
Intracapital	30

This system provides personal bonuses, which is only fair as the individuals involved have taken personal risk and deferred income. At the same time it gets around the major drawbacks of bonuses by empowering people inside the corporation to a greater degree than their bonuses empower them to act outside. Let us say that there is a profit of $10 million: $6 million goes to the general fund, $1 million is

292

divided among the intrapreneurs as a bonus, and $3 million is available for funding new ideas and new enterprises.

An individual intrapreneur with a one-tenth share would receive a bonus of $100,000 and have discretionary spending authority over an intracapital fund of $300,000. He or she would thus feel very strongly the tangible trust of the corporation and be empowered to do new things to a degree that would greatly reduce the need to leave.

4. Certain Likely Contingencies Must Be Dealt With in Advance. What happens if an intrapreneur is removed from the management team? (Does he or she have any bonus or intracapital interest in the future performance or current equity of the venture he helped found? If yes, what?) What happens if the venture is reintegrated into a pre-existing business unit?

5. Earned Reward and Earned Autonomy Must Not Be Trifled With. If the corporation lets an intrapreneur take personal risks and, more important, put in years of work in part to receive agreed-upon rewards, trifling with these rewards will produce uncontainable disillusionment not only in that individual but in all intrapreneurs reached by the story.

Here, in the form of a hypothetical example, is how intracapital serves corporations and intrapreneurs alike.

Working in the labs of Consolidated Rubber, Faith, an engineer, develops a new compound with extraordinary wear characteristics. Unfortunately it doesn't grip the road well enough to be sold to tire companies, and Faith thinks it may take years to improve it enough so it can meet all the specifications of the tire industry. She has high hopes for doing so but knows realistically that if she sets that goal, then works for years without meeting the specifications, she will lose funding and the new technology will die. But Faith is more than a technologist. She is an intrapreneur. She knows a little about running shoes because she is a moderately dedicated marathoner and runs fifty miles a week. She decides to build high-mileage heel inserts, has a pair made and cut into the sole of her running shoes, and tests them for 2,000 miles. They make a satisfying impact with just the right amount of slide. Best of all, they don't wear out. Faith knows she's on to something.

Faith soon meets with a friend from manufacturing and they discuss the probable costs, concluding that they can make such inserts for six cents apiece. Armed with that information, Faith soon arranges a business trip—paid for with intracapital left over from a past success—to meet with designers at a large running shoe manufacturer. Carrying a couple of handmade inserts and her own shoes, she shows them to the chief designer. He is very interested in the heels and asks about cost and delivery dates. Faith soon has a sample order for 100 sets, with the manufacturer considering an exclusive manufacturing arrangement with her.

At this point Faith assembles a team with another rubber chemist, Fred; a fabrication engineer, Carol; and the marketing expert, Al, who will also do the bookkeeping and shipping. Her boss's boss is excited both by the running shoes and the long-term potential tire market. She agrees to be sponsor and protector for the team.

Quickly they write up a business plan showing the need for $500,000 to address the new opportunity: $50,000 for market research to make sure they have a good idea, and $450,000 if it becomes clear, as they suspect, that they could manufacture the heel inserts for under ten cents a pair and sell them in quantity for over $3.00. Faith agrees to invest $50,000 of her intracapital for the test if the corporation will give her a letter of intent stating that if the test is successful, the corporation will either put up the $450,000 or sell her the rights for $10,000. Their plan offers the following disbursement of profits:

The corporation	75 percent
Profit share for team	5
Intracapital	20

The last two (Profit share and Intracapital) were divided among the team as follows:

Faith	20 percent
Fred	10
Al	10
Carol	10
Sponsor	5
Reserve for future team members	45
	100 percent

This plan means that for every $100 in profit, the corporation gets $75, Faith gets a bonus of 20 percent of 5 percent or $1, and each of the other team members gets a bonus of 10 percent of 5 percent or 50¢. The team would get $20 for intracapital to reinvest individually or as a team. To lower the risk they decide to give the manufacturer a one-year exclusive in exchange for a guaranteed order of $500,000.

At the end of the first year, Faith and her team had sold 100,000 sets at $5.00 per pair. This is what their simplified statement would look like:

Cost of goods sold	$ 50,000
Sales expenses	10,000
Research expense	100,000
Team salaries	240,000
Other General and Administrative	400,000
	$600,000
First year net loss	$100,000

In the second year, sales increased to 200,000 pairs, but the team invested heavily in a new product—wear-resistant rubber linings for industrial polishing equipment. This unanticipated market proved far larger than the one for running shoes. They broke even.

In the fifth year, variations on the new high-wear rubber formula are in use for conveyor belts and experimental tank treads as well as the polishing equipment. Faith's intraprise has turned into a $20 million business, with a profit of $2.5 million.

The business began to outgrow Faith's interest in it. She feels it is time to go back to the lab, creating new businesses. Her intraprise becomes her employer's Abrasion Resistant Rubber Division. The corporation values it at 20 times earnings, or $50,000,000. The cash and intracapital are apportioned according to the original agreement and come to:

The team's share:	
Intracapital	$10,000,000
Bonus	2,500,000
Faith's share (20 percent):	
Intracapital	$2,000,000
Bonus	500,000

She goes back to the lab a fully empowered engineer, eager to launch a new intraprise.

FREEDOM CHITS

To do their jobs, intrapreneurs imagine new business opportunities for the corporation and blunder their way through to making them happen, learning as they go. They need freedom to do this efficiently. When they are breaking new ground there are almost never enough hard facts to justify their decisions, just best guesses on the basis of everything they have learned to date. In their own areas, theirs are probably the best guesses available to the corporation.

Perhaps the most personal form of freedom is the freedom to direct what one does with one's own time. Many research facilities in places like Bell Labs, IBM, Du Pont, as well as at a host of smaller companies, formally recognize the right of every researcher to a small portion of his own time for exploratory projects; 15 percent is common.

But it is generally difficult to use the 15 percent because of pressing official priorities. Managers give the most innovative people their most desperate crises. Unintentionally, the reward given to effective innovators is to be loaded down with orders to put out fires, not the freedom to select and work on interesting long-term innovative projects. What is needed is a form of intracapital that effectively gives top innovators more exploratory time.

When I asked Brian Ehlers what he felt would be an appropriate reward, he said, "A sabbatical—what I need is a year off to come up with something new." IBM has recognized intrapreneurs' need for control of their own time. The IBM fellowship, a senior award for innovation, gives it in full measure—five years of time and support to start something new.

A few companies are experimenting with exploratory time as a reward. People who do something highly innovative are given free time to explore new ideas of their own choosing.

INTRACAPITAL BONDS

The way to get started with the concept of autonomy as a reward is to introduce it gradually. The most effective first step we have found to date is the issuance of development bonds as a reward for minor innovations and innovative suggestions. Development bonds can be printed by a company in $100 denominations, entitling the bearer to spend $100 of corporate funds on any developmental corporate objective of the recipient's choice.

Development bonds have an interesting side effect: They not only reward innovation and empower employees but, if transferrable, they can also become the currency of a low-level intracorporate service economy. For example, an employee from outside the labs who needs access to the electron microscope may "buy" access with an intracapital bond. The labs can then use that bond to buy something they need. Since the erosion of divisional boundaries is a driver of innovation, the side effect of this new currency may be substantial cross-fertilization and innovation.

INTRACAPITALISM

If we view the U.S. or other capitalist nations as among the largest of organizations, we see that to a very large degree these very large organizations have decided to trust those who accumulate capital to use it productively. They may act to prevent abuses like pollution and price fixing, but they don't worry too much about capitalists making poor business decisions, losing money, and thereby squandering national resources. If capital is primarily used for conspicuous consumption, as it is in some nations, capitalism will not survive. At its best capitalism is a system for placing control of resources in the hands of those who have, according to the rules of the game, employed them most productively. This system has proved a driver of efficiency and innovation in truly large organizations such as whole societies. It is beginning to prove equally effective in somewhat smaller organizations such as large multinational corporations.

In a way, it is surprising that in a business community where there is great faith in the ability of the free enterprise system to produce innovation, we don't use free enterprise within large organizations. Instead, our largest businesses follow an internal pattern far more like a vast socialist state than like a free market. No wonder we are coming up short in innovation.

One Hundred Dollar Development Bond

THIS DEVELOPMENT BOND AUTHORIZES THE BEARER TO
SPEND ONE HUNDRED DOLLARS ON BEHALF OF

Not to be deducted from any budget other than Intracapital Account.

Not valid for cash awards, bonuses, etc., for bearer's personal use.

Valid for any purpose beneficial to the corporation including:

Training	Research & Development
Equipment	Market Research
Patents	Prizes
Business Travel	Or any other
Consultants	legitimate business
Public Relations	purpose.

CHAPTER 12

Putting to Rest the Fears of Anarchy

The first reaction many people have to the idea of an intrapreneurial corporation is that is it out of control—perhaps even anarchic. But this is not so. Quite to the contrary—in every meaningful way, intrapreneurial corporations are better controlled than their hierarchical counterparts.

THE KOLLMORGEN EXPERIENCE

In the late 1960s, Photocircuits Corporation was a rapidly growing, quarter-billion-dollar producer of periscopes, circuit boards, high-performance motors, and high-speed wiring robots that tried the traditional centralized control system. They built a powerfully centralized management as well as a sophisticated computerized system for warehousing and inventory control. Kollmorgen bought the growing company in 1970. Chairman Robert Swiggett says, "We probably had the most advanced MRP [materials requirements planning] and inventory control system in the world. It kept track of and scheduled every order, traced the materials needed, scheduled work and the allocation of people. The system was so good that IBM printed a forty-four page brochure on it to show others how to use their model 360 computer. The system made sure that everything was where it had to be on time. The trouble was that despite all that, customers were having to wait longer for their orders and inventories were rising. It didn't make sense. Kollmorgen had reached the pinnacle of planning and everything was going to hell."

The company had a giant organization for each functional specialty such as marketing, engineering, and manufacturing. Each order had to wend its way through each of these giant functional organizations and then move on to the next. At each transition, information was lost and the customer and his needs became more abstract.

Scrapping Centralized Controls

In utter despair, Bob and his brother Jim, who headed manufacturing, began thinking about things that worked. Reaching back into the past, Bob remembered the beginnings of his first intrapreneurial venture in a small leaky building, where he led a dedicated team that made a series of fundamental inventions and processes, creating the printed circuit board industry. Jim thought about a later time in the business when the prototype facility was established, run by a small autonomous team whose original purpose was to speed up the process of making prototype boards to bid on orders. But this team was so much faster and more efficient than the formally controlled manufacturing organization that it became a short-run production center as well and one of the most profitable parts of the company.

With great courage and pragmatism, the Swiggett brothers decided to go with what worked. They threw out the organization chart and the computerized control system.

They divided the company into small product teams, each of which had full responsibility for a product line—engineering it, manufacturing it, selling it, etc. Each group had their own profit and loss statement and their own balance sheet, and they were judged on their return on assets employed, which created a strong pressure to use less working capital. As a result, each product team became very clever about being frugal with inventory and receivables. Within eighteen months, inventories were down to half of what they had been with centralized planning and on-time deliveries and customer satisfaction had climbed steadily from 65 percent to over 95 percent.

After seeing the results of radical decentralization, Bob Swiggett says emphatically, "Never make the mistake of believing there are necessarily economies of scale in a service-oriented business."

At first glance, the Kollmorgen system seems like an abdication of control. Yet the company is really a confederation of intrapreneurs, each of whom has great control over his or her own destiny. In fact, this company of intrapreneurial teams is a quarter-billion-dollar corporation with a staff of 5,000 in 27 locations.

Managing Kollmorgen's Resources

Judging by performance, Kollmorgen's resources are under better control than those of most of their competitors. They have grown at a compounded rate of 18 percent over the last ten years and doubled their earnings per share every year. Their 1984 sales will be well over $300 million.

The Kollmorgen system controls resources better because the system more effectively focuses employees' minds on frugality and customers. Each customer matters to the small group of people making up a product team, who concentrate their attention on a narrow market niche with a limited number of customers.

When decisions are shunted to the top of an organization, top management may have only a few minutes to make a decision on how to spend $10 million. On the other hand, an autonomous business unit doing $10 million a year can spend days making up its mind about a $100,000 decision because it will have a significant effect on their little business. The chances are a decentralized team will make a better and more timely decision than would be made by a multilevel decision system. As a result, the decentralized team system takes better care of the company's resources.

A Better Breakdown of Financial Results

At Kollmorgen, when top management breaks down the financial results of the corporation, they are particularly interested in which profit centers are doing well and which are in trouble. This way of breaking down the aggregate results is useful because it leads to questions top management should be asking, such as:

- Do we have the right intrapreneurs running our business units?
- What business trends explain the patterns of relative growth rates and profitability of our business units?
- How can we change our overall vision of where the company is headed to take advantage of what we are learning from these patterns of growth?

In contrast, traditional financial breakdowns can lead to dangerous results. For instance, I have watched cost-conscious CEOs pick out of the financial statements the fact that their corporations spent 1½ percent of sales on travel and, based on that, issue edicts for each division to cut their travel budgets by 20 percent.

While it may be appropriate for the CEO to tell the divisions that cost cutting is needed, it is the height of foolishness to decide at the corporate level which costs to cut. Only the people on the scene really know where the fat is. Centralized edicts too often end up cutting the muscle and leaving the fat.

DECENTRALIZING CONTROL

Many centralized companies with highly sophisticated control systems are, in fact, out of control. As one intrapreneur put it after a "midnight requisition" of a major piece of capital equipment needed by his team, "Nothing is as out of control as a large control system."

In almost every corporation, there exist large numbers of hard-boiled characters who no longer believe the platitudes that emanate from the corporate staff. They know the system backward and forward and know how to acquire what they need to get the job done, regardless of what the official system dictates. Whether he knows it or not, the CEO has turned large chunks of the corporation's assets over to these people and their informal network of swapping favors and equipment. All he can do under the current system is hope the corporation has chosen the right people.

Fitting the System to the Task

Intrapreneuring is a more timely and effective way of conceptualizing the control task, not an abdication of control. Existing control systems are breaking down because they are so clearly a poor fit with the nature of most people's work. The result of the poor fit between system and task is enormous waste. There is the waste of finding ways around the system that consumes perhaps half of the total human energy of many organizations. Then there are the attitudes such systems produce: great tolerance of waste as long as "it's no skin off my nose."

Seeing the waste, some call for *more* centralized controls; but the waste is not being created by inadequate controls. It is being created by removing the sense and fact of control from the only people close enough to the problem to do something about it.

Old systems appropriate to one type of work break down in the face of more sophisticated work. Slavery has worked for agricultural societies but it isn't free enough for the industrial era. A close look at the patterns of slavery in the American South shows that prior to the Civil War traditional master-slave relationships were already breaking down in the cities. The basic problem was one of freedom and control. The kind of cooperation required by an industrial society stretched beyond the limits of the master-slave relationship.

Most attempts to use slaves in factories failed because many slaves passively resisted by pretending to be as whites expected—so obediently stupid that machinery was destroyed in a manner suggesting no blame. In a few places such as the Tredegar Iron Works in Richmond, slave labor in factories did succeed, but there we find the slaves were paid salaries to work. The system, called somewhat bitterly "buying your own time," was one in which slaves rented themselves from their masters and then resold their labor to the factory at a higher rate.

Leaving aside reflections on man's inhumanity to man, the meaning of this strange system is this: The traditional master-slave relationship with too little freedom and too little reward produced a level of performance inadequate to the industrial era. Only when slaves were offered incentives and freedoms approaching those of a free citizen could they be motivated to do factory work effectively.

Just as slavery was inadequate in the Industrial Age, so the freedoms and rewards of the traditional employee are inadequate to the Innovation Age.

The strongest control the Tredegar Iron Works had on a slave was to allow him to earn money to purchase his freedom. Many wage slaves are doing just that today, working hard to earn the money and experience they need to become free of their employers. From the companies' points of view a better system of control would be one in which intrapreneurs work toward more freedom inside the company, not toward escaping from it.

A Control System for the Innovation Age

Control systems for the Innovation Age will focus on conserving and efficiently using the most important resources of the corporation—the brains of the people in that organization. It will be designed to stop the waste of human resources by giving people the opportunity to act.

An intracapital system provides many of the bases needed for such a control system, but even in the Innovation Age the more mundane sorts of controls, such as financial controls, will also be in effect.

There are two very different kinds of financial control functions in every corporation: first, keeping track of how money is spent; second, controlling before the fact how it will be spent in an attempt to prevent wrong decisions.

Keeping track of how money has been spent is accounting, an information-gathering process that is necessary to keep score, prevent fraud and embezzlement, and provide input for business judgment. It becomes oppressive only if it involves the intrapreneur in too many time-consuming reporting activities.

Controlling the intrapreneur's business decisions in advance by the use of a system of financial approvals has little to do with the requirements of accounting; rather, it seeks to second-guess the business judgment of the intrapreneur. Intrapreneurs work best with a minimum of controls of this kind.

There is a third form of control that seeks not to second-guess intrapreneurs but only to ensure that they operate within their budgets and approval levels. This is no different nor more damaging than a bank that makes sure you have funds available before cashing your check.

Confusing these forms of control is the source of much fear about losing control of intrapreneurs. Of course, managers must keep track of how money is spent and prevent intrapreneurs from overdrawing their spending authority, but that doesn't mean managers have to make their business decisions for them.

Preserving Quality Without Excessive Controls

One of the corporation's legitimate concerns is maintaining its quality standards and reputation. Some fear that unchanneled intrapreneurs will care so much about their innovations and getting to market rapidly that they will neglect to ensure adequate quality. This logic then serves to justify a plethora of controls.

The assumption that intrapreneurs cannot be trusted to meet high quality standards is by and large false if the corporation has reason to trust its intrapreneurs and their teams on the basis of their track records. In most cases, it will be enough to remove rewards from those who create minor quality failures and provide help to those who ask for assistance in achieving quality. In some situations it may be best to have some inspection before products go out done by employees other than members of the intrapreneurial team. But companies such as Kollmorgen have found that trusting their people works. Customer satisfaction increased when they gave business teams the responsibility for their own quality control.

In large functional organizations, where each person is part of a vast machine responsible for only part of a business, it is easy for quality to drop. A manufacturing person may be fixated on cost reduction or an engineer on performance. But an intrapreneur thinks deeply about customer satisfaction, usually in rather idealistic terms. Quality is unlikely to be sacrificed.

Computers and Controls

We haven't really rethought corporate organization to match the new information tools. In many cases the new tools are simply too powerful for old patterns and attitudes. One division manager explains:

> My sector executive vice-president knows my numbers before I do. He sits at his desk with his new computer terminal, pulling up monthly breakdowns of our results. In the past I could hide a new project for years. Now, at the touch of a button, he calls up that project's complete P&L, and begins asking questions I don't have time to answer.
>
> Years ago I ran this division, and was responsible for my P&L. That was fine, but now staffs at each level above me can see each tiny piece of this business separately, and I have to justify all of it. The result's I'm no longer running a business.

Because of computers, we need much smaller staffs than we used to have. To prevent overcontrol we must take into account the new efficiency of computer-enhanced executives. Above the division level, ten divisions, instead of five, could report to the group executive. This—plus giving these executives much smaller staffs—will keep them so busy that they won't have time to overcontrol the divisions.

Making Reporting Simpler

Starting a new business is time consuming enough. There simply isn't time to spend long hours explaining the business to people who want to know about it. One entrepreneur who left Intel said, "If I wanted to do a new product at Intel, I had to visit all those committees, and that made it extremely awkward to do new things."*

Managers should be careful not to overburden a new intraprise with excess reporting. A good policy is to require minimal written reports and insist that anyone wanting further information gather it by going to the location of the intraprise and seeing for themselves. That way, they gather data with more sense and use an hour of their time for each hour they take from the intrapreneurs. The one-to-one principle states:

> Anyone who wishes to know what's going on with an intraprise can go and visit it. If a senior executive wishes to spend an hour of his time learning about it, the team will match his hour one to one with someone to show him around. What they won't do is prepare dog and pony shows or reports except for the occasional and brief scheduled reports which were promised in the business plan.

At Xerox's East Rochester skunkworks they do not permit overhead projections or any other fancy presentations. Waving hands and a chalkboard are all that are allowed. This prevents time and money from going into internal presentations and leaves more time for thinking about the real customers. As many as seventy intrapreneurs share one secretary to help them with their paperwork.

---

* "Big Business Tries to Imitate the Entrepreneurial Spirit," *Business Week*, April 18, 1983, p. 80.

Milestones

Intrapreneurs set measurable goals and intermediate targets for themselves. Once approved, these self-determined goals should be the focus of the corporation's control. Since innovation never happens as planned, the milestones should be deliberately conservative and very general, such as "A prototype demonstrating feasibility should be completed by February 15," or "Customers respond well to a market test before third quarter 1985." Sales and profit figures make good milestones once the project is ready for them. Lengthy specification of milestone targets limits the flexibility of the new business and suggests a precision inappropriate to the early phases of a venture.

THE VENTURE-CAPITAL CONTROL SYSTEM

Over the last fifty years the venture-capital community has evolved a pattern for controlling investments that meets both their fiduciary responsibility to investors and their entrepreneurs' need for freedom. One of the most important parts of the venture-capital control system is selection of the right entrepreneurs, ones who are capable of self-control. But the venture capitalist is more than an unusual type of investor who specializes in finding and putting money into good start-ups. A New Jersey venture capitalist says that in his firm they spend about 15 percent of their time finding and selecting ventures, 60 percent working with the ones they have invested in, and 25 percent selling the ones that succeed (which in their case is twenty-eight out of the last thirty-two). The firm spends from five to twenty man-hours per week with each venture in their portfolio of investments.

Given the closeness of the relationship it is surprising that entrepreneurs can retain their autonomy. The secret to the venture capitalist's partnership with entrepreneurs is a clear definition of roles. Between major commitments of

309

funds, as long as things are going well, the venture capitalist may advise, question, and disagree, but basically the entrepreneur runs the business and has the final say. However, the venture capitalist is not a fool. When things go wrong, the venture capitalist moves in and takes over.

At the core of the venture-capital control system are measurable threshold conditions that, when they occur, trigger reductions in freedom for the entrepreneurs. For example, most venture capital deals include loans as well as investment in stock. If the venture team fails to make a loan payment on time, that generally triggers a clause which gives control to the venture capitalists.

THE FREEDOM LEVER

It probably was not done consciously at first, but this control system is almost diabolically clever, because it grabs the entrepreneur at the core of his being, his need and desire for freedom. At the same time it allows the venture capitalist, who in reality is holding the ax over his head, to come as a friend. Having established the conditions under which the entrepreneur will lose control, the venture capitalist works side by side with him as a powerful adviser. Both are on the same team because neither wants the venture capitalist to take over.

In the Innovation Age, *control systems will be based primarily on selecting and empowering the right people to manage resources, not on building elaborate controls to make sure inadequate people do what they are supposed to.* This imposes a new responsibility on managers. They must have the wisdom to select good intrapreneurs and the toughness to move them out if they don't work out. Synergy will be found less by ordering people to cooperate than by allowing them to find mutually beneficial ways to do so. But for this to happen, the systems in place must reward those who cooperate to produce the greater benefit to the corporation.

310

In the Innovation Age the primary task of the head office of a large corporation is twofold. First, it must lead by creating a clear picture of the kind of corporation everyone should be struggling to build. This picture should include a very general vision of where the company might be headed. (Like any strategy, it may change with circumstances.) A good example is the statement of the famous technical leader of 3M, Richard P. Carlton, who summed up his complex philosophy by saying:

> If you get an idea and the idea is basically new, if you can coat it on 3M equipment in an efficient way to meet a demonstrable need, then you've probably got something worthwhile.°

This simple statement gave a generation of 3M intrapreneurs a great way to check whether their ideas fit with 3M's overall strategy. More importantly, intrapreneurs need to know how the company thinks about basic issues like quality, service, customers, profit, capital investment, and the like. Frito Lays' 99.5 percent service level and Procter & Gambles's insistence on having superior products give clear signals to intrapreneurs what management wants.

Bob Swiggett of Kollmorgen defines the first task of leadership:

> After all, what is the role of a leader? Is it to kick someone in the ass or to create a vision and let them go for it? The role of a leader is a servant's role. It is supporting his people, running interference for them. It is coming out with an atmosphere of understanding and trust and love. You want people to feel that they have complete control over their own destiny at every level. Tyranny is not tolerated here. People who want to manage in the traditional sense are cast off by their peers like dandruff.

Once a vision is in place, the second great task of

° Tim Raymond in *Our Story So Far: Notes from the First 75 Years of 3M Company*, Minnesota Mining and Manufacturing Company, St. Paul, Mn., 1977, pp. 112–113.

leadership is to create the rules of the game so that self-determined players end up serving their own interests best when they serve the corporation well. We have made great progress in building up rule by law in our societies as a whole; it is time to turn to that task in our corporations. In large firms we have passed the point of complexity where anyone can do a good job ruling by fiat. Finding ways to integrate more self-determined efforts is our only choice.

The Renaissance Corporation

To survive, the corporation of the future must radically change from today's corporation. If one were to create the new Renaissance Corporation right now, one could use as a model the organization of whole societies that, centuries ago, faced and successfully dealt with the problems now plaguing corporate organizations. In the Renaissance Corporation, we can see our future and the ways to attain it.

ORGANIZATION AND FREEDOM

Organizations—whether corporations or nations—face predictable problems in balancing necessary structures and freedom of action as they grow larger and more complex. Societies have grown from tribal, follow-the-leader organizations through more organized monarchies to decentralized feudal empires to centralized bureaucracies. Corporations have grown in a parallel manner from entrepreneurial leadership through functional bureaucracy to divisional decentralization and the growth of corporate staffs. But how corporations can take the next step to greater productivity and, as it turns out, greater freedom is actually quite clear.

The next step is to institute more effective forms of "interactive decentralization," relying more on voluntary customer-vendor relationships than on commands.

In some industries these next steps are already visible. Consider projects of enormous complexity and scale, such as space missions. Many assume that these great projects illustrate the supremacy of centralized planning. In truth, the production of a space shuttle is achieved through a hybrid of centralized planning and a radically decentralized system whose relationships are the voluntary relationships of vendors and custo-

mers—not the hierarchical relationships of bosses and subordinates. These voluntary relationships, which are basically
entrepreneurial/intrapreneurial hybrids, are the first steps to
the corporation of the future.

No single organization yet devised could manage all the
details of something as complex as a space shuttle, so NASA
passes the responsibility to its vendors. In turn the vendors
break up the responsibility and pass pieces of it on to their
vendors. Computerized project planning and project management tools are largely focused on managing vendor relationships and seeing that all vendors are on schedule with their
respective parts of the job. For example, Rockwell subcontracts
the construction of the disposable tank to Martin Marietta,
which subcontracts the mounting pad to AVCO. And so it
goes. There are probably 20,000 companies in the United
States involved in producing the shuttle.

There are good economic reasons for working this way.
There is a severe loss of power faced by integrated hierarchical
organizations, which Norman Macrae, deputy editor of the
Economist, identified as far back as 1976:

> It is gradually becoming clear that ownership of the means
> of production is no longer a source of economic or political
> power, and may indeed now be a source of economic and
> political powerlessness. It is easy for an organization to take
> action against sub-contractors by cutting off contracts; it is
> no longer easy to pass down orders to direct employees.
> Where it has hitherto been fashionable for a company to
> boast how many workers it employs, it will be fashionable
> henceforth to boast how much work it has contracted out
> to others all round the world.*

Building the space shuttle is a task of great complexity—but
with an unusually simple market, a single government organization. In complex markets, contractors outperform centrally
planned production even more because they can adapt to a

---

* "The Coming Entrepreneurial Revolution: A Survey," *The Economist,* Dec.
25, 1976, p. 42.

variety of customers with changing needs and tastes.

There seems no rhyme or reason to the Italian garment industry, which is composed of innumerable tiny companies, each performing tasks so specialized we don't even have names for them in English. However, the results of this fragmented network of voluntary relationships are garments that set world standards for quality and style. By contrast, the centrally planned Soviet garment industry produces poor quality and out-of-date clothes. They have great difficulty getting a good match between the sizes they produce and the sizes demanded in the market. No human institution yet devised is as effective at coordinating complexity as the free market.

Both for customer and employee, the benefits of decentralizing production into human-scale units is well understood. But leaders of large corporations have difficulty imagining how they would manage so many small units because they think in the pattern of feudal empires. Large organizations based on rule by command—rather than on voluntary choices disciplined by market forces—will eventually exhaust their leaders.

The corporate officers and staffs of successful large organizations will increasingly see their roles shift from one of telling others what to do to that of creating the rules by which free people in their organizations can perform on their own inspiration. By structuring an internal marketplace that pushes intrapreneurs and employees toward the objectives of the corporation, leaders can preside over organizations of great complexity that also attain a high level of responsiveness. They can do this without exhausting themselves and their staffs with efforts to judge the unjudgable, plan the unplannable, and control the uncontrollable.

History makes it quite clear that, in very large systems, free people, ruled by a market that guides them toward supplying what others want, will outperform hierarchically run systems.

One of the great puzzles of history exemplifies this

principle. In A.D. 1000 the Chinese were technically and scientifically far ahead of Western civilization. Starting with the Renaissance, the West suddenly started moving ahead. Why? The great British historian Joseph Needham spent a lifetime studying this question. His conclusion: Starting with the Renaissance, the West developed a less hierarchical social and economic system.*

The shift away from servility toward *individual* freedom was fundamental to the Renaissance. Replacing serfdom with freer middle-class vendor/customer relationships was fundamental to developing the independence of mind and action necessary to make use of new ideas from the Islamic world and, through it, the classical Greek culture. That freedom produced a flowering of art, craftsmanship, music, courtly love, science and industry, and, alas, the arts of destruction and war. Whatever man sought to do, freedom brought new ways to do it better.

Following the Renaissance, there was a long period of active debate on the best ways to organize society. In the salons and through the revolutions of France, and to a greater extent in the coffeehouses and on the battlefields of England, workable compromises between liberty and power were forged. When France opted for the central planning of mercantilism, her great economy was nearly ruined. A far less wealthy England experimented with a greater degree of laissez faire and a constitutionally limited government and became the seat of the industrial revolution and the wealthiest nation on earth.

We have now reached a point in time when such lessons as these from *The Wealth of Nations* can be applied to the wealth of corporations. Our big corporations have become so big that finding ways to apply the concepts of individual liberty and free *intra*prise inside them will produce a renaissance of innovation and productivity. Unfortunately, merely

---

* Joseph Needham, *Science and Civilization in China*, Cambridge University Press, New York, vol. 5, sec. 4, 1980, p. xxxvii.

wishing to do so will not accomplish that result.

According to Peter Drucker, the people running General Motors some years ago saw that decentralization is an application of the concepts of constitutional government and the rule of law.* But GM's efforts have not lived up to its liberal ideals, for elsewhere Drucker is moved to say: ". . . the very large divisions of General Motors are run much like the units in a planned economy. They resemble remarkably, in their interior organization, the Russian 'trusts' with their 'socialist competition' regulated by base pricing as described in the most authoritative book on Russian industrial management."†

The freedom supplied by the decentralization of General Motors was adequate to displace monarchical Ford as the number-one automaker. The change was about as progressive as the Magna Charta was in its time. It gave a few great barons greater freedom but did nothing to liberate the serfs or create a middle class. Having increased the freedom of an aristocracy, we must turn our attention to the creation of the next great step in liberation, the creation of an intrapreneurial "middle class." This new class can exist only if the corporation encourages and establishes freer internal markets. In addition, there can be no middle class without the basic tools of freedom: ownership and capital.

INTRACAPITAL AND FREE INTRAPRISE

Intracapital may prove to be the key ingredient in making decentralization work. The conduct of a business unit or intraprise in a large diversified firm differs from the operation of an entrepreneurial business in many ways. Among them is a fundamental difference in accounting procedures that causes, or contributes to, many of the problems large organizations currently suffer from.

* Peter Drucker, *The Concept of the Corporation*, NAL, New York, 1983, p. 107.

† Ibid., p. 108.

Given the amount of trouble our accounting systems cause us, it may be difficult to understand how good they are. Without our current accounting systems, we would have great difficulty understanding concepts like return on investment, amortization, and joint stock ownership. We could not calculate or precisely understand earnings, cash flow, or net worth.

James Greer Miller, is the author of *Living Systems,* which at 1,102 pages is a great work by weight alone, but which is also recognized as a breakthrough in systems theory. In it Miller describes the basic functional structures of any living organism, whether a bacterium, a person, General Motors, or the planet. One of these functional structures is the "reservoir," in which organisms store food, fuel, water, money, energy, or other sustenance. For businesses, the reservoir of capital is a key to survival.*

While an independent business generally has a reservoir in the form of net worth and liquid reserves, a business unit of a diversified firm has almost no reserves of its own. All reserves belong to the corporation. As a result, the business unit has a tendency to become short-sighted and cautious.

One may say that business units can draw on the capital resources of the corporation as a whole, but one must admit that they have no inherent right to do so, and the extent to which their corporate parent will favor them and their prospects is never known. This uncertainty creates dependency and an overdeveloped urge to please. The basis of adulthood is independence; the inability to earn freedom leads to endless dependency.

In business, independence and freedom cannot exist without a reservoir of capital. Without capital, you are forced to produce immediate success and constant results or your venture will starve. Without capital, there is no basis for daring because one has nothing to sustain oneself through the period of investment and risk.

Business units such as intraprises do in practice have

---

* James Greer Miller, *Living Systems,* McGraw-Hill, New York, 1977.

some capital in the form of fixed assets, trade secrets, and good will that produces income which can then be diverted into innovation without the corporation's knowledge. They have political capital in the form of personal trust and expectations about the future performance of the unit. But they cannot earn and own liquid reserves beyond their annual budgets. All other reserves are the property of the corporation.

Imagine for a moment that in the free-market economy all bank accounts were the property of the federal government. Managers would be rewarded for depositing more than they withdrew, but would have no balance of funds under their control. Rather, the government would accept all deposits and carefully control all checks, allowing some to spend more than they deposited and requiring others to spend less.

Several dislocations would probably result. The managers of businesses, unable to store value from past successes, would seek to produce steady and predictable earnings so as to please the government and maintain continuity in expenditures. They would learn to abhor surprises and mistakes and to avoid experimentation. Innovation would serve little purpose since the benefits of sudden breakthroughs might well be confiscated by the government. On the bright side, promising developments might just get labeled growth businesses and be granted more expenditures than revenues.

Since they would have no capital of their own, and would be in competition for favor with managers of other businesses, they would become fiercely competitive with one another whether or not they were in competition in the marketplace. Without the ability to earn capital there is no sense that marketplace performance alone will result in security and resources, so every other part of the organization becomes a potential enemy.

Many large corporations show the short-sightedness and turf-consciousness that this capital-free system tends to produce. Giving freedom as a reward gives corporate citizens a chance to grow up. Allowing small business units to retain a portion of their earnings as capital and to build up liquid assets that the unit manager controls (like the CEO of an independent business), will eliminate many of the problems big business has in achieving speed, flexibility, innovativeness, and a strong sense of self-determination.

The average corporate citizen is eager to rise and thus eager to please his bosses. The result of this is that once an erroneous idea is established no one dares challenge it. Most organizations have no one to tell the emperor he has no clothes, and so they need intrapreneurs. Once they are secure in their intracapital and maverick role, intrapreneurs can afford to speak out. In fact, by character they are likely to speak out whether they can afford to or not. Such open honesty will make everything work better.

THE FUTURE IS INTRAPRENEURIAL

Right now business has a great deal to learn from the way society governs itself. It will take decades to formulate ways to apply to the smaller cultures of our giant organizations the minimally hierarchical patterns we have evolved for conducting the lives of our freer nations. Nonetheless, those organizations can eventually return the favor by experimenting with and perfecting new forms for establishing responsible freedom. It is no secret that issues such as pollution, job creation, foreign competition, meaningful work, and equal opportunity plague our efforts to make economic freedom work.

On a micro level, corporations face all these same issues. To date they have been organized to face them in the pattern of a socialist nation. The corporation owns the means of production and takes care of its employees. Though there are differences in compensation, these are not proportional to differences in contribution. In effect our businesses are showing the world that they do not believe free enterprise can work except perhaps on the largest scale. Over the next few decades great leaders will experiment with increasing courage in making a free intraprise system work inside their organizations.

They will have a freer hand and better environment for experimentation with economic systems than any head of state. Out of these experiments will come solutions for capitalism's current difficulties in such areas as pollution and human resources, but which will nevertheless allow enormous economic freedom.

Intrapreneurship is not just a way to increase the level of innovation and productivity of organizations, although it will do that. More importantly, it is a way of organizing vast businesses so that work again becomes a joyful expression of one's contribution to society.

A Last Word to the CEO

The United States of America became a great nation by extending freedom to its people. Our forefathers believed that freedom was not only good for the soul, but the source of the wealth of nations. Today, the wealth of large corporations is as dependent on the freedom of its people as the wealth of this country was then.

We often complain about the erosion of the free enterprise system. We wonder how socialist leaders believe they can achieve high productivity by having their bureaucratic governments run their industries. But if you are the CEO of a large firm, you have probably inherited or chosen a system of governing your organization that bears little relationship to the system of freedoms that you know are essential to the innovation and growth of those large organizations we call nations.

Consider, in fact, that your company has larger revenues than many small countries—and you are, therefore, the president of a kind of small nation. Your predecessors ruled it through a typical hierarchy: Freedom of speech was limited and no one could individually own capital or property. But the seeds of the American revolution are stirring in you. Were you governing a small nation, you would probably try a bit more freedom. It is time to do so in the "nation" that you do rule—your company—for a better bottom line and for the fulfillment of your employees.

It takes great courage, and few will attempt even the small steps toward this new form of freedom. But those who make it work will be rewarded not only with a growing, wealthy corporation but with the knowledge that they used their position to serve freedom. You could be one of them.

Intraprise Plan Guidelines

This section is designed to stimulate the intrapreneur's thinking about a new business idea. It is similar to the checklist an airplane pilot uses before taking off. Use it to be sure the intraprise you are planning has all the necessary parts. Find the questions in each section most important to your business idea and concentrate on them. If you can't answer some important questions, find someone who can. Then consider making them a part of your team.

    I.   Executive Summary
    II.   The Product, Service, or Process Improvement
   III.   Corporate Fit
   IV.   The Marketing and Sales Plan
    V.   Operations Plan
   VI.   Summary of Risks
  VII.   Targets/Milestones
 VIII.   Financial Statements
   IX.   Managerial Issues

I. EXECUTIVE SUMMARY

Even though it comes first, the last thing you write into your business plan is the executive summary. It may be the section that makes or breaks your idea, and it should be carefully constructed.

If your business plan is a selling tool you should know who will read it and what their "hot buttons" are. Tailor the plan to them.

In your writing, treat the reader as a peer. Don't beg or propitiate. Don't give the impression that you think your reader is ignorant about your specialty. Avoid exaggeration, but don't be afraid to share your hopes for the project. Present the facts well and your hopes will be easily understood and shared.

The executive summary should be brief. It should cover the following:

- A short description of the product or service.
- A profile of the customers to be served.
- Their needs and how the product satisfies them.
- The fundamental reason the intraprise ought to succeed. You want a lesson for success so strong that you can succeed even if there are setbacks.
- The fundamental reason why your particular company will be good at the business, e.g., fit with existing products, distribution patterns, manufacturing compatibilities, or match with corporate strategy. Senior executives usually feel the responsibility to maintain coherent strategy. Know their central themes and fit your idea into them.
- Use of corporate facilities, technologies, and marketing and what further investments are required.
- The expertise of your team (it is not always politic to name the team members in an *intra*preneurial plan).
- The qualitative potential for revenues and profits you hope to make.
- The future opened up by this beginning:
  Next-generation products
  The new businesses it leads to
  New market footholds

It is the contents of this summary that, presumably, have been concept tested and pre-sold numerous times before by you and your sponsor. The total content of the plan shows management that you have thoroughly thought through the business, and that you're willing to put your whole being behind it.

Suppose you are the intrapreneur behind the video cassette system. Your excecutive summary needs to make clear what the product is, what it does and how it would be used.

It might have included the following:

> Our product is a tape recorder for home recording and playback
> of TV programming. The recording medium will be a small (17
> X 8.8 centimeters) cassette that will run for 30 minutes. We
> believe it will be primarily used for recording special events
> like football games and favorite shows. It will also be used to
> play taped versions of movies, which we expect will be widely
> available as soon as the movie industry responds to this new
> market. This new product will address several needs:
>
> - The need to enjoy movies in the privacy of the home,
>   particularly movies that people wish to see many times or
>   would be embarrassed to see in movie theaters;
> - The ability to see favorite shows that are broadcast when
>   one is away from home.

**Having described your product you might then go on to
describe your customers, showing how the company's experience can be used to understand them.**

> Our initial customers will be affluent and gadget-oriented. They
> will be primarily male, single, under 40, and the owners of
> expensive stereo systems. We understand these customers and
> how to address their needs because we have been in the stereo
> market for years.

**What needs does the product serve? How is it better than the
competition you expect to face in the future?**

> Our competition for home recording of TV shows will initially
> be live TV. We have the advantage of catching shows customers
> might otherwise miss, either because they are away from home
> or are interrupted. An additional advantage is that when watching
> recorded shows they can fast forward through commercials. Our
> competition for cassette movies is primarily broadcast TV, cable
> TV, and movie theaters. The cassette format allows you to see
> a favorite movie anytime without commercials and without
> leaving home. We have placed prototypes in the homes of other
> employees, and the results are encouraging except that they are
> using them so much the machines are wearing out.

Our greatest competition will not be movies and TV but other companies who copy this idea. We believe Mutsushita may choose to enter this market and could be a formidable competitor. However, we believe that the head start we have, in addition to our ability to upgrade our product rapidly, will allow us to maintain a dominant market position.

Will it sell through existing market channels?

The video cassette recorders will sell through our existing distribution channels in both high fidelity and TV electronics shops.

Does it make use of an established corporate technology base?

Sony has always been a leader in recorder technology and this is a good opportunity to apply that technology to an exciting new market.

Why should it succeed?

We have identified a consumer need and tested it in the homes of employees. The users love it. We understand the customers and distribution and have strong name recognition with both. We are leaders in the required technologies and have a working prototype. Projected manufacturing costs will allow us to fix a price that market tests suggest customers will be willing to pay.

Your executive summary should cover the basics of your business proposition and contain the necessary overview information that will ensure that the whole plan is read and favorably acted upon. It should provide a brief but convincing case of why the company should invest in your idea and your team.

This provides some intrapreneurial business plan guidelines. There are countless other checklists in the literature. But it is important to remember to adapt your format to your business. Use this appendix and other references only as a starting point. In developing your outline put the most important sections first. If you don't, they may never be read.

II. THE PRODUCT, SERVICE, OR PROCESS IMPROVEMENT

Describe the product or service and how you envision its use. To make sure it is clear, test your description on several people who don't know the business very well. Use pictures if possible. You are the best judge of how much detail to include in this section. If it makes sense, showing is usually better than telling; if you have a prototype or artist's rendition of a potential final design, then a page or two of text may be plenty. Don't go into great detail on technical specifications in this section. Detailed design strategies and product specifications should appear in an appendix. Nonetheless, it should contain more detail than the executive summary, including:

Basic and unique features, their value and their use

Basic performance specifications (including any regulatory requirements)

Basic design strategy and technology (for products, particularly if proprietary)

Delivery system (for services)

Basic competitive advantage in the context of the industry and the specific customer

The models and companion products (are there consumables like razor blades?)

Customization opportunities?

As you write this and every other section of the business plan, show how the product relates to the overall strengths and strategies of the company. Executives will keep asking the question, "But why us?" so keep answering it.

One of the tensions in writing a business plan is deciding in which section to put some of your basic ideas. To describe the product you must, to a degree, describe the needs it

327

serves. Then when you describe the customer and his needs, you will have to describe them again. Minor redundancy is OK, but I suggest you put most of the material on needs in the marketing plan.

What is the development status of your first product or service?

Concept

Prototype

Field-tested pilot

Final design

Full-scale production or delivery

What are your current manufacturing approach, your cost/volume relationships, key equipment, key raw materials, manufacturing capabilities and other relationships, key development and manufacturing issues? What future products or services could be line extensions or spin-offs in the next five years? This is an often neglected area.

A plan for each major additional product or service should include a list of the steps needed to get it ready for market; the cost of each step in dollars, man-hours, and elapsed time; the kinds of people needed; and who will do what. Add this to your events table to make sure no one is in three places at once (two may be acceptable for intrapreneurs). Then develop a realistic budget and timetable for each task.

Later you may face a situation where there appears to be a failure of either courage or vision. Even when the first generation is a success, the company may be unwilling or unable to develop new versions. Perhaps this attitude arises from relief: "We took the scary step, and luckily it worked. But we're not foolish enough to cross that shaky bridge a second time." Or it may be a form of complacency: "We've got this wonderful thing here. Everyone loves it, it's selling like hotcakes, it's profitable as hell. Why argue with success?"

First-generation products are rarely the money makers; there is little point in beginning unless you commit to future generations as well. By the time the first generation hits the market, the second-generation product must be well under way or a competitor will beat you to it.

Product-generation timing varies from industry to industry, with the degree of patent and trade secret protection, the number of competent competitors, etc. The basic lesson is clear: Don't build a one-product business strategy. Describe second- and third-generation products and the evolution of your services in your business plan and build R&D funding into your early budgets to begin producing them.

If you propose running a personal image consulting service in the department store that employs you, you might also suggest how the service could broaden as it grows. A second or third generation could be a school for successful dressing, licensed perhaps under the store's name.

Your duty is to see that your intraprise has a future.

III. CORPORATE FIT

Almost no corporation has a hand so light that intrapreneurs don't at times feel the weight of bureaucracy and the cost of being part of a large organization. If intrapreneuring is to make more sense than entrepreneuring, the venture must benefit in some way from the association with the corporation as a whole.

Some intrapreneurial ideas are so dependent on being part of the corporation that they make sense only in that context. A good example of this type is a business that finds a use for the company's waste or discards. Such an idea treads on no one's toes, competes with no one's pride or product, and generally makes money using something people used to have to pay to have removed. This could involve turning the leftovers of an internal abrasive-processing plant into a lucrative wire-saw business, as one intrapreneur has done. A publishing intrapreneur packages book ideas that her house is not interested in and sells them elsewhere. Such ventures have few enemies within and pose no temptation for the intrapreneur to leave since the business is dependent on the corporation for its inputs.

No matter what type of venture you have selected, this section of the business plan gives you a chance to point out all the ways in which your venture supports the corporate strategy and the goals of top management. Art Fry pointed out that Post-it Notes fit 3M's distribution channels, preference for consumables, proprietary technology, and traditional strength in coatings. With all these strategic pluses, he was able to overcome the fact that Post-it Notes were almost impossible to manufacture.

This part of the plan also allows you to position your product or services so as to minimize any potential conflicts. Furthermore, it gives you a chance to sharpen your political skills and prepare your responses to potential adversaries.

Although corporate values and politics vary greatly, intrapreneurial ventures everywhere must navigate between the Scylla of fit with corporate strategy and the Charybdis of avoiding close competition with existing activities.

You should never lose track of the fact that you are still part of your company. In this section of the plan you should mention all the parts of the company to which you will turn for support as well as listing the internal services you will provide. Some of these transactions will be completely informal; others will involve transfer payments.

The more synergy you note in your business plan, the stronger will be the rationale for keeping your business inside the corporation instead of spinning it off.

IV. THE MARKETING AND SALES PLAN

If you are not a marketing specialist, gathering market data and describing the market may seem difficult. In many cases it isn't. Even so, you should consider approaching someone in your company's marketing department for advice. In doing so you may gain a valuable sponsor or team member; by working with that person informally you can see if you want to work together more closely as the intraprise grows.

With or without help, intrapreneurs have to understand their markets personally. The more you do the work yourself, the more visceral your feel for the market will be. Get advice on *how* to do it, but do a good part of the research yourself.

Marketing has been described by many as the common killer—the key reason for failure. Too often, the technical and manufacturing problems are overcome, but the product is a marketing flop. In some corporations the marketing plan and an economic justification are the only formal documents required for program approval.

Your Customers

Many intrapreneurs find it easy to describe their product or service, but harder to identify the customers and their needs. If this is true of you, spend more time talking to and working with potential customers.

The easiest kind of marketing plans to write are ones in which a few customers constitute an adequate market. This is often true of large industrial customers. When Al Marzocchi was developing fiberglass tire cords it wasn't hard to define who his potential customers were in terms of companies. There are only a few major tire companies. Once he had a relationship with Armstrong Tire, he worked with them to develop the product that was later sold to other tire companies. If you have a situation like this, put in your plan the names of specific companies, their sizes and potentials as customers, and the key people inside them who have to be sold.

More generally, consider the following:

- The overall customer group or industry you are serving
- The segments of that industry you will serve
- The size of the industry and its segments

- The needs of the customers in those segments that you will serve
- Trends in the size of the industry and its segments
- Trends in the needs or perceived needs in your market segments

If you are selling an internal process or service improvement, your customers are the users inside the company. List them and their needs and their fears relative to the new process or service.

If you face a complex market in which it is difficult to identify prospective customer groups, get help from a marketing professional. You will need someone on your team who can segment markets and identify each segment's demographics and needs.

The Competition

If your product is truly unique, you may be tempted to say that it has no competition. Don't! No new human needs have been established recently; all products compete. They merely represent different ways of delivering the same benefits. When you clearly understand the benefits of your product or service you can easily find out who else serves the same needs. When possible, describe the major competitors—their products, volume, market share, competitive strengths and weaknesses, distribution, technology, how you are different. Then explain why you think they are vulnerable to your plan and how they might respond to your intrusion on their turf.

You may find all this rather overwhelming if you haven't done it before, but it is really not hard, especially if you find a friendly librarian. Begin looking for competitors in the *Thomas Register*. Also, many industries have syndicated resource services that keep up-to-the-minute information on volume and share for all major competitors. For retailing, it is *Sheldon's*; for groceries, *Sami*; for pharmaceuticals, *The Grey Sheet*. Someone in marketing in your industry can tell you who keeps track of it. Before you spend money on syndicated reports, call the industry trade association and look at recent back issues of the appropriate trade journals. Gale's *Encyclopedia of Associations,* available in any library, is a good place to start.

After a stint in the library, go to where the products that interest you are sold. Ask the buyers how they got them and follow the chain back to the initial vendors. You will be surprised by what you can learn by asking, especially if you share with others what you already know. Be sure to ask people about their competitors' style of operation and strategies. They will be more willing to tell you about others in the industry than about themselves.

A good way to summarize the section on competition is a chart showing the major competitors, their characters and personalities, the advantages and disadvantages of your offerings compared to theirs, the segments in which you believe you beat them, and their capacities for competitive responses.

The Position(s) of Your Products or Services

Describe the ways in which your potential customer will think of your product. Explain those aspects that will make your customer choose your product, rather than the others available. You must establish two broad areas of superiority:

Your product must address needs not fulfilled by existing products.

Your product must benefit your customers more than those they are currently using.

When you have established that the need exists, and that its benefits make it desirable, write a *brief* statement. Emphasize your product's unique characteristics, as some of the companies mentioned in this book might have touted their products or services:

- "A cheaper, more accurate way to put conductive elements on a circuit board" (Du Pont's Riston®)
- "A nonvolatile memory that can go anywhere a microprocessor goes" (Intel's bubble memory)
- "Shipping within 24 hours of receipt of order; questions concerning all orders answered immediately" (NBI Supplies)
- "A mixed-size wire-saw abrasives mixture at a superior price" (Norton Abrasives)

Marketing Communication

Intrapreneurs, like first-time lovers, tend to ramble on about their loves. Since the world can't remember all that you'd like to report, you must be brief and focus on what's "unique"—whether that involves being cheaper, more accurate, more convenient, or whatever. In the School for Intrapreneurs in Tarrytown, New York, one of the exercises is to have students create an advertisement for their product with a ten-word headline, a picture, with no more than fifty words of copy. Most complain that it is impossible; their ideas are too complex. Yet by the end of the session they have learned the essence of their own ideas and have become far more articulate about them. The ad becomes an important internal selling tool as well as the basis for discussions with customers.

Once you have a succinct, unique selling proposition, you can determine the correct medium to convey it:

Word of mouth

Direct personal selling

Direct mail

Brochure

Print advertising

Radio and TV

Press releases and articles

Sales representatives

As a starting point, ask potential customers how the message should be conveyed. They will tell you which methods reach them best.

Sophisticated or innovative products whose benefits are poorly understood, as well as most services, specialities, and intangibles, generally require personal selling. An element of human trust is needed to offset the risk of buying when it's hard to know what one is getting. Specialty chemicals almost always are sold by a technically aware sales force. Intangibles like insurance are still largely sold face to face. (Will your product require a lot of personal selling?)

A word of caution on public relations: A new product or service is news for only a short time. Don't issue press releases before you are ready to serve the demand they create. Time your press releases so they will do the most good and then quickly follow up on the results. Sometimes you can design a series of press releases, each containing new information.

A press release can also be used for internal as well as external effect. One sponsor of an advanced video game feared that, despite his efforts, the program would soon be canceled. In a last-ditch effort, he gave an interview to *The New York Times* describing the great technical progress of the project and his hope that a joint-venture partner would soon appear. Management howled for his head and called his ploy inexcusable: What did he, a scientist, know about marketing and how dare he so tip the corporation's hand? But the project, which before had little chance of surviving, is alive today. Of course he could have lost his job. Fortunately for innovation, the courageous sponsor takes those risks. It is just this kind of zeal that makes him or her such an asset to his company.

Your understanding of the customer's needs, unique selling proposition, and medium of communication should be applied to four distinct tasks:

Generating leads

Interesting prospects in buying

Closing sales

Distribution

Think through each of these steps and test your pitch on friendly potential customers:

Why should they identify themselves as prospects?

Why should they become more interested?

Why should they close the deal?

Does the delivery system match the promise, e.g., speed, follow-up service?

Does the proposition make sense for distributors?

Check the things you want to say at each step against your product specification and design. Do the words and pictures match?

Distribution and Sales

In your sales and marketing plan, describe thoroughly how your product will be distributed and how you will influence it each step of the way. Are selling aids needed? Brochures? Point-of-sale displays? Training? Be sure these aids are included in your marketing and sales cost estimates.

If you are using your own sales force, estimate calls per day, number of calls per sale, average initial sale, and average repeat sale. Estimate sales cost per dollar of sales and the average time from lead generation to delivery of the product or service. You will find these numbers very useful later when making financial projections. If you are planning to use an existing company sales force or an outside sales representative, figure out how worthwhile it is for them to push your product.

When a product first goes to market it often needs a highly informed and enthusiastic sales force. For the initial penetration, a small sales force reporting directly to the intrapreneurial team may be preferable to a much larger divisional or corporate sales force that neither cares about nor understands the new product.

Market Research

One of my most consistent findings is that most successful intrapreneurs do their own market research. The information you need to design a product or a service and its associated market strategy doesn't come from reading someone else's market-research report. Reports influence only the logical part of your nature. When you deal directly with customers, their expressions and gestures and intonations enter your brain at a deeper level. The experience of trying a variety of pitches and product variations, and getting the subtle sensory feedback of face-to-face contact, makes an astonishing amount of information available to guide both intuitive strategy and creative product design. Of course, these insights can rarely be explained on an analytical level, but intrapreneurs let them guide their actions. Do your own market research.

When Stuart Sando took over marketing for the Intel bubble memory venture, his first act was to pack the entire team, including the engineers, out on a series of forty in-depth customer interviews. They emerged with a radically new strategy that overwhelmed the competition. While others tried to make mass memories for giant computers, Intel provided a nonvolatile memory that could go anywhere a microprocessor could go. This gave them their design strategy—hardy bubble memories that could take vibration and extreme variations in temperature, and that came equipped to interface with microprocessors. After visiting many customers, they had no difficulty stating how their strategy differed from the competition's.

Sales Projections

You may find that your seniors question your sales projections more strenuously than almost any other aspect of your plan and well they should. Market research is least effective on highly innovative products or services. For instance, market research studies demonstrated no need for power steering, or for central air conditioning for homes. Almost no one understood how to use Post-it Notes until they tried them for a while. Whenever possible, test innovative products in use.

If you can find some highly creative market researchers in the company, work closely with them to find ways to estimate your potential market. If not, take heart: many good ideas do not test well at first. Under these unpromising conditions, remember that a business begins with a customer. If you are far enough along in your intraprise, sell some of your products (or services). If you can't do that, get your customers to help you design your offering. Have your customers write you letters saying how interested they are in what you are doing. Get them talking with the people in your organization who will decide the fate of your business.

When you have defined your strategy for lead generation, positioning, selling, closing, and order fulfillment, it is time to look at the dynamics of the system. You may be surprised at how long it takes to fill the marketing pipeline. That time lag has very serious cash-flow implications.

How long does it take from the time you begin to generate leads all the way through billing, and collection? In many businesses it is over six months; it could be as long as a year. Can you cut down that time? What about collecting deposits from your initial customers? Progress payments? Faster delivery?

After thinking this through, build a realistic plan for meeting each volume and market-share goal. Find out what the company's tolerance for negative cash flow is and plan accordingly. Then go back and adjust your goals and the cards on your event-flow table.

V. OPERATIONS PLAN

The Steps

List in detail the steps necessary to make the product or deliver the service. Can you see where the bottlenecks and problems are? Figure out the man-hours per unit for each step. Pick three different volume levels and design a process appropriate to each level.

Capital Equipment

List the capital equipment you will need for each of the three production levels. You may be tempted in the early stages of an intrapreneurial venture to recommend investing heavily in equipment to reduce labor costs. This may seem like a good idea, but it should be pursued with caution because it may also reduce your options. Workers are much more flexible than a complex machine designed to do a specific task. It may be wiser to accept a lower profit along with lower risk until you are sure exactly where the market is, and only then invest in fancy equipment or tooling. The danger of premature investment is not just that the investment is useless if you are wrong, but that you will not be permitted to get rid of the equipment and will find yourself locked into an inferior process or product.

Many service businesses require little capital. This was true of new services like the consumer certificate of deposit and simplified checking. Other services, like transportation, are quite capital-intensive. Some of these, like overnight delivery, cannot be started on a small scale, as they make sense only with a large area of coverage. But in services, as in products, the intrapreneur should seek to make small beginnings, so as to prove the viability of the business before making large capital investments.

There are strong forces in the accounting practices of

many firms that reward making what in reality are poor business decisions. Overhead is often allocated as a percentage of labor, even though the bulk of the overhead comes from other areas, such as the cost of financing or depreciation of capital equipment. This means that the system discriminates against labor-intensive strategies and encourages capital spending. The effect of this distortion is not small. In many mature industries, overheads may exceed actual labor costs by a factor of five, meaning that if an employee actually costs $10 an hour he or she will be billed to the intraprise at $50 to cover capital equipment not being used by the intrapreneur. Since start-ups are and should be labor-intensive, their costs are often calculated fictitiously high.

For underutilized plants, the same overhead must be carried by a smaller volume, so there is an even greater discrimination against labor-intensive enterprises. The result is paradoxical—the emptier a plant is, the more difficult it is to justify bringing new products into it.

Management can increase the utilization of capacity by a more carefully thought through system of overhead allocation. Intrapreneurs should fight for fair overhead allocation, or even a temporary exemption from it during the start-up period.

The IBM personal computer, for example, was relieved not only of IBM controls and policy during its early phase, but was also relieved of the normal overheads until after it was established and able to handle them. To justify special treatment, show the net effect of your intraprise on the profitability of the division or firm, not just the calculated profit using the full burden rate. Many companies have begun experimenting with freeing new intraprises from the corporate overhead during start-up.

The operations plan should include a facilities plan, which states how you will use whatever space you finally occupy, and lists of overhead expenses at various stages of the venture (including corporate overhead and any overhead items directly billed to the venture). Consider the following:

Rent and utilities

Office supplies

Administrative staff or time

Postage, telex, messengers, communications

Insurance

Fringe benefits (perhaps 30 percent of salaries)

Legal, accounting, bookkeeping

Find a way to define how corporate overhead will be handled that doesn't crush your venture.

The Make/Buy Decision

For intrapreneurs, the issue of internal versus external manufacturing is often a hot one. There can be enormous pressures to buy internally, but frequently the internal facilities are not set up for short runs or rapid turnaround.

If Don Estridge at IBM hadn't gotten permission to use outside vendors on the personal computer, it might have taken years to introduce the IBM PC. If Hulki Aldikacti hadn't been able to use his suppliers imaginatively, we would still be waiting for the Fiero.

The Design/Manufacturing Interface

One of the great pitfalls in launching a new product is the design/manufacturing interface. Initially, many intrapreneurs think about product design and the market and neglect manufacturing. Hard experience proves that this is a major mistake. A great many products fail first in manufacturing, when miscalculated costs force prices too high, and underestimated machine times cause delivery delays. That is not a marketing failure. Have good manufacturing people on your team in the design phase and listen to them.

Quality

What are your goals for quality?

Reject rates

Customer complaint levels

Rework

Customer satisfaction levels

How do you plan to achieve and maintain quality?

Supplies quality

Internal process quality

Measurement of quality

Motivation

Operator responsibility

Have your quality goals been integrated into every aspect of this plan?

Production Details

The production plan may include:

Facilities

Floor plans

Weekly production per square foot, per person, per machine, per truck or whatever the sensible unit is

Capital equipment plans (for production of the product or delivery of the service)

Tooling timing

Cost and time required for each planned scale-up.

Location

One point that is often intensely debated is whether the intraprise should be located outside of corporate facilities or remain inside. Moving into lower-overhead space has the additional advantage of separating you from bureaucratic oversight. Yet staying close to the informational umbrella of the corporation also has its appeal. Of course, corporate policy has a lot to do with which is best. A company that has a successful history of intrapreneuring is more likely to have a culture that minimizes the drawbacks of proximity. On the other hand, an organization that is about to take the plunge for the first time may find separate quarters are needed to create the autonomy that may be necessary for success.

VI. SUMMARY OF RISKS

Few intrapreneurial business plans contain a good summary of risks, even though this is a standard practice for entrepreneurial plans. If it is not customary in your corporation, delete this section from your formal plan, but prepare it for yourself. After all, it is your career that's at stake.

Your task in describing risks is to identify what might go wrong. Begin by listing possible threats and barriers, and then figure out which are most likely to cause problems. When possible, figure a way around the barriers. Be imaginative.

Some possible risks:

Competitive response: copying your innovation, stepped-up advertising and sales effort, etc.

New technology overtaking yours

Foreign competition

Technical failure of your innovation

Service difficulties

Customer rejection: because of price, unfamiliarity, unpleasant associations, fears, loyalty to old brands, etc.

Unpredictable events, such as bad weather, economic downturn, or a scare as with Tylenol.

Ask others to help you with this section. It is easy to get help to figure out why a venture will not work.

VII. TARGETS/MILESTONES

The month-by-month targets are derived from the events table described at the end of Chapter 6. In exchange for substantial autonomy, the intraprise must promise results. The milestones it establishes should be general in nature, having to do with major growth and profit (or loss) objectives.

The basic contract the intraprise should make with the corporation is that as long as it doesn't exceed its limits of either time or money, the intrapreneurs will be allowed considerable autonomy to run the business. Set your goals flexibly. Rather than promise:

At the end of one year: (1) cumulative losses will be less than $125,000 and (2) sales will be over $250,000.

you could say:

We will achieve $250,000 in cumulative sales before cumulative losses exceed $125,000.

VIII. FINANCIAL STATEMENTS

The value of financial planning is to discipline your vision with dollars. It's detailed work, but actually much, much simpler than the technical activities of many intrapreneurs. It has always been quite surprising to see brilliant technical people stymied by financial statements. If you're comfortable with bits and bytes or can plough through an expense report, I guarantee that you can become comfortable with financial statements.

Finding a Friendly Accountant

Most corporations have made it incredibly easy to get financial assistance by surrounding you with an army of accountants. It is important to become associated with at least one accountant, especially if he or she is the one who assembles the budgets and reports your number progress to management. Management normally does not look at all the numbers. They rely on their accountants and controllers to report on major variances from the expected. Since you, as an intrapreneur, will constantly have major variances, an accountant in an adversary position can make your life miserable.

Obviously, it is best to make a financial person your friend or, at least, to render him or her neutral. The best way to do this is to remove all suspicions. Controllers, probably more than managers, hate surprises. Have them involved in your financial preparations. Let them understand your assumptions. Keep them informed of events as you learn them.

A friendly controller can be an unbelievably important protector. But don't let them force you into excessive detail or sway you from a customer-oriented approach.

Budgets

An expense budget is simply your best guess of what you plan to spend in a particular area, such as engineering salaries or materials, within a specific time period, such as a year. A sales-revenue budget is how much product you expect to ship to customers, a bookings budget is how many orders you expect to get (not necessarily the same as revenue), a capital budget is how much you expect to spend on equipment, etc. Budget preparation and monitoring are time-consuming activities in all corporations. If the corporation is on a January-December fiscal reporting schedule, annual budgets begin to be prepared for the following year sometime in August or September. As an intrapreneur you may find you have increased responsibility for preparing budgets.

If you're forecasting or proposing numbers beyond one year, then terms like pro-forma are used, but this is just a fancy buzzword for projected statements. Economic justification forms often require projections for the next five or ten years.

The preparation and eventual monitoring of budgets related to your intraprise make you visible. It is best to delay being visible for as long as possible. Some of the methods used are:

- Charge the expense of the initial investigations to three or four different, unrelated projects where it will make only a very small dent in each.
- Borrow people, equipment, and expenses from other people's departments.
- Utilize purchase orders for the purchase of outside services, not just for materials and equipment (sometimes, there are fewer accounting controls on purchase orders than on internal spending).

Eventually, you'll have to prepare an annual budget and total program estimated cost. As the project grows you will have to show the economic justification for it.

To plan your budget during the preincome phase of your intraprise, do the following:

1. Establish the basic things that have to happen before you get your product or service to market. These should already be present in narrative form in the earlier sections of your business plan. Get them into chart form, showing the ten or twenty important steps you have to take.

2. Decide on completion dates for each of those steps, and state them as milestone targets to measure your progress toward commercialization.

3. Build a plan of the steps you must take to achieve each milestone.

4. Estimate the cost of each of those steps and the date you will incur it.

5. Add 20 to 100 percent to all estimates, depending on how well you know what you are doing. If you are working from some actual past performance numbers, as opposed to starting from scratch, you can use a smaller fudge factor.

6. Add up the money and staff you will need in each month. List it neatly.

When you have done all that, you have a budget. If you had to make changes in the earlier section of the business plan to make it all hang together, be sure to go back and change those sections.

Revenues

The size and timing of the projected revenue numbers are the most important and the most uncertain financial numbers you will have to present. "How big is the market?" "How much can we sell?" You're going to have to answer based on all the work previously described in the plan. Many corporations fail to conduct sensitivity analyses to see how variations in sales volume or major cost categories will effect the venture. For your own peace of mind, you should find out what happens financially if things don't turn out exactly as planned.

Important Numbers

Most managers (and corporations) have particular numbers that get the most attention, such as:

Annual sales volumes

Annual sales growth

Return on sales

Return on capital employed

Gross profit

Pretax profit

Payback

Inventory turns

Find an accountant who knows which numbers matter to the decision makers who matter to you, and learn how they are calculated. Generally, for each number there are threshold conditions which "good businesses" meet. These might be "payback in 2½ years" or "30 percent pretax return on capital employed." Working with your accountant, go back and forth between calculating gross numbers that satisfy these threshold conditions and detailed, itemized, bottom-up projections. When you find a realistic plan that satisfies the ratios, makes sense from an itemized standpoint, and builds a business, your financial planning is well on its way.

IX. MANAGERIAL ISSUES

When venture capitalists evaluate venture opportunity, the most important factor is the venture team. As much as 80 percent of the investors' decision is based on the team and only 20 percent on other factors such as the quality of the concept and the rest of the business plan. The reason for this is that good management can make a mediocre plan succeed, but almost no idea or plan can save a poor venture team. Despite these facts, corporate business plans rarely include the single most important section, a description of the venture team.

In a way this is not surprising. Once when my associates and I were hired to help an important intraprise write a business plan we suggested that the plan include a venture team. The champions and would-be intrapreneurs of the plan were nervous but went along despite their forebodings.

When management got the plan they exploded at the effrontery of the intrapreneurs suggesting personnel to implement the plan. The team was told that was the prerogative of senior management. We were promptly dismissed for encouraging the would-be intrapreneurs. The plan was handed off to "more suitable" managers and soon died. I learned from that experience.

A year and a half later, to my great surprise and pleasure, the venture was successfully launched by the original team. After the official project had died, the first team, inspired by their original act of daring, and undaunted by management, revived the idea and surreptitiously developed it until its potential could no longer be ignored. This time, management allowed them to carry it forward to success.

As an intrapreneur, you must decide whether or not to include a venture team in your business plan. If your employer will not allow you to form a venture team, you might do well to consider a new employer.

In describing the venture team, you need to put special

emphasis on the relationship between each member's background and skills and the requirements of the business. You will need an explanation of why each of you is personally committed to the venture. There should also be a list of key resource people who will consult with or sponsor the venture, though in some cases sponsors can be more effective if they are unofficial. You should also have the answers to two basic questions in order to protect those you hope to recruit for your team:

1. Will your corporation free members from other departments to join you?

2. Are team members "loaned" to an intraprise, with the promise that if the project fails they will be welcomed back in their department of origin? Would they at least be welcomed back somewhere in the corporation?

Organizational Form

A good organizational form can give great strength to an intraprise, and a poor one can undo it. There is no right place for an intraprise to report—that depends on the circumstances and the nature of the venture—but there are general principles to follow.

It is best to have the venture team report to its leader and the leader report to a strong sponsor. When you reach the stage of formality that calls for a business plan, the team members should not report to the various organizations from which they had come.

What functional area the leader reports to is not important as long as there is not a multilevel decision process above him. Whomever the leader talks to must be authorized to approve the purchases, personnel transfers, marketing strategies, etc., necessary for the smooth and rapid development of the business. In some companies the easiest way to stop the buck is to have intrapreneurs report to a board. If this is the direction your company takes, I strongly recommend having at least one member who has experience with intrapreneurs or entrepreneurs, preferably an outsider.

To establish a new venture, two organizational characteristics are generally effective: (1) You must create a freewheeling atmosphere in which anyone can talk back to anyone and the opinions of everyone are respected and (2) there must be a quick way to resolve issues and get on with it.

This section of the business plan should have an organization chart, a description of the authority and responsibilities of the team members, and the person or board to which they report. It should contain job descriptions that are purposely vague. Most intrapreneurs aren't fond of job descriptions.

Bibliography

Abernathy, William J., Kim B. Clark and Alan M. Kantrow, *Industrial Renaissance*, Basic Books, New York, 1983.

Bannock, Graham, *The Economics of Small Firms: Return from the Wilderness*, Blackwell, Oxford, England, 1981.

Baty, Gordon B., *Entrepreneurship: Playing to Win*, Reston, Reston, VA 1974.

Baumbach, Clifford and Joseph R. Mancuso, *Entrepreneurship and Venture Management*, Prentice-Hall, Englewood Cliffs, NJ, 1975.

Bell, Daniel, *The Coming of Post Industrial Society*, Basic Books, New York, 1976.

Bennis, Warren G., *Changing Organizations*, McGraw-Hill, New York, 1966.

Braudel, Fernand, *The Wheels of Commerce: Civilisation and Capitalism, 15th–18th Century*, vol. 2, Harper & Row, New York, 1979.

Burns, James MacGregor, *Leadership*, Harper & Row, New York, 1978.

Chandler, Alfred D., Jr., *The Visible Hand: The Managerial Revolution in American Business*, Harvard University Press, Cambridge, MA, 1977.

————, *Strategy and Structure*, M.I.T. Press, Cambridge, MA, 1962.

Collins, Orvis and David Moore, *The Organization Makers*, Meredith, New York, 1970.

———— with Darob B. Unwalla, *The Enterprising Man*, Michigan State University Press, East Lansing, MI, 1964.

Deal, Terrence E. and Allan A. Kennedy, *Corporate Cultures*, Addison-Wesley, Reading, MA, 1982.

de Bono, Edward, *Lateral Thinking*, Harper & Row, New York, 1970.

de Vries, Manfred Kets, "The Entrepreneurial Personality: A Person at the Crossroads," *Journal of Management Studies*, vol. 14, 1977.

Dible, Donald M., *Up Your Own Organization*, The Entrepreneur Press, 1974.

Drucker, Peter, "Our Entrepreneurial Economy," *Harvard Business Review*, vol. 62, no. 1, 1984.

————, *The Concept of the Corporation*, NAL, New York, revised, 1975.

Fast, Norman D., "Pitfalls of Corporate Venturing," *Research Management*, March 1981.

————, "A Visit to the New Venture Graveyard," *Research Management*, March 1979.

Gardner, John W., *Self-Renewal: The Individual and the Innovative Society*, Harper & Row, New York, 1964.

Hanan, Mack, *Venture Management*, McGraw-Hill, New York, 1976.

Hawken, Paul, *The Next Economy*, Holt, Rinehart & Winston, New York, 1983.

Hayes, R. H., and W. J. Aberanthy, "Managing Our Way to Economic Decline," *Harvard Business Review*, July–August, 1980.

Hill, Chris T., and James Utterback, eds., *Technological Innovation for a Dynamic Economy*, Pergamon Press, Chelmsford, NY, 1979.

Hunt, Inez, and Wanetta W. Draper, *Lightning in His Hand: The Life of Nikola Tesla*, Omni Publications, Hawthorne, CA, 1964.

Kidder, Tracy, *The Soul of a New Machine*, Little, Brown, Boston, 1981.

Lao Tsu, translated by Gia-fu Feng and Jane English, *Tao Te Ching*, Vintage Books, New York, 1972.

Lawler, Edward E., III and John A. Drexler, Jr., *The Corporate Entrepreneur*, Center for Effective Organizations, University of Southern California, Graduate School of Business, Los Angeles, CA, 1980.

Macrae, Norman, "The Coming Entrepreneurial Revolution: A Survey," *The Economist*, December 25, 1976.

————, "Intrapreneurial Now," *The Economist*, April 17, 1982.

Maidique, M. A., "Entrepreneurs, Champions, and Technological Innovation," *Sloan Management Review*, Winter 1980.

———— and Robert H. Hayes, "The Art of High Technology Management," *Sloan Management Review*, Winter 1984.

Mancuso, Joseph R., *How to Start, Finance and Manage Your Own Small Business*, Prentice-Hall, Englewood Cliffs, NJ, 1978.

McClelland, David C., "Achievement Motivation Can Be Developed," *Harvard Business Review*, November–December 1965.

————, *The Achieving Society*, Van Nostrand, New York, 1961.

———— and David H. Burnham, "Power Is the Great Motivation," *Harvard Business Review*, March–April 1976.

———— and David Winter, *Motivating Economic Achievement*, Free Press, New York, 1969.

Miller, James Greer, *Living Systems*, McGraw-Hill, New York, 1977.

Needham, Joseph, *Science and Civilisation in China*, Cambridge University Press, New York, 1980.

Ogilvy, James, *Many Dimensional Man*, Harper & Row, New York, 1979.

Pascale, Richard Tanner and Anthony G. Athos, *The Art of Japanese Management*, Simon & Schuster, New York, 1981.

Peters, Thomas J., and Robert H. Waterman, Jr., *In Search of Excellence*, Harper & Row, New York, 1983.

Quinn, James Brian, *Strategies for Change: Logical Incrementalism*, Irwin, Homewood, IL, 1980.

————, "Technological Innovation, Entrepreneurship, and Strategy," *Sloan Management Review*, Spring 1979.

Rind, Kenneth W., "The Role of Venture Capital in Corporate Development," *Strategic Management Journal*, John Wiley & Sons Ltd., vol. 2, April 1981, pp. 170–180.

————, "Dealing with the Corporate Venture Capitalists," *Guide to Venture Capital Sources*, 7th ed., Stanley E. Pratt, ed. Capital Publishing Corp., Wellesley Hills, MA., revised 1984, pp. 42–44.

Roberts, E. B., "Generating Effective Corporate Innovation," *Technology Review*, October/November, 1977.

————, "What It Takes to Be an Entrepreneur . . . and to Hang on to One," *Innovation*, no. 7, 1969.

————, "New Ventures for Corporate Growth," *Harvard Business Review*, July–August 1980.

Schumacher, E. F., *Small Is Beautiful*, Harper & Row, New York, 1973.

Schumpeter, Joseph, *The Theory of Economic Development*, Harvard University Press, Cambridge, MA, 1934.

Shapero, Albert, "The Entrepreneurs: Corporate Heroes or Lousy Managers?" *The Wharton Magazine*, Wharton School, University of Pennsylvania, vol. 3, no. 1, Philadelphia, PA, 1978.

Smith, Adam, *Selections from The Wealth of Nations*, Henry Regnery Company, Chicago, IL, 1953.

Taffi, Donald J., *The Entrepreneur: A Corporate Strategy for the Eighties*, AMACOM, New York, 1981.

3M Company, *Our Story So Far: Notes on the First 75 Years of 3M Company*, Minnesota Mining and Manufacturing Company, St. Paul, MN, 1977.

Timmons, Jeffrey A., Alexander Smollen and L. M. Dingree, Jr., *New Venture Creation*, Irwin, Homewood, IL, 1977.

Toffler, Alvin, *Previews and Premises*, William Morrow, New York, 1983.

————, *The Third Wave*, William Morrow, New York, 1980.

Vesper, Karl H., *Entrepreneurship and National Policy*, Heller Institute for Small Business Policy Papers, Chicago, IL, 1983.

————, *New Venture Strategies*, Prentice-Hall, Englewood Cliffs, NJ, 1980.

von Hippel, Eric, "Successful and Failing Internal Corporate Ventures: An Empirical Analysis," *Industrial Marketing Management*, vol. 6, no. 3, July 1977, pp. 163–174.

————, "Users as Innovators," *Technology Review*, vol. 8, no. 3, January 1978.

Wade, Richard C., *Slavery in the Cities: The South 1820–1860*, Oxford University Press, New York, 1964.

Weaver, Peter, *You, Inc.*, Doubleday, New York, 1973.

White, Richard M., Jr., *The Entrepreneur's Manual*, Chilton Books, Radnor, PA, 1977.

Wilson, Claude, Jr., *The Wilson Concept for Management*, (unpublished monograph, copyright, 1963).

Acknowledgments

The task of nurturing authors can be particularly irksome. While they require a great deal of protection from distractions, they appear ungratefully shiftless, spending much of their time pacing or staring out the window and offering only the lame excuse that they are thinking. Libba, my wife, dealt with this situation, which could have produced great resentment, by making writing this book her project as well. She stayed up all night with me finding passages that needed work and organizing my tasks. She argued the logic with me until I saw the skipped steps. She checked facts and figures. She soothed intrapreneurs' fears that their stories would get them fired. And in addition she took over most of my household duties and the running of my business (as well as her own). Although she refused to be named co-author, without her this book would not be.

My heartfelt thanks to Marco, Alex and Marianna, who patiently and understandingly endured two years without much of a father. For them most of all I am glad the writing is finished.

How can I express the appreciation I have for Sarah Davison and Yel Hannon, who not only typed and commented on innumerable drafts, but kept everything else on an even keel. Scores of times they worked through the night to meet our schedule. Clearly they are driven to excellence from within. Yel prepared the diagrams for the book as well. Four brilliant Yale students helped Yel and Sarah with production and research: Brenda Taylor, Chip Hourihan, Ann Mackie and Allison Rutledge-Parisi.

Dan Shurman helped me set up my first interviews for the book. Nahid Aryannejad, Didi Major, Dailey Jessup, and Marianna Kastner searched the data bases and libraries and produced several feet of useful articles.

Without my editor, Harriet Rubin, and an assisting editor, Jonathan Kastner, who knows when or what poor imitation of a book might have emerged. They endured my stubborn resistance to good editing and took the more difficult path of trying to teach me to write so that I could do more of the fixing in my own voice. Production editor Gail Gavert, emerging editor John Michels and Harper & Row's all-star production team avoided a delay of several months by working night and day to push the book through in time.

Only those who know her can appreciate Mary Schoonmaker's ability as a muse and supporter. Her understanding of the stages of authorship put in perspective my struggles and fears, and prepared me for each new crisis before it occurred.

I owe special tribute to Ken Stahl who read the early manuscripts and saved us from many errors. He hinted at new ways to think about the challenge of intrapreneuring and allowed me to believe I had invented them myself. He was relentless in his encouragement. I also extend my thanks to Virginia Simpson for her help and contributions.

Nils Dailey helped simplify the freedom factors and the business planning sections. Abbas Nadimfard helped me with several early projects, as did the other members of the New Directions Group, and gave me time to start the book. Annie Goheen and Walter Bloch pushed me into my earliest literary attempt, which gave me the taste for writing.

I especially want to thank all the intrapreneurs whose stories pushed me toward many of the basic ideas in this book. Some of the stories I heard could not be repeated, yet they contained lessons I have found other ways to tell. To those intrapreneurs who have given up their anonymity and allowed their stories to be published, I owe a special debt. This book may excite the "immune system" of their corporations and slow them down in the future. (In business as in physics, we cannot observe without changing the thing we are observing.) None wanted the notoriety, yet they each let us convince them that the value of their story to other intrapreneurs outweighed the cost of letting it be told. More than protecting themselves, they were all concerned that they might put their colleagues at risk. On the other hand, all wanted to share the credit with so many of their colleagues that we felt the stories would have been unreadable, and we regretfully had to simplify the personnel.

I am also grateful to the courageous legal and public relations people who allowed these stories to be told. No intrapreneur could have appeared in this book if their corporations had lacked the good sense and the humor to realize that stories of intrapreneurs bucking their systems was a sign of health, not a source of embarrassment.

When we were all much younger, Lew Randall and Jim Stein shared with me the trials and triumphs of working in Silicon Valley. Their articulate stories shaped my thinking and years later led to many of the insights of intrapreneurship. Then when I returned to them for help in writing *Intrapreneuring*, they helped me track down dozens of intrapreneurs with crucial stories to tell.

When I was a student in the School for Entrepreneurs, Hershel Kranitz taught the psychology of the entrepreneur brilliantly.

Bill and Vieve Gore of Gore Associates and Bob Swiggett of Kollmorgen showed me that the conscious creation of an environment for intrapreneurs can pay off handsomely for everyone.

My thanks also to Tom Peters and Bob Waterman for speeding the change to a climate of avid interest in intrapreneurship, and to Gustaf Delin, Sven Atterhed and Lennart Bosjo of The Foresight Group for their pioneering work in establishing the first School for Intrapreneurs in Sweden. Their encouragement was invaluable.

Special thanks go to:

Jim Adams	Larry Britt	Norman Hochgraf
Jules Arbose	Napier Collyns	Alan Mendelson
David Belle Isle	Peter Dunston	Gary Pint
Bob Bigliano	Bob Gubrud	Jim Porter
Wes Boyd	Art Hill	Mik Sawka
		Dick Smith

Index